A Year in the Word

Catholic Bible Journal

A YEAR IN THE WORD

CATHOLIC BIBLE JOURNAL

MEG HUNTER-KILMER

Nihil Obstat
Msgr. Michael Heintz, Ph.D.
Censor Librorum

Imprimatur
✠ Kevin C. Rhoades
Bishop of Fort Wayne-South Bend
April 22, 2022

The *Nihil Obstat* and *Imprimatur* are official declarations that a book is free from doctrinal or moral error. It is not implied that those who have granted the *Nihil Obstat* and *Imprimatur* agree with the contents, opinions, or statements expressed.

27 26 25 24 23 22   1 2 3 4 5 6 7 8 9

Our Sunday Visitor Publishing Division
Our Sunday Visitor, Inc.
200 Noll Plaza
Huntington, IN 46750
www.osv.com
1-800-348-2440

ISBN: 978-1-63966-023-0 (Inventory No. T2763)
1. RELIGION—Biblical Studies—Bible Study Guides.
2. RELIGION—Biblical Commentary—General.
3. RELIGION—Christianity—Catholic.

eISBN: 978-1-63966-024-7

Cover design and Interior design: Amanda Falk
Cover art: AdobeStock

Printed in the United States of America

To my students at Holy Spirit Prep and Maur Hill-Mount Academy. Teaching you, learning from you, listening to you, encouraging you, praying with you, laughing with you, and loving you has been one of the great joys of my life.

One-Year Reading Plan

DAY	READINGS		
❑ 1 ✓	1 John 1:1—3:10	Psalm 1	Matthew 1:1–17
❑ 2 ✓	1 Jn 3:11—5:21	Ps 2	Mt 1:18–25
❑ 3 ✓	Genesis 1–3	Ps 3	Mt 2:1–12
❑ 4 ✓	Gn 4–5	Ps 4	Mt 2:13–23
❑ 5 ✓	Gn 6–8	Ps 5	Mt 3
❑ 6 ✓	Gn 9:1—11:26	Ps 6	Mt 4:1–17
❑ 7	Gn 11:27—13:18	Ps 7	Mt 4:18–25
❑ 8	Gn 14–15	Ps 8	Mt 5:1–12
❑ 9	Gn 16–17	Ps 9	Mt 5:13–26
❑ 10	Gn 18–19	Ps 10	Mt 5:27–37
❑ 11	Gn 20–21	Ps 11	Mt 5:38–48
❑ 12	Gn 22–23	Ps 12	Mt 6:1–18
❑ 13	Gn 24:1—25:18	Ps 13	Mt 6:19–34
❑ 14	Gn 25:19—26:35	Ps 14	Mt 7
❑ 15	Gn 27–28	Ps 15	Mt 8:1–17
❑ 16	Gn 29–30	Ps 16	Mt 8:18–34
❑ 17	Gn 31–32	Ps 17	Mt 9:1–17
❑ 18	Gn 33–34	Ps 18	Mt 9:18–38
❑ 19	Gn 35–36	Ps 19	Mt 10:1–15
❑ 20	Gn 37–38	Ps 20	Mt 10:16–33
❑ 21	Gn 39–40	Ps 21	Mt 10:34—11:1
❑ 22	Gn 41–43	Ps 22	Mt 11:2–19
❑ 23	Gn 44–45	Ps 23	Mt 11:20–30
❑ 24	Gn 46–48	Ps 24	Mt 12:1–14
❑ 25	Gn 49–50	Ps 25	Mt 12:15–37
❑ 26	Philippians 1:1—2:18	Ps 26	Mt 12:38–50
❑ 27	Phil 2:19—4:23	Ps 27	Mt 13:1–30
❑ 28	Exodus 1–3	Ps 28	Mt 13:31–53
❑ 29	Ex 4:1—6:27	Ps 29	Mt 13:54—14:21
❑ 30	Ex 7–8	Ps 30	Mt 14:22–36

❑ 31	Ex 9–11	Ps 31	Mt 15:1–20
❑ 32	Ex 12–14	Ps 32	Mt 15:21–39
❑ 33	Ex 15–16	Ps 33	Mt 16:1–12
❑ 34	Ex 17–18	Ps 34	Mt 16:13–28
❑ 35	Ex 19–20	Ps 35	Mt 17:1–13
❑ 36	Ex 21–22	Ps 36	Mt 17:14–27
❑ 37	Ex 23–24	Ps 37	Mt 18:1–20
❑ 38	Ex 25–27	Ps 38	Mt 18:21–35
❑ 39	Ex 28–29	Ps 39	Mt 19:1–15
❑ 40	Ex 30–31	Ps 40	Mt 19:16–30
❑ 41	Ex 32–33	Ps 41	Mt 20:1–16
❑ 42	Ex 34–36	Ps 42	Mt 20:17–34
❑ 43	Ex 37–38	Ps 43	Mt 21:1–17
❑ 44	Ex 39–40	Ps 44	Mt 21:18–32
❑ 45	Romans 1–2	Ps 45	Mt 21:33–46
❑ 46	Rom 3–4	Ps 46	Mt 22:1–14
❑ 47	Rom 5–6	Ps 47	Mt 22:15–33
❑ 48	Rom 7–8	Ps 48	Mt 22:34–46
❑ 49	Rom 9–10	Ps 49	Mt 23
❑ 50	Rom 11–12	Ps 50	Mt 24:1–28
❑ 51	Rom 13–14	Ps 51	Mt 24:29–51
❑ 52	Rom 15–16	Ps 52	Mt 25:1–30
❑ 53	Leviticus 1–3	Ps 53	Mt 25:31–46
❑ 54	Lv 4–5	Ps 54	Mt 26:1–25
❑ 55	Lv 6–7	Ps 55	Mt 26:26–56
❑ 56	Lv 8–10	Ps 56	Mt 26:57–75
❑ 57	Lv 11–13	Ps 57	Mt 27:1–26
❑ 58	Lv 14–16	Ps 58	Mt 27:27–66
❑ 59	2 John, 3 John	Ps 59	Mt 28
❑ 60	Lv 17–18	Ps 60	Mark 1:1–13
❑ 61	Lv 19–20	Ps 61	Mk 1:14–31
❑ 62	Lv 21–23	Ps 62	Mk 1:32–45
❑ 63	Lv 24–25	Ps 63	Mk 2:1–17
❑ 64	Lv 26–27	Ps 64	Mk 2:18–28

❑ 65	1 Corinthians 1–3	Ps 65	Mk 3:1–19
❑ 66	1 Cor 4–6	Ps 66	Mk 3:20–35
❑ 67	1 Cor 7–9	Ps 67	Mk 4:1–25
❑ 68	1 Cor 10–11	Ps 68	Mk 4:26–41
❑ 69	1 Cor 12–13	Ps 69	Mk 5:1–20
❑ 70	1 Cor 14–16	Ps 70	Mk 5:21–43
❑ 71	Numbers 1–3	Ps 71	Mk 6:1–29
❑ 72	Nm 4–5	Ps 72	Mk 6:30–56
❑ 73	Nm 6–7	Ps 73	Mk 7:1–23
❑ 74	Nm 8:1—10:10	Ps 74	Mk 7:24–37
❑ 75	Nm 10:11—12:16	Ps 75	Mk 8:1–26
❑ 76	Nm 13–14	Ps 76	Mk 8:27–38
❑ 77	Nm 15–16	Ps 77	Mk 9:1–32
❑ 78	Nm 17–18	Ps 78	Mk 9:33–50
❑ 79	Nm 19:1—22:1	Ps 79	Mk 10:1–31
❑ 80	Nm 22:2—24:25	Ps 80	Mk 10:32–53
❑ 81	Nm 25–26	Ps 81	Mk 11:1–14
❑ 82	Nm 27–28	Ps 82	Mk 11:15–33
❑ 83	Nm 29–30	Ps 83	Mk 12:1–27
❑ 84	Nm 31–32	Ps 84	Mk 12:28–44
❑ 85	Nm 33–34	Ps 85	Mk 13:1–23
❑ 86	Nm 35–36	Ps 86	Mk 13:24–37
❑ 87	2 Corinthians 1–3	Ps 87	Mk 14:1–21
❑ 88	2 Cor 4–6	Ps 88	Mk 14:22–52
❑ 89	2 Cor 7–9	Ps 89	Mk 14:53–72
❑ 90	2 Cor 10–11	Ps 90	Mk 15:1–20
❑ 91	2 Cor 12–13	Ps 91	Mk 15:21–47
❑ 92	Deuteronomy 1–3	Ps 92	Mk 16
❑ 93	Dt 4–5	Ps 93	Luke 1:1–38
❑ 94	Dt 6–8	Ps 94	Lk 1:39–80
❑ 95	Dt 9–11	Ps 95	Lk 2:1–21
❑ 96	Dt 12–14	Ps 96	Lk 2:22–52
❑ 97	Dt 15–17	Ps 97	Lk 3:1–22
❑ 98	Dt 18–20	Ps 98	Lk 3:23–38

❑ 99	Dt 21–23	Ps 99	Lk 4:1–13
❑ 100	Dt 24–26	Ps 100	Lk 4:14–44
❑ 101	Dt 27–28	Ps 101	Lk 5:1–26
❑ 102	Dt 29–30	Ps 102	Lk 5:27–39
❑ 103	Dt 31–32	Ps 103	Lk 6:1–26
❑ 104	Dt 33–34	Ps 104	Lk 6:27–49
❑ 105	Galatians 1–3	Ps 105	Lk 7:1–28
❑ 106	Gal 4–6	Ps 106	Lk 7:29–50
❑ 107	Joshua 1–3	Ps 107	Lk 8:1–25
❑ 108	Jo 4–6	Ps 108	Lk 8:26–56
❑ 109	Jo 7–9	Ps 109	Lk 9:1–27
❑ 110	Jo 10–12	Ps 110	Lk 9:28–50
❑ 111	Jo 13–16	Ps 111	Lk 9:51–62
❑ 112	Jo 17–19	Ps 112	Lk 10:1–24
❑ 113	Jo 20–22	Ps 113	Lk 10:25–42
❑ 114	Jo 23–24	Ps 114	Lk 11:1–28
❑ 115	Ephesians 1–3	Ps 115	Lk 11:29–54
❑ 116	Eph 4–6	Ps 116–117	Lk 12:1–34
❑ 117	Judges 1–3	Ps 118	Lk 12:35–59
❑ 118	Jgs 4–6	Ps 119:1–48	Lk 13:1–17
❑ 119	Jgs 7–9	Ps 119:49–88	Lk 13:18–35
❑ 120	Jgs 10–12	Ps 119:89–136	Lk 14
❑ 121	Jgs 13–16	Ps 119:137–176	Lk 15:1–10
❑ 122	Jgs 17–19	Ps 120–121	Lk 15:11–32
❑ 123	Jgs 20–21	Ps 122	Lk 16:1–15
❑ 124	Ruth	Ps 123	Lk 16:16–31
❑ 125	1 Samuel 1–3	Ps 124	Lk 17:1–19
❑ 126	1 Sm 4–7	Ps 125	Lk 17:20–37
❑ 127	1 Sm 8–10	Ps 126	Lk 18:1–14
❑ 128	1 Sm 11–12	Ps 127	Lk 18:15–43
❑ 129	1 Sm 13–14	Ps 128	Lk 19:1–27
❑ 130	1 Sm 15–16	Ps 129	Lk 19:28–48
❑ 131	1 Sm 17	Ps 130	Lk 20:1–19
❑ 132	1 Sm 18–20	Ps 131	Lk 20:20–47

❏ 133	1 Sm 21–23	Ps 132	Lk 21:1–19
❏ 134	1 Sm 24–25	Ps 133	Lk 21:20–38
❏ 135	1 Sm 26–28	Ps 134	Lk 22:1–38
❏ 136	1 Sm 29–31	Ps 135	Lk 22:39–71
❏ 137	2 Sm 1–3	Ps 136	Lk 23:1–32
❏ 138	2 Sm 4–6	Ps 137	Lk 23:33–56
❏ 139	2 Sm 7–10	Ps 138	Lk 24:1–35
❏ 140	2 Sm 11–12	Ps 139	Lk 24:36–53
❏ 141	2 Sm 13–14	Ps 140	John 1:1–18
❏ 142	2 Sm 15–17	Ps 141	Jn 1:19–51
❏ 143	2 Sm 18–20	Ps 142	Jn 2:1–12
❏ 144	2 Sm 21–22	Ps 143	Jn 2:13–25
❏ 145	2 Sm 23–24	Ps 144	Jn 3:1–21
❏ 146	Colossians 1–2	Ps 145	Jn 3:22–36
❏ 147	Col 3–4	Ps 146	Jn 4:1–42
❏ 148	1 Kings 1–2	Ps 147	Jn 4:43–54
❏ 149	1 Kgs 3–5	Ps 148	Jn 5:1–30
❏ 150	1 Kgs 6–8	Ps 149	Jn 5:31–47
❏ 151	1 Kgs 9–11	Ps 150	Jn 6:1–21
❏ 152	1 Kgs 12–14	Proverbs 1	Jn 6:22–59
❏ 153	1 Kgs 15–16	Prv 2	Jn 6:60–71
❏ 154	1 Kgs 17–18	Prv 3	Jn 7:1–13
❏ 155	1 Kgs 19	Prv 4	Jn 7:14–36
❏ 156	1 Kgs 20–22	Prv 5	Jn 7:37–52
❏ 157	1 Thessalonians 1–3	Prv 6	Jn 7:53—8:11
❏ 158	1 Thes 4–5	Prv 7	Jn 8:12–30
❏ 159	2 Kings 1–2	Prv 8	Jn 8:31–59
❏ 160	2 Kgs 3–4	Prv 9	Jn 9
❏ 161	2 Kgs 5–6	Prv 10	Jn 10:1–21
❏ 162	2 Kgs 7–8	Prv 11	Jn 10:22–42
❏ 163	2 Kgs 9–10	Prv 12	Jn 11:1–54
❏ 164	2 Kgs 11–13	Prv 13	Jn 11:55—12:36
❏ 165	2 Kgs 14–15	Prv 14	Jn 12:37–50
❏ 166	2 Kgs 16–17	Hosea 1	Jn 13:1–20

❑ 167	2 Kgs 18–19	Hos 2	Jn 13:21–38
❑ 168	2 Kgs 20–21	Hos 3	Jn 14
❑ 169	2 Kgs 22–23	Hos 4	Jn 15:1–10
❑ 170	2 Kgs 24–25	Hos 5:1–14	Jn 15:11–17
❑ 171	2 Thessalonians	Hos 5:15–7:2	Jn 15:18—16:4a
❑ 172	Amos 1–3	Hos 7:3–12	Jn 16:4b–15
❑ 173	Am 4–6	Hos 7:13–8:14	Jn 16:16–33
❑ 174	Am 7–9	Hos 9	Jn 17
❑ 175	Micah 1–3	Hos 10	Jn 18:1–27
❑ 176	Mi 4–5	Hos 11	Jn 18:28–40
❑ 177	Mi 6–7	Hos 12:1–13:1	Jn 19:1–30
❑ 178	1 Timothy 1–3	Hos 13:2–14:1	Jn 19:31–42
❑ 179	1 Tim 4–6	Hos 14:2–10	Jn 20:1–18
❑ 180	1 Chronicles 1–3	Proverbs 15	Jn 20:19–31
❑ 181	1 Chr 4–6	Prv 16	Jn 21:1–14
❑ 182	1 Chr 7:1—9:34	Prv 17	Jn 21:15–25
❑ 183	1 Chr 9:35—11:47	Prv 18	Matthew 1:1–17
❑ 184	1 Chr 12–14	Prv 19	Mt 1:18–25
❑ 185	1 Chr 15–17	Prv 20	Mt 2:1–12
❑ 186	1 Chr 18–20	Prv 21	Mt 2:13–23
❑ 187	1 Chr 21–22	Prv 22	Mt 3
❑ 188	1 Chr 23–25	Prv 23	Mt 4:1–17
❑ 189	1 Chr 26–27	Prv 24	Mt 4:18–25
❑ 190	1 Chr 28–29	Prv 25	Mt 5:1–12
❑ 191	2 Timothy	Prv 26	Mt 5:13–26
❑ 192	2 Chronicles 1–2	Prv 27	Mt 5:27–37
❑ 193	2 Chr 3–5	Prv 28	Mt 5:38–48
❑ 194	2 Chr 6–7	Prv 29	Mt 6:1–18
❑ 195	2 Chr 8–9	Prv 30	Mt 6:19–34
❑ 196	2 Chr 10–12	Prv 31	Mt 7
❑ 197	2 Chr 13–15	Isaiah 1	Mt 8:1–17
❑ 198	2 Chr 16–18	Is 2	Mt 8:18–34
❑ 199	2 Chr 19–21	Is 3	Mt 9:1–17
❑ 200	2 Chr 22–23	Is 4	Mt 9:18–38

❑ 201	2 Chr 24–25	Is 5	Mt 10:1–15
❑ 202	2 Chr 26–27	Is 6	Mt 10:16–33
❑ 203	2 Chr 28–29	Is 7	Mt 10:34—11:1
❑ 204	2 Chr 30–31	Is 8	Mt 11:2–19
❑ 205	2 Chr 32–33	Is 9	Mt 11:20–30
❑ 206	2 Chr 34–36	Is 10	Mt 12:1–14
❑ 207	Zephaniah	Is 11	Mt 12:15–37
❑ 208	Titus	Is 12	Mt 12:38–50
❑ 209	Nahum	Is 13	Mt 13:1–30
❑ 210	Philemon	Is 14	Mt 13:31–53
❑ 211	Habakkuk	Is 15	Mt 13:54—14:21
❑ 212	James 1–3	Is 16	Mt 14:22–36
❑ 213	Jas 4–5	Is 17	Mt 15:1–20
❑ 214	Jeremiah 1–2	Is 18	Mt 15:21–39
❑ 215	Jer 3–4	Is 19	Mt 16:1–12
❑ 216	Jer 5–6	Is 20	Mt 16:13–28
❑ 217	Jer 7–8	Is 21	Mt 17
❑ 218	Jer 9–10	Is 22	Mt 18:1–20
❑ 219	Jer 11–12	Is 23	Mt 18:21–35
❑ 220	Jer 13–14	Is 24	Mt 19:1–15
❑ 221	Jer 15–16	Is 25	Mt 19:16–30
❑ 222	Jer 17–18	Is 26	Mt 20:1–16
❑ 223	Jer 19–20	Is 27	Mt 20:17–34
❑ 224	Jer 21–22	Is 28	Mt 21:1–17
❑ 225	Jer 23–24	Is 29	Mt 21:18–32
❑ 226	Jer 25–26	Is 30	Mt 21:33–46
❑ 227	Jer 27–29	Is 31	Mt 22:1–14
❑ 228	Jer 30–31	Is 32	Mt 22:15–33
❑ 229	Jer 32–33	Is 33	Mt 22:34–46
❑ 230	Jer 34–35	Is 34	Mt 23
❑ 231	Jer 36–37	Is 35	Mt 24:1–28
❑ 232	Jer 38–39	Is 36	Mt 24:29–51
❑ 233	Jer 40–42	Is 37	Mt 25:1–30
❑ 234	Jer 43–44	Is 38	Mt 25:31–46

❑ 235	Jer 45–47	Is 39	Mt 26:1–25
❑ 236	Jer 48–49	Lamentations 1	Mt 26:26–56
❑ 237	Jer 50–51	Lam 2	Mt 26:57–75
❑ 238	Jer 52	Lam 3	Mt 27:1–26
❑ 239	Baruch 1:1—3:8	Lam 4	Mt 27:27–66
❑ 240	Bar 3:9—5:9	Lam 5	Mt 28
❑ 241	Bar 6	Isaiah 40	Mark 1:1–13
❑ 242	Tobit 1–3	Is 41	Mk 1:14–31
❑ 243	Tb 4–6	Is 42	Mk 1:32–45
❑ 244	Tb 7–11	Is 43	Mk 2:1–17
❑ 245	Tb 12–14	Is 44	Mk 2:18–28
❑ 246	Ezekiel 1–3	Is 45	Mk 3:1–19
❑ 247	Ez 4–5	Is 46	Mk 3:20–35
❑ 248	Ez 6–8	Is 47	Mk 4:1–25
❑ 249	Ez 9–11	Is 48	Mk 4:26–41
❑ 250	Ez 12–13	Is 49	Mk 5:1–20
❑ 251	Ez 14–16	Is 50	Mk 5:21–43
❑ 252	Ez 17–18	Is 51	Mk 6:1–29
❑ 253	Ez 19–20	Is 52	Mk 6:30–56
❑ 254	Ez 21–22	Is 53	Mk 7:1–23
❑ 255	Ez 23–24	Is 54	Mk 7:24–37
❑ 256	Ez 25–26	Is 55	Mk 8:1–26
❑ 257	Ez 27–28	Is 56	Mk 8:27–38
❑ 258	Ez 29–30	Is 57	Mk 9:1–32
❑ 259	Ez 31–32	Is 58	Mk 9:33–50
❑ 260	Ez 33–34	Is 59	Mk 10:1–31
❑ 261	Ez 35–36	Is 60	Mk 10:32–53
❑ 262	Ez 37–39	Is 61	Mk 11:1–19
❑ 263	Ez 40–42	Is 62	Mk 11:20–33
❑ 264	Ez 43–44	Is 63	Mk 12:1–27
❑ 265	Ez 45–46	Is 64	Mk 12:28–44
❑ 266	Ez 47–48	Is 65	Mk 13:1–23
❑ 267	1 Peter 1–2	Is 66	Mk 13:24–37
❑ 268	1 Pt 3–5	Daniel 1	Mk 14:1–21

❑ 269	Haggai, Zechariah 1–2	Dn 2	Mk 14:22–52
❑ 270	Zec 3–6	Dn 3:1–45	Mk 14:53–72
❑ 271	Zec 7–9	Dn 3:46–100	Mk 15:1–20
❑ 272	Zec 10–11	Dn 4	Mk 15:21–47
❑ 273	Zec 12–14	Dn 5	Mk 16
❑ 274	Esther A–2	Dn 6	Luke 1:1–38
❑ 275	Est 3–C	Dn 7	Lk 1:39–80
❑ 276	Est D–5	Dn 8	Lk 2:1–21
❑ 277	Est 6–E	Dn 9	Lk 2:22–52
❑ 278	Est 8–F	Dn 10	Lk 3:1–22
❑ 279	Ezra 1–2	Dn 11	Lk 3:23–38
❑ 280	Ezr 3:1—4:23	Dn 12	Lk 4:1–13
❑ 281	Ezr 4:24—6:22	Dn 13	Lk 4:14–44
❑ 282	Ezr 7–8	Dn 14	Lk 5:1–26
❑ 283	Ezr 9–10	Wisdom 1	Lk 5:27–39
❑ 284	Nehemiah 1–3	Ws 2	Lk 6:1–26
❑ 285	Neh 4–5	Ws 3	Lk 6:27–49
❑ 286	Neh 6–7	Ws 4	Lk 7:1–28
❑ 287	Neh 8–9	Ws 5	Lk 7:29–50
❑ 288	Neh 10–11	Ws 6	Lk 8:1–25
❑ 289	Neh 12–13	Ws 7	Lk 8:26–56
❑ 290	Judith 1–3	Ws 8	Lk 9:1–27
❑ 291	Jdt 4–5	Ws 9	Lk 9:28–50
❑ 292	Jdt 6–7	Ws 10	Lk 9:51–62
❑ 293	Jdt 8–9	Ws 11	Lk 10:1–24
❑ 294	Jdt 10–11	Ws 12	Lk 10:25–42
❑ 295	Jdt 12:1—14:10	Ws 13	Lk 11:1–28
❑ 296	Jdt 14:11—16:25	Ws 14	Lk 11:29–54
❑ 297	Malachi, Obadiah	Ws 15	Lk 12:1–34
❑ 298	Joel	Ws 16	Lk 12:35–59
❑ 299	Jonah 1–2	Ws 17	Lk 13:1–17
❑ 300	Jon 3–4	Ws 18	Lk 13:18–35
❑ 301	Job 1–3	Ws 19	Lk 14
❑ 302	Jb 4–7	Sirach Foreword, 1	Lk 15:1–10

❑ 303	Jb 8–10	Sir 2	Lk 15:11–32
❑ 304	Jb 11–14	Sir 3	Lk 16:1–15
❑ 305	Jb 15–17	Sir 4	Lk 16:16–31
❑ 306	Jb 18–19	Sir 5	Lk 17:1–19
❑ 307	Jb 20–21	Sir 6	Lk 17:20–37
❑ 308	Jb 22–24	Sir 7	Lk 18:1–14
❑ 309	Jb 25–28	Sir 8	Lk 18:15–43
❑ 310	Jb 29–31	Sir 9	Lk 19:1–27
❑ 311	Jb 32–34	Sir 10	Lk 19:28–48
❑ 312	Jb 35–37	Sir 11	Lk 20:1–19
❑ 313	Jb 38–39	Sir 12	Lk 20:20–47
❑ 314	Jb 40–42	Sir 13	Lk 21:1–19
❑ 315	2 Peter	Sir 14	Lk 21:20–38
❑ 316	Ecclesiastes 1–3	Sir 15	Lk 22:1–38
❑ 317	Eccl 4–6	Sir 16	Lk 22:39–71
❑ 318	Eccl 7–8	Sir 17	Lk 23:1–32
❑ 319	Eccl 9–12	Sir 18	Lk 23:33–43
❑ 320	Song of Songs 1–4	Sir 19	Lk 23:44–56
❑ 321	Sg 5–8	Sir 20	Lk 24:1–35
❑ 322	1 Maccabees 1–2	Sir 21	Lk 24:36–53
❑ 323	1 Mc 3–4	Sir 22	John 1:1–18
❑ 324	1 Mc 5–6	Sir 23	Jn 1:19–51
❑ 325	1 Mc 7–8	Sir 24	Jn 2:1–12
❑ 326	1 Mc 9–10	Sir 25	Jn 2:13–25
❑ 327	1 Mc 11–12	Sir 26	Jn 3:1–21
❑ 328	1 Mc 13–14	Sir 27	Jn 3:22–36
❑ 329	1 Mc 15–16	Sir 28	Jn 4:1–42
❑ 330	Jude	Sir 29	Jn 4:43–54
❑ 331	2 Maccabees 1–2	Sir 30	Jn 5:1–30
❑ 332	2 Mc 3–4	Sir 31	Jn 5:31–47
❑ 333	2 Mc 5–6	Sir 32	Jn 6:1–21
❑ 334	2 Mc 7–8	Sir 33	Jn 6:22–59
❑ 335	2 Mc 9–10	Sir 34	Jn 6:60–71
❑ 336	2 Mc 11–12	Sir 35	Jn 7:1–13

❑ 337	2 Mc 13–14	Sir 36	Jn 7:14–36
❑ 338	2 Mc 15	Sir 37	Jn 7:37–52
❑ 339	Acts 1:1—2:13	Sir 38	Jn 7:53—8:11
❑ 340	Acts 2:14—3:26	Sir 39	Jn 8:12–30
❑ 341	Acts 4–5	Sir 40	Jn 8:31–59
❑ 342	Acts 6:1—8:3	Sir 41	Jn 9
❑ 343	Acts 8:4—9:43	Sir 42	Jn 10:1–21
❑ 344	Acts 10–11	Sir 43	Jn 10:22–42
❑ 345	Acts 12–13	Sir 44	Jn 11:1–54
❑ 346	Acts 14:1—15:35	Sir 45	Jn 11:55—12:19
❑ 347	Acts 15:36—16:40	Sir 46	Jn 12:20–36
❑ 348	Acts 17–18	Sir 47	Jn 12:37–50
❑ 349	Acts 19–20	Sir 48	Jn 13:1–20
❑ 350	Acts 21:1—22:29	Sir 49	Jn 13:21–38
❑ 351	Acts 22:30—24:27	Sir 50	Jn 14
❑ 352	Acts 25–26	Sir 51	Jn 15:1–10
❑ 353	Acts 27–28	Hebrews 1	Jn 15:11–17
❑ 354	Revelation 1	Heb 2	Jn 15:18—16:4a
❑ 355	Rv 2	Heb 3	Jn 16:4b–15
❑ 356	Rv 3	Heb 4	Jn 16:16–33
❑ 357	Rv 4–5	Heb 5	Jn 17
❑ 358	Rv 6–7	Heb 6	Jn 18:1–27
❑ 359	Rv 8–9	Heb 7	Jn 18:28–40
❑ 360	Rv 10–12	Heb 8	Jn 19:1–30
❑ 361	Rv 13–14	Heb 9	Jn 19:31–42
❑ 362	Rv 15–16	Heb 10	Jn 20:1–18
❑ 363	Rv 17–18	Heb 11	Jn 20:19–31
❑ 364	Rv 19–20	Heb 12	Jn 21:1–14
❑ 365	Rv 21–22	Heb 13	Jn 21:15–25

Introduction

"Scripture is like a river," St. Gregory the Great said, "broad and deep. Shallow enough here for the lamb to go wading, but deep enough there for the elephant to swim."

When I picked up my Bible the day after the Lord won my heart on a confirmation retreat, I was hardly even a lamb. Only thirteen years old, I'd considered myself an atheist just the week before. But the Holy Spirit had done some heavy lifting that weekend, and I found myself — quite unexpectedly — ready to live for Jesus.

God wrote one book, I reasoned, so I'd better read that. I threw in the *Catechism* for good measure and set off running. Wandering, rather. Stumbling. Dragging my feet through begats and cubits. Grimacing at genocide. Shaking my head over what certainly looked like misogyny. Getting distracted for a few months before grabbing my beat-up Bible again and picking up where I'd left off.

It took me five years to read the Bible from Genesis to Revelation.

I understood almost nothing.

But I knew it was the word of God. And I'd had moments, glimpses of the glory that would come if only I sought the Lord, if only I let his word change me. "The word of God is living and effective," Hebrews tells us, "sharper than any two-edged sword, penetrating even between soul and spirit, joints and marrow, and able to discern reflections and thoughts of the heart" (Heb 4:12). I wanted to be pierced, wanted my heart broken open by the Lord. I'd seen my Protestant friends wax poetic over the beauty of Scripture, and I wanted that same love of the word of God.

So I started again, this time with a schedule that would take me through the whole Bible in a year. And at the end of that year, I started again. Then again. All the while, I was studying theology, hearing Scripture preached at Mass each day, praying the Rosary and meditating on its mysteries, attending Bible studies, praying the Liturgy of the Hours. I was encountering Scripture in different contexts, in different translations. I began memorizing it, meditating on it, preaching on it.

Before I knew it, the word of God was running through my veins, tugging at the edges of my mind, speaking hope and conviction and life-changing love into my weak and weary heart. And as I read the Bible in its entirety year after year, as I marked up my Bible with highlighting and underlines and notes full of information gleaned from modern commentators and Church Fathers and prayer — above all else, prayer — I began to *know* the God I had met all those years earlier.

I saw how he had worked through Judith, how he had given hope to Joseph, how he had answered Sarah and Tobit. I heard his proclamations of undying love in Isaiah and Hosea and Ezekiel and the Song of Songs. I read about him in the Gospels and held these things in my heart, learning (like Mary) to gaze at him, to wonder at his perfect infant body and his strong carpenter's hands and his smile lines and his scars. I saw myself in the woman caught in adultery, the man born blind. I ignored him with Peter, followed him with Peter, corrected him with Peter, denied him with Peter, repented with Peter. I stood beside Paul and learned to rejoice in affliction, to be weak so that Christ might be strong.

When I was a lamb, opening my Bible for the very first time, I found truth. I found mystery. I found a love letter from the God who had always seemed so distant. And though I'm far from what Saint Gregory would consider an elephant in Scripture study, when I began my twentieth time through the Bible this year, I pulled out my pencil yet again. Because when I encounter God in his word, he is always working, always calling me to conversion and surrounding me with love and delighting me with connections I never saw before. Sometimes, it's all I can do to trudge through the passages I haven't been able to find meaning in; but every once in a while he shows me just a glimmer of his radiance even in the descriptions of sacrifices or temple adornments, and I remember: This is no dead text but the living word of God, an invitation to stand in awe before the God of the Universe and enter into intimacy with the Bridegroom Messiah.

There is very little in my life that I'm more grateful for than that inspiration to begin reading the Bible each year, simply because being in the word of God every day — over and over again, even the parts I would very much rather avoid — has made me the Lord's far more than I ever thought possible.

The first time I read through the whole Bible, I started at Genesis and read until Revelation. It took me five years. Every subsequent time, I've managed it in a year. The problem with my initial cover-to-cover approach (among others) was that I'd get bogged down in Leviticus or Ezekiel, and it was hard to motivate myself to keep going. You may have tried this yourself. Almost everyone I know who's picked up the Bible at Genesis has put it down before Joshua. You need something to break up the cubits and begats, something to keep you going when Ezekiel is watching wheels in wheels or when prophets keep spouting oracles against various nations you don't know. Not that it's not all inspired; I'm just not always in a place where I find it inspiring. What I need is a schedule, something that mixes in some of the easier books while still leading me through the harder ones.

This schedule does just that, leading you through the Bible in its entirety (and the Gospels twice). We'll move chronologically through the Old Testament, but in between the harder books such as Leviticus or 2 Chronicles, we'll read epistles or books such as Ruth and Jonah as carrots dangling in front of us to keep us moving. Each day, we'll also read from a book that's more poetic (like Psalms or Lamentations or Hebrews) and needs to be read more slowly. We'll read half a chapter of a Gospel each day as well, so that even when our first two readings seem dense or dry, we've got the words of Jesus beckoning us and inviting us to keep going.

On each page of this journal, you'll see the citations of the day's readings. I invite you to pull out your Bible, along with a pen or pencil and highlighter. As you read, make notes in the margins and highlight verses that move you, things you'll want to notice in the future. Then come back to this journal to read my reflections, which try to make sense of difficult passages or draw connections or share the beautiful things the Spirit has taught me in these verses. Below those reflections you'll find space where you can jot down notes on the reading or write a response to the Lord or meditate on what you've read.

Each day also features a short verse from the day's readings (or even a fragment of a verse). On days when you aren't able to read all three readings in their entirety, take this one verse to meditate on for the day, then return to the full readings the following day. You might also consider reading the day's verse first thing in the morning and making it your meditation for the day, returning to it in your brief moments of inactivity or allowing it to guide you at times of frustration or grief. Having sat with that verse for a few hours before you open up your Bible for the day might open you up to new insights in your reading.

While I've arranged this in a one-year schedule, there is no particular virtue in accomplishing this feat in 365 days. If you want to take two days for each set of readings, that's lovely. If you work diligently for a few weeks and then set this journal aside for a year, feel free to pick up right where you left off. Open it up weekly for your holy hour or sporadically if that works best for you. However you use it, this journal exists to invite you into the word of God, to help you understand it, and to encourage you to persevere. I very much hope that, whether you're a lamb or an elephant, you find yourself refreshed by the living water given to you through the Scriptures.

A note about versions, translations, and numbering

Except where otherwise stated, this journal will use the text and numbering from the New American Bible, Revised Edition (NABRE). Most of the time, verses cited will correspond exactly to their equivalent in other translations. Occasionally (especially in the Psalms) different translations have slightly different numbers. If the referenced verse in your Bible doesn't match the reflection, look at the verse just before and just after. Personally, I use an older version of the New American Bible (NAB), which more closely matches the texts we hear at Mass, but as long as you're using a Catholic Bible, you're on the right track. I recommend any wide-margin option from a Catholic publisher. (For study purposes, the Ignatius Study

Bible is excellent, but only the New Testament is available.) We will occasionally use some non-Catholic translations in this journal because they are particularly beautiful or shed light on some element of the text, but if you're Catholic, it's best to have a Catholic Bible as your main Bible.

Having a Catholic Bible means that your footnotes will reflect Catholic teaching and that your translation won't be made with non-Catholic theology in mind; all translation is interpretation, after all, and Catholics who want to read Scripture from within the heart of the Church will want to trust that it was translated from the heart of the Church. Above all, having a Catholic Bible ensures that your Bible will have all seventy-three books that have been included in the Catholic canon of Scripture since at least the fifth century. Seven of these books were removed by various Protestant denominations during the Protestant Reformation; Catholics refer to these books as the Deuterocanonical books, while Protestants call them the Apocrypha. For Protestant readers of this book, Tobit, Judith, 1 and 2 Maccabees, Wisdom, Sirach, and Baruch will be unfamiliar, hidden treasures loved by Christians of old. If your faith tradition doesn't accept these texts as Scripture, spend time with them anyway, recognizing them as beautiful texts written by faithful Jews who were seeking the Lord in the centuries before the coming of Christ.

If you want to learn more about the Bible

This journal is not a systematic explanation of all of Scripture. If you'd like a more robust overview of each individual book, *You Can Understand the Bible* (Peter Kreeft) is invaluable. *Walking with God* (Tim Gray and Jeff Cavins) provides an excellent overview of the story of salvation history, making it easier for you to understand how each reading fits into the big picture. The best book I've ever read on the Gospels was *To Know Christ Jesus* (Frank Sheed) — truly, reading that book changed my life. For deeper dives on individual New Testament books, I've found the Catholic Commentary on Sacred Scripture to be very helpful, especially the volumes by Mary Healy. *Bound for Freedom* (Göran Larsson) is an excellent commentary on Exodus, while *Christ in the Psalms* (Patrick Henry Reardon) draws beautiful connections between the Psalms and the Messiah. Finally, *Fire of Mercy, Heart of the Word* (Erasmo Leiva-Merikakis, all four volumes) is an incomparable meditation on the Gospel of Matthew.

1 | *1 John 1:1—3:10*
Psalm 1
Matthew 1:1–17

"See what love the Father has bestowed on us that we may be called the children of God." (1 Jn 3:1)

It's always tempting to skim a genealogy, even when it's the list of the ancestors of God-made-man. But nothing in Scripture is there by accident, and reading Matthew's list prayerfully may show you more than you expect. Matthew doesn't confine himself to the heroes of ancient Israel — the admired among Jesus' ancestors. No, he specifically highlights four women, each calling to mind the scandal of her adultery or career or religion or assault. Even David, the man after God's own heart (1 Sm 13:14), was an adulterer and a murderer. And wise Solomon's lecherous ways led to a division among God's people that has never been repaired. After him, a list of kings, mostly wicked. Then fourteen generations of nobodies, as the People of God wondered whether he was still on their side. But God was working. Through generations of sin and drudgery, God was working, laying the groundwork in the midst of faithlessness and scandal, for his coming into the world. He's working in your life, too.

2 | *1 John 3:11—5:21*
Psalm 2
Matthew 1:18–25

"Children, let us love not in word or speech but in deed and truth." (1 Jn 3:18)

The First Letter of John is a miserable book to read if you're trying to silence your conscience. Especially if you've been trying to convince yourself that it's okay to hate someone (or a vague group of people). John makes it very clear that if you hate your brother (or ignore your brother's needs), you can't truly love God. Most of us know this theoretically, but ruminating on the first letter of Saint John demands that we confront our petty jealousies, our selfish attitudes, our prejudices. Saint Jerome tells us that at the end of his life, Saint John preached the same homily at every Mass: "Little children, love one another!" That's the plea of this letter, an entreaty that we love, whatever the cost. Love isn't a feeling, of course, or it wouldn't be commanded. Love is a choice to work for the good of the other, to recognize people's suffering instead of dismissing them for whatever reason. Who am I refusing to love right now? How can I work to change that today?

3 | *Genesis 1–3*
Psalm 3
Matthew 2:1–12

"God looked at everything he had made, and found it very good." (Gn 1:31)

God saw how good it was. Imagine God delighting in the act of creation over the course of billions of years, never growing bored but marveling at each new star and species and cell. Then imagine him directing that wonder at you, looking at you as he looked at sinless Adam and Eve and calling you "very good." This story is designed to teach us far deeper truths than we might at first imagine when we read it as a timeline and not the beginning of a love story. God is speaking here not of a strict accounting of the minutes of creation but of the goodness of the world, created from nothing. God brought order out of chaos to make a home for his people, created in his image and likeness. The second creation story (in Gn 2) similarly shows us a world created for our good by a God who made us for relationship with one another and with him. The Fall damaged those relationships, but even in the wake of Adam and Eve's sin, God promised redemption (Gn 3:16). Compare the two creation stories. What truths is each trying to tell?

4 | *Genesis 4–5*
Psalm 4
Matthew 2:13–23

"The Lord hears when I call out to him." (Ps 4:4)

Again, we find ourselves wading through a sea of unfamiliar names — this time in Genesis. Time and again, Scripture will proclaim a list of begats, prompting many Christians to skip past the Old Testament in favor of the more accessible parables or epistles. But while many of these lists are filled with people about whom we know nothing at all, the very act of reading those names, of remembering their existence, reminds us that we matter. Each of those men was a unique person, desperately loved and eternally willed by God. The lists were canonized in Scripture not just because the Israelites had a particular fondness for genealogy, but also so that the Spirit could tell us that each person matters. You matter. When you feel insignificant, God sees you and delights in you.

5 | *Genesis 6–8*
Psalm 5
Matthew 3

"All who trust in you will be glad / and forever shout for joy." (Ps 5:12)

Noah spent years — perhaps decades — building the ark. It would have seemed idiotic in a land with so little rain, and it must have earned him a great deal of ridicule. But his building was preaching, warning people of the coming flood and attempting to draw them to repentance. He was called to do something that seemed insane so that he could save his family and invite all the world to salvation. None but his family listened and were saved, but Noah's faithfulness saved his life (and the lives of every person who followed after). John the Baptist received his fair share of ridicule and was ultimately imprisoned and murdered for his faithfulness to an uncomfortable call. But in the darkness of his prison cell, I expect he remembered this moment: when the voice of the Father proclaimed his love for the Son. Meanwhile, the Spirit in the form of a dove reminded the people of Noah's dove, proclaiming that Jesus was the home they were seeking and the one who would inaugurate a new creation. How is God calling you to be a fool for him? Are you willing to obey, even if it bears no evident fruit?

6 | *Genesis 9:1—11:26*
Psalm 6
Matthew 4:1–17

"Have pity on me, LORD,
for I am weak." (Ps 6:3)

The great beauty of the psalms lies not in their lyricism but in the authenticity of their authors, particularly in the pain and shame and rage that comes through again and again. They're so powerfully human, so real, without the veneer of piety that often covers our suffering because we're afraid that God can't handle our pain. But God honors those honest prayers; indeed, he canonizes them as Scripture for people to pray down through the centuries. They give us permission to pray as we need to: haltingly, stuttering and overwhelmed, sometimes brimming with anguish and exhaustion. Maybe you're not ready yet to submit to God. Maybe you can't ask for his will to be done. Maybe all you can do is stand before your crucified God and rage against him. Maybe your sorrow is too great for any words of trust. Still, that is a good prayer. Because you're offering him your heart, whether you're allowing him to heal and transform it or not. Every honest prayer is a gift of our hearts to God. How blessed we are to know that he wants not immaculate piety but our true selves.

7 | *Genesis 11:27—13:18*
Psalm 7
Matthew 4:18–25

"Go forth from your land, your relatives, and from your father's house to a land that I will show you." (Gn 12:1)

Though he went forth from his land and his father's house at God's command, Abram was not inclined to trust God completely. Instead of leaving all his kin (as God commanded), he brought Lot along. Lot's presence became an obstacle to Abram, who wasn't given the land God had promised him until Lot was gone (Gn 13:14–17), and who was eventually dragged into local rivalries and battles (Gn 14) by a cousin who shouldn't have been there in the first place. Abram failed to trust God to provide during the famine, so he abandoned the promised land for Egypt, where he lied to Pharaoh and endangered Sarai. There too he likely met Hagar, against whom he would later sin so grievously because of his refusal (once again) to trust God (Gn 16). Each time Abram failed to trust God fully, there were consequences. Abram's story shows us God's faithfulness in the midst of our refusal to trust. Like him, when we grasp at control and refuse to trust God, we always end up making trouble for ourselves.

8 | *Genesis 14–15*
Psalm 8
Matthew 5:1–12

"Lord God, what good will your gifts be, if I keep on being childless?" (Gn 15:2, NAB)

Abram's first prayer was a raw, vulnerable complaint against God — one that resonates strongly in everyone who has tried to follow the Lord. What good are your blessings, we so often ask, if you don't give me what I really want? God's response was unsurprisingly enigmatic. He told Abram that his descendants would be as the stars in the sky. What we often miss about this verse is that the sun hadn't set yet; it set in verse 12. Abram was being asked to trust in what he couldn't see. God provided evidence of his faithfulness by enacting a covenant with Abram; but instead of asking Abram to walk between the split carcasses (to say, "If I break this covenant, let me be like these slaughtered animals," as we will see in Jer 34:18), God passed between them, to say that if Abram (or his descendants) broke the covenant, God would be destroyed. It's a promise that he fulfilled when he let us nail him to the cross.

9 | *Genesis 16–17*
Psalm 9
Matthew 5:13–26

"You are the God who sees me." (Gn 16:13, NIV)

The heroes of the faith, as found here in Genesis, were flawed yet still chosen. This is a significant characteristic of the Hebrew Scriptures. Ancient mythological texts tended to depict a culture's great kings and founders as perfect. Israel, on the other hand, acknowledged that her heroes were deeply flawed. The text doesn't run from that or even excuse it, though we often assume their behavior must be approved because it's in the Bible. But most of the time what we struggle to accept isn't being put forward as a model by the text; it's just a grimacing account of what actually happened. As with many other events in Scripture, Abraham's treatment of Hagar ought to disturb us. Still, God ultimately brought good for her out of the whole vile situation. "You are the God who sees me," she said, speaking hope into the lives of survivors down through the ages. God saw her and cared for her. He made a nation of her descendants. But in doing so, he didn't abandon Abraham and Sarah because they were cruel and faithless (and broken and suffering). He remained faithful.

10 *Genesis 18–19*
Psalm 10
Matthew 5:27–37

"If your right eye causes you to sin, tear it out and throw it away." (Mt 5:29)

Lot was *not* a hero. He first appeared as evidence of Abram's unfaithfulness (Gn 12:1–4). Then he took the better portion of land that should have been Abram's (13:10–12). After that he got caught up in a war he could have avoided and dragged Abram into that, too (14:12–16). And in his last appearance in Scripture, he was drunk and sleeping with his daughters. He may have been "righteous" relative to the men of Sodom and Gomorrah (2 Pt 2:7–8), but that is a very low bar. Which means when we read of his plan to save strangers by sending his daughters out to be sexually assaulted, there is nothing in the text requiring that we approve of this selfish, callous cruelty. Lot wasn't saved because he was virtuous; he was saved as a favor to Abraham (19:29). Not everything Scripture recounts is proposed as good and holy. If it strikes you as horrific, it may be because the author thought it was horrific, too.

11 | *Genesis 20–21*
Psalm 11
Matthew 5:38–48

"So be perfect, just as your heavenly Father is perfect." (Mt 5:48)

Matthew 5:48 tells us to "be perfect." The parallel text in the Gospel of Luke (6:36) says "be merciful" or "be compassionate" rather than "be perfect." It's tremendously consoling to realize that when Jesus invites us to perfection, it doesn't mean being immaculate; it means sharing in God's nature, which requires mercy. It's also incredibly challenging, because while perfection seems an unattainable standard, mercy isn't. Though forgiveness may seem impossible at times, it's not a feeling. Mercy starts with our choices and then transforms our feelings. And we can all choose — a thousand times a day, if necessary — to forgive again. How have you failed be merciful as the Father is merciful? Can you meditate on that not as a condemnation but as an invitation?

12 | *Genesis 22–23*
Psalm 12
Matthew 6:1–18

"The promises of the LORD are sure." (Ps 12:7)

For many of us, the story of Isaac's sacrifice is so familiar that we forget to be horrified at Abraham's willingness to slaughter his son. We've been told to admire his obedience, so we overlook what that obedience entailed. But when we consider that God commanded murder, the whole scene begins to look far more like a cautionary tale of religious extremism than a sweet parable of obedience. Here's what we have to remember: God had promised Abraham that he would have descendants *through Isaac* (see Heb 11:17–19). Abraham had refused to trust God before, but he had learned his lesson and he knew: Isaac would survive this day. God would be faithful. Maybe he would prevent Isaac's death. Maybe Isaac would be raised from the dead. But at the end of the day, Isaac would be alive. This is why Abraham was able to trust despite the horror of what was asked of him, despite the three full days he had to change his mind. That's why we can trust, too. Whatever God asks (and it can be a lot), he has promised us eternity. He's promised us himself.

13

Genesis 24:1—25:18
Psalm 13
Matthew 6:19–34

"As for me, I trust in your merciful love." (Ps 13:6, Revised New Jerusalem Bible)

The progression of this psalm is so powerful: first anguish and desperation, then pleading. Finally (though we're given no indication that the psalmist's circumstances have changed), he sings of trust and joy. The feelings of abandonment and sorrow likely persist, but the psalmist chooses to trust and rejoice. Because trust and joy aren't feelings. They're choices we can make even in great suffering. The prayer of Jesus calls us to the same kind of trust, particularly with the petition, "Give us this day our daily bread." Many of us spend considerable time grieving over anticipated sorrow that may or may not come to pass. But even if it does, we're not better prepared for it for having suffered it for years ahead of time. Let this petition teach you to suffer only the present pain, not wallowing in the ugliness of the past or anticipating the sorrow sure to come. Instead, ask for today's bread and live in today's hunger rather than borrowing trouble.

14 | *Genesis 25:19—26:35*
Psalm 14
Matthew 7

"The poor have the L*ORD* *as their refuge." (Ps 14:6)*

The brief account of Rebekah and Isaac's twenty-year struggle with infertility makes those twenty years of suffering seem paltry, as though they could fairly be summarized as, "Rebekah was sterile. Isaac prayed. Rebekah got pregnant." Perhaps Isaac and Rebekah had begged God for a child every day of those two long decades, feeling so bitterly the long-unanswered prayer and never realizing that God was answering their prayer in his own time, waiting until the right moment to give them their longed-for children. Or perhaps Isaac truly hadn't prayed for a child for those first twenty years, thinking he could handle the problem without God's help. How often do we do that? Fight for years to make things work and never surrender it to the Lord? Not just beg but really surrender, trusting him even if his will doesn't line up with ours? When Isaac submitted, his prayer was answered. That may not happen to us — at least not the way we hope — but prayer changes things, not least because it changes us.

15 | *Genesis 27–28*
Psalm 15
Matthew 8:1–17

"He stretched out his hand and touched him." (Mt 8:3)

I once heard a bishop tell a story of working in New York at the beginning of the AIDS epidemic. He was called in to minister to a man with AIDS who told him that the hardest part of the disease was that nobody had touched him without gloves on in months. "All I want is for someone to touch me like a normal human being." Terrified of this unknown disease, the young priest didn't do it. Thirty years later, preaching on Jesus touching the leper, he said, "It's the greatest regret of my life. That man died without feeling another loving touch, and it's my fault." Who are the lepers you're refusing to touch?

16 | *Genesis 29–30*
Psalm 16
Matthew 8:18–34

"The LORD saw my misery." (Gn 29:32)

Oh, the grasping and suffering of these poor, broken women in Genesis, desperate to be loved, to be fruitful, to be secure. It must have broken the Father's heart to watch them hurt one another (and themselves) this way. I want to hold them and tell them — tell you — you are loved. Regardless of your relationship status or quality. You are bearing fruit, even if your home and arms (and bank account and resumé and portfolio) are empty. You may never see the fruit your life is bearing, but God is working it all for good. I love these sisters because I see so much of myself in both of them. Which one do you identify with more?

17 | *Genesis 31–32* *Psalm 17* *Matthew 9:1–17*

"I did not come to call the righteous but sinners." (Mt 9:13)

Jacob is not my favorite biblical figure. He might not even be my favorite son of Isaac. He was deceptive and rather lecherous, a lying polygamist whose favoritism nearly got one of his children killed. But I love him here. I love that he had every reason to fear for his life and the life of everyone he loved, but still he followed God. I love that his trust was tenuous, that he had a thousand safety nets, but he still followed. Whatever was literally happening when he wrestled with an angel, I think this is what God is trying to tell us: It is heroic to wrestle with God. The name *Israel* comes from this wrestling with God, which proves that loving God doesn't make us glib and saccharine, accepting all he sends with a pasted-on smile. We can struggle, as long as in the struggling we follow.

18 | *Genesis 33–34*
Psalm 18
Matthew 9:18–38

"The crowds were amazed and said, 'Nothing like this has ever been seen in Israel.'" (Mt 9:33)

In the last two chapters, Jesus healed a leper, healed a paralyzed servant, healed Peter's mother-in-law, calmed a violent storm, healed two demoniacs, healed a paralytic, healed a woman who had been sick for twelve years, raised a dead girl, healed two blind men, and healed a mute man — in addition to going around curing all the sick and possessed at least twice. That's the context for the crowds' amazement. Try to imagine the feeling of freedom and release and hope they would have been experiencing. Have you ever felt such astonishment at God's power and mercy?

19 | *Genesis 35–36*
Psalm 19
Matthew 10:1–15

"The law of the LORD is perfect, / refreshing the soul." (Ps 19:8)

The psalmist's delight in the law may surprise you. We who have a limited (and possibly prejudiced) view of the law of Moses tend to see it as a series of impossible demands, arbitrary expectations that force the law's followers into failure and hypocrisy, making calculating legalists of its most devoted adherents, while the rest are left feeling like failures. This is a profoundly unchristian view. Remember, the same God who made the law sent his Son to save all people. The giving of the law must, then, have been an act of love from the God who is love. Reading the Old Testament on the law makes that abundantly evident. It's described as a tremendous gift and a source of delight. "The law" is more than rules, of course: It's God's covenant with his people. But it is also rules, and the Israelites chose to find the rules a source of joy. What would it look like for you to embrace God's commandments as refreshing, wise, enlightening, precious, and sweet? Even sexual morality? Even the demands of justice and charity? Even the requirement that your heart be pure and generous, not angry or lustful or envious?

20 | *Genesis 37–38*
Psalm 20
Matthew 10:16–33

"May the Lord grant all your prayers." (Ps 20:6, Revised Grail translation)

Today's psalm is my favorite psalm, especially in the Grail translation:

> May the Lord answer in time of trial. / May the name of Jacob's God protect you. / May he send you help from his shrine / and give you support from Zion. May he remember all your offerings / and receive your sacrifice with favor. May he give you your heart's desire / and fulfill every one of your plans. / May we ring out our joy at your victory / and rejoice in the name of our God! / May the Lord grant all your prayers.

Ask the Spirit to sing this blessing over you. Which part is hardest for you to imagine or accept? Now pray this prayer over an enemy or someone you struggle to love. What blessing is hardest to ask for them?

21 | *Genesis 39–40*
Psalm 21
Matthew 10:34—11:1

"Whoever does not take up his cross and follow after me is not worthy of me." (Mt 10:38)

Joseph must have felt absolutely forsaken — betrayed, enslaved, sexually harassed, falsely imprisoned, and forgotten. We tend to gloss over all this to get to the end of the story, reveling in his beautiful statement of faith, which we'll read later in Genesis 50:20: "Even though you meant harm to me, God meant it for good, to achieve this present end, the survival of many people." But that acceptance and surrender is so much more beautiful when you sit with him in the years of feeling abandoned, choosing to trust God in spite of his silence. Jesus speaks in today's Gospel passage of the need to carry our crosses, and few are more painful than the call to be faithful through years of spiritual darkness, through uninterrupted suffering while God seems distant. How do you trust God when it seems he's abandoned you?

22 | *Genesis 41–43*
Psalm 22
Matthew 11:2–19

"He did not hide his face from me, / but heard when I cried to him." (Ps 22:24, NRSV)

Many of us are familiar with the passion part of this psalm — the part Jesus recited from the cross — but we often neglect the triumph that follows the suffering here. Jesus didn't quote Psalm 22 merely to show how his passion had been foretold, but also to point to the victory that would come through his suffering. Verse 25 shows how the Father had not abandoned him. Verse 27 points to the Eucharist, verse 28 to the conversion of the Gentiles, and verse 30 to the resurrection of the dead. The subtlety of these prophecies makes their fulfillment all the more stunning. But even read outside the context of the passion, it's a beautiful prayer. The psalmist started with a feeling of utter isolation from God but prayed through the anguish and arrived at a place of prayer. What suffering do you need to bring before the Lord for resurrection?

23 | *Genesis 44–45*
Psalm 23
Matthew 11:20–30

"Do not be distressed, and do not be angry with yourselves for having sold me here." (Gn 45:5)

The healing Joseph must have experienced is just incredible: to be able to acknowledge the evil his brothers had done and not only refuse to hate them but even to be grateful for what resulted from it! To insist that they not blame one another! To embrace them and weep! O Lord, give us such healing. What sin or suffering in your life has God so thoroughly redeemed that you can praise him for it now? What sin or suffering are you certain he can't redeem?

24 | *Genesis 46–48*
Psalm 24
Matthew 12:1–14

"The Son of Man is Lord of the sabbath." (Mt 12:8)

When objecting to Jesus' Sabbath healings, the Pharisees weren't just being legalistic. They were trying to avert a catastrophe like the one they had survived centuries earlier. Jews in the sixth century B.C. had broken the Sabbath and been deported to Babylon for it (Jer 17:19–27; Neh 13:17–18). Some who opposed Jesus here may genuinely have been concerned about faithfulness to the law and the threat to national security that might come of disobedience. And yet, every single healing that Jesus initiated took place on the Sabbath. Clearly, he was trying to make a point that the day God has set aside for rest and worship ought to be a gift and not a burden, an invitation to worship and justice and charity, not to legalism. Do you experience Sunday as gift?

25 | *Genesis 49–50*
Psalm 25
Matthew 12:15–37

"I long for your deliverance, O Lord!" (Gn 49:18)

Lying on his deathbed, Jacob was trying to finish his life's work. He promised the coming rule of the tribe of Judah (Gn 49:8–10) and even uttered a curse (49:7) that God would turn to good as the tribe of Levi scattered throughout Israel to serve as priests for the sanctification of the People of God. But the line that strikes me most isn't declared with authority but gasped in pain and exhaustion: the longing for deliverance that Jacob uttered as an aside in 49:18. For Jacob death was a deliverance, though he had no idea what might lie beyond the veil. For all his faults, he had served the Lord and trusted that whatever was coming, God would protect him. What a prayer.

26 | *Philippians 1:1—2:18*
Psalm 26
Matthew 12:38–50

"Life is Christ, and death is gain." (Phil 1:21)

Paul's attitude in his letter to the Philippians is reminiscent of Joseph the Patriarch in yesterday's reading (Gn 50:20), rejoicing at his imprisonment because of the good God was able to do through it. In Paul's case, it meant not only that he got to preach the Gospel to prisoners but also that he was able to preach to guards who then brought the Gospel to Caesar's own household (Phil 4:22). It's incredible the work that God can do through circumstances that we decry. Paul understood this, describing even death as gain for those who live in Christ. What would it look like to live as though that were true? As you read Philippians, keep an eye out for what Paul has to say about joy and about suffering.

27 | *Philippians 2:19—4:23*
Psalm 27
Matthew 13:1–30

"I have learned the secret of being content in any and every situation ... whether living in plenty or in want." (Phil 4:12, NIV)

I have had everything and I have had nothing, Paul says, and I'm telling you, the only thing that brings joy is Jesus. He was writing to a Roman colony originally formed of veterans. Its citizens were given a special privilege of Roman citizenship — an honor that was very unusual outside of Rome itself. To these people who prided themselves on their loyalty, Paul spoke of Jesus as Lord (and thus a threat to Caesar). To these people who prided themselves on their Roman citizenship, he spoke of their true citizenship in heaven (Phil 3:20). To these people who honored Paul but disdained the enslaved — and to their slaves — he called himself a slave (1:1). All this so that he might remind them that only the love of Jesus brings true joy. Not wealth or honor or status — just Jesus. What needs to change in your life for you to experience detachment like this?

28 | *Exodus 1–3*
Psalm 28
Matthew 13:31–53

"Out of joy [he] goes and sells all that he has and buys that field." (Mt 13:44)

Because of his joy. When we give up everything for the Lord, we do it not because we're compelled by shame or duty or ecclesial edicts, but because we've been transformed by joy. The call to discipleship is an invitation to carry your cross, yes, but it begins in love, is sustained by peace, and ends in glory. It's heavy and it's hard and it costs the whole world, but that's true of every love affair. This image is all the more powerful in light of Moses' encounter with God, especially in Exodus 3:7–8. Read it in the second person: I have witnessed *your* affliction and heard *your* cry. But Moses resisted. Consider how many times the great hero of the Exodus objected to God's call. He didn't think he was good enough to serve God *because he didn't trust God.* Do I love God like it's a love affair? Do I live like it's worth everything — like *he's* worth everything? Or am I half-hearted and grudging or shame-faced and put-upon or so full of self-congratulation that I've forgotten to be in love?

29 | *Exodus 4:1—6:27*
Psalm 29
Matthew 13:54—14:21

"I will take you as my own people, and I will be your God." (Ex 6:7)

The Old Testament can be hard to read, but when you're really letting the Spirit speak, there's so much beauty. Look at the promises God made in Exodus 6:6–7. He was speaking to people who were so overcome by helplessness and exhaustion that God's efforts to set them free infuriated them. "I will free you … I will deliver you … I will redeem you," he promised, coming as their redeemer to liberate them physically and spiritually, to bring them into freedom so that they might worship him. And then he promised to take them as his people and to be their God, covenant language that calls to mind Ruth 1:16 and Song of Songs 6:3. Though they refused to trust him, he would not give up on them. He just kept offering them hope, offering them himself. What hope and promise is God speaking into the hopeless places in your life?

30 | *Exodus 7–8*
Psalm 30
Matthew 14:22–36

"Immediately Jesus stretched out his hand and caught him." (Mt 14:31)

It can be very distressing to read about God hardening Pharaoh's heart. It sounds as though God forced Pharaoh to act a certain way and then punished him for it. But the ancients spoke of the will of God in a much more active way than we do. We would say, "He allowed Pharaoh's heart to be hardened." Pharaoh freely rejected God after every plague — after every demonstration of God's great power. Still, God tried to win Pharaoh's heart, reaching out his hand again and again to this man of little faith. The ten plagues were a battle; the battleground was Pharaoh's heart, as God sought to win over Pharaoh and thus all of Egypt. What signs and wonders has God worked in your life that your hardened heart has refused to recognize or remember? Where have you hardened your heart against the word of God?

31 | *Exodus 9–11*
Psalm 31
Matthew 15:1–20

"You heard my voice, my cry for mercy, / when I pleaded with you for help." (Ps 31:23)

Does Exodus 10:16 sound familiar? It's what the prodigal son said when he came back to his father (Lk 15:18). When Pharaoh said it, he wasn't at all repentant — just trying to get out of trouble. So when Jesus used this language in the parable, it was a strong indication that the prodigal son wasn't truly sorry either — just sick of being hungry. Still, the father welcomed him home. God does not care what brings you back to him; he just wants you to come back. Once you've come home, he'll sort out the details.

32 | *Exodus 12–14*
Psalm 32
Matthew 15:21–39

"The Lord will fight for you; you have only to keep still." (Ex 14:14)

Do you see the echoes of creation in the story of the exodus? Water, wind, dry land, divided water, light, darkness — a new creation was being wrought by the redemption of Israel. But the story points forward as well as backward. The People of God were saved through the sacrifice of an unblemished lamb. They were marked with its blood and saved from death, delivered from slavery to Egypt (which always represents sin in the Bible), and brought into the promised land, just as we were saved by the blood of the Lamb and delivered from slavery to sin. The lamb was sacrificed at twilight; when the Lamb was crucified, darkness covered the earth. They ate its flesh just as we eat his flesh. The exodus is the central moment in the Old Testament because it points most directly to the paschal mystery (the passion, death, and resurrection of Christ). By the new exodus accomplished on Calvary, God brought about a world made new, saved from death and set free from the bondage of sin even more fully than in the first exodus from Egypt.

33 | *Exodus 15–16*
Psalm 33
Matthew 16:1–12

"My strength and my refuge is the LORD, / and he has become my savior." (Ex 15:2)

At this point in Exodus, only a month had passed since God had upended the entire natural order for the good of his people. He'd parted the Red Sea so they could cross through on dry ground, and already they were grumbling about God not providing for them because they wanted a snack. There is no mention of their asking God for other food — just of their complaint. This becomes a pattern in the Pentateuch (the first five books of the Hebrew Scriptures); take note of how often you see the word *grumble* in Exodus and Numbers (and then in John 6, too, in connection with different bread from heaven). If only we weren't exactly the same. If only we weren't constantly closing our eyes to the miracles of God's providence and complaining about his refusal to give us things we often haven't even asked for. Point fingers at the Israelites as we may, there's not one fault of theirs that isn't mirrored in our lives.

34 | *Exodus 17–18*
Psalm 34
Matthew 16:13–28

"Whoever wishes to come after me must deny himself, take up his cross, and follow me." (Mt 16:24)

Peter had the most triumphal moment of his life, proclaiming Jesus to be the Son of God and receiving the keys to the kingdom as a result. But when Jesus followed this by explaining what it meant to be the Son of God — that the cross was part of his ministry and would be part of following him — Peter took Jesus aside to insist that the cross wasn't necessary. He rebuked the one he had just proclaimed to be the Messiah and came crashing down from rock to stumbling-stone. But his failures didn't disqualify him; they just meant Jesus had to remind him that to gain the crown, he would have to carry the cross. Peter was a slow learner on this front, but Jesus never gave up on him. Not even when Peter denied Jesus in his hour of greatest need. Jesus won't give up on you. And he won't give up on the person you're most inclined to write off, either. Nobody is beyond redemption.

35 | *Exodus 19–20*
Psalm 35
Matthew 17:1–13

"You will be my treasured possession among all peoples, though all the earth is mine." (Ex 19:5)

The cloud of Exodus 19 is familiar to us from Israel's flight out of Egypt (Ex 14:19–20). This cloud symbolized the presence of God and continued to lead the Israelites in the Book of Exodus. It also covered Moses on Sinai while he spoke to the Lord (Ex 24:15–18). A similar cloud surrounded Jesus, Moses, and Elijah at the Transfiguration (Mt 17:5), making God's presence manifest to Peter, James, and John. Today's passage from Exodus describes the very first Pentecost, when the cloud of God's presence came down upon Sinai as God drew near to his people. Jewish tradition says that God made a marriage covenant with his people when he came to them on Sinai (present in the cloud) and revealed his love. This encounter with God was the purpose of the Passover: God had liberated his people so that they could be in relationship with him. This is the message of Moses' appearance at the Transfiguration, shrouded in a cloud: Through Jesus, God gives us a new exodus, a new Pentecost, and a new marriage feast between the bridegroom Messiah and his people.

36 | *Exodus 21–22*
Psalm 36
Matthew 17:14–27

"Your justice is like the highest mountains; / your judgments, like the mighty deep." (Ps 36:7)

As we begin to read from the Law, there are a few important points to keep in mind: 1) This culture was very different from ours. What seems cruel to us was often a dramatic limitation of violence. In Genesis 34, Simeon and Levi murdered a whole town because their sister had been raped. "An eye for an eye" would have limited them to commensurate punishment. Often the Law seems unjust to us because we don't know enough of the context to understand it.* 2) Slavery in the ancient world was very different from chattel slavery in the Americas. Note Exodus 21:9, where a slave must be treated like the master's daughter. 3) Above all, the Law was intended to protect people and teach them God's love. See especially the tenderness of 22:20–26, where God shows his care for the weak. While reading rules and punishments and descriptions of ceremonies, always ask yourself: What does this tell me about God's love? Scripture is always teaching the love of God, but sometimes you have to look harder than others.

* The idea in Exodus 22:15–16 is that, if this relationship was consensual, neither of them had to be punished; they could just get married. If it was a case of assault that couldn't be proven, the woman could tell her father to refuse the man. She didn't have to marry him but at least had some financial compensation. As we'll see in Deuteronomy 22:25 (where it's clearly assault), the man was executed for it. These laws were intended to protect survivors, and they were much more successful than laws in other societies at the time, most of which said women who were "defiled" must be killed. Though at first glance some of these laws might be quite distressing, it's possible to read them in a much more positive light.

37 | *Exodus 23–24* *Psalm 37* *Matthew 18:1–20*

"Take delight in the L*ORD / and he will give you the desires of your heart." (Ps 37:4, RSV2CE)*

Psalm 37:4 is beautiful — and perilous. Too often people read this promise as a declaration that those who love God will get what they want. "If you desire something, God will give it to you," they insist. That's a dangerous mentality, not merely because it's not true. It also sets us up to treat God as a butler, making our relationship with him entirely transactional until he "fails" us and leaves us doubting his goodness or his very existence. The psalmist is saying that if we delight in the Lord, if he is the desire of our hearts, then we will receive him. This is no prosperity Gospel, but a promise that God will be near you when you seek him. That's much more consoling than the idea that God will give us whatever we want, however ill-advised. If God is God, then he knows better. It might not always be easy to believe that when we feel so deeply a need that he has chosen not to satisfy, but it's always true.

38

Exodus 25–27
Psalm 38
Matthew 18:21–35

"They are to make a sanctuary for me, that I may dwell in their midst." (Ex 25:8)

Even if you find descriptions hard to read, try not to skim Exodus's description of the Ark of the Covenant. Keep this in mind: God delighted in fashioning the place where he would dwell with his people. This points forward to the Incarnation (Ex 25:8 says God will "dwell in their midst," a foreshadowing of Emmanuel, God with us). It points to the Eucharist in the tabernacle (25:30 talks about the bread of the presence). It points back to the garden and forward to heaven (compare 25:18–20 with Gn 3:24, then compare Ex 30:1–3 with Rv 9:13). And it points to the Temple, which points to you (1 Cor 6:19–20), reminding you that you are perfect, beautiful, made exactly to order because the Lord delights in you and longs to dwell in you. As with all of creation, that was the purpose of the Ark of the Covenant: for God to love his people and draw them to love him. Nothing in Scripture is wasted. Just because a certain passage isn't speaking to you right this moment doesn't mean it can't.

39 | *Exodus 28–29*
Psalm 39
Matthew 19:1–15

"And now, LORD, for what do I wait? / You are my only hope." (Ps 39:8)

Jesus tells us himself that some things were allowed in the Old Testament to prepare us gradually for what would eventually be expected. As with many things in God's plan, there was a gradual revelation of truth as regards marriage. After the Fall, polygamy was allowed, as was divorce (though as a protection for women who might want to remarry, it was required that their husbands give them a bill of divorce). Later polygamy was prohibited among the Jewish people. Finally, divorce was banned for the followers of Christ. Doing all that at once would have been too much — the people would likely have scoffed and ignored it all had they been expected to go from a society of polygamy and divorce to an understanding of marriage that required exclusivity and indissolubility. God does this in our lives, too, gradually revealing a call or pulling us gently away from disordered behavior. Have you seen it in your life?

40 | *Exodus 30–31*
Psalm 40
Matthew 19:16–30

"I delight to do your will, my God." (Ps 40:9)

What a beautiful example of testimony we see in Psalm 40:2–4. The psalmist tells how he's suffered, how the Lord saved him, and the joy he now has. Why does he tell it? To give praise to God and to witness to his goodness so that people will "look on in awe" (40:4, NAB). We need to pray through our own testimonies so that (for the glory of God and the salvation of souls) we can share this story:

1. I was …
2. God did …
3. Now I'm …

Can you share your testimony? Whether or not there's a moment of dramatic conversion, your story is a story of God's love. Write it out here so you can share it with others in the future.

41 | *Exodus 32–33*
Psalm 41
Matthew 20:1–16

"You have found favor with me and you are my intimate friend." (Ex 33:17)

The worship of the golden calf was no silly sin but a tragedy, called the second fall in Jewish tradition. If God's covenant with Israel at Sinai was considered a wedding, this episode shows the bride sleeping with another bridegroom just after the wedding. And while it's clear that Israel's motivation was fear and worry and uncertainty, the sin of rejecting God remained. God's response may look like an enraged refusal to fulfill his promise to protect his people, but I think he was inviting Moses to be an intercessor here, a type* of Jesus and a witness of the power of prayer. This incident also showed how the Lord had transformed Moses since his series of refusals before the burning bush (Ex 3–4). Look particularly at 33:14–16. It looks as though Moses was responding irrationally to God's decision to go with Israel. In reality, God said (v. 14) that he would go with Moses (singular), and Moses responded by insisting that God accompany all of Israel. Moses was no longer primarily concerned with himself. That's enormous growth.

* When used in reference to Scripture, the word *type* means a foreshadowing or prefigurement of a New Testament reality. Thus the manna is a type of the Eucharist, David a type of Jesus, and Eve a type of Mary.

42 | *Exodus 34–36*
Psalm 42
Matthew 20:17–34

"The LORD, the LORD, a God gracious and merciful, slow to anger and abounding in love and fidelity." (Ex 34:6)

This selection from Exodus feels terribly familiar, doesn't it? Like it's nearly an exact repetition of what we just read? That's no accident. This repetition shows Israel that nothing of God's goodness was held back after their fall. Their restoration wasn't to a shadow of the former covenant; it was a complete restoration. Because God is faithful even when we aren't. Read these repetitive descriptions as God rereading his old love letters aloud to an unfaithful wife, looking lovingly at her even as she weeps and shakes her head. Read the renewal of his promise to you, his love poured over you anew each time you go to confession.

43 | *Exodus 37–38*
Psalm 43
Matthew 21:1–17

"Why are you cast down, my soul; / why groan within me? / Hope in God; I will praise him still, / my savior and my God." (Ps 43:5, Grail translation)

I *love* the refrain in today's psalm (and yesterday's). Hearing the psalmist lament his life and then pull himself together and remind himself that God is God and there is hope and no reason to despair — and then do it again? And again? There's nothing more relatable. That spiritual self-talk is such a powerful witness: It's OK that you're miserable. But remember the goodness of God! But it's OK that you're still miserable. Thomas Merton called it "the joy of a soul that knows how to hope in the hour that would otherwise seem nothing but despair." Once again, we see that joy and hope are choices, not feelings. There are no pleasant feelings in these two psalms, just choices. In his misery, the psalmist chooses joy and hope. So can we.

44 | *Exodus 39–40*
Psalm 44
Matthew 21:18–32

"Moses did just as the Lord had commanded him." (Ex 40:16)

"As the Lord had commanded Moses," Exodus says again and again — forty times in these two chapters. It might feel needlessly repetitive, but every line of this was an act of obedience, a choice to do God's will even when it seemed excessive or unnecessarily specific. The author makes it clear that every bit of it was an attempt to be faithful after the disaster of the golden calf (and before the disasters of repeated defiance that would follow). This is poetry, proclaiming the healing that followed the renewal of the covenant. In 40:16, we're told, "Moses did just as the Lord had commanded him." This sentiment is repeated seven times. Only *then* was God's presence manifested in the Dwelling. He was always with them, but they were only able to sense and follow him when they were obedient.

45 | *Romans 1–2*
Psalm 45
Matthew 21:33–46

"The daughter of the king is clothed with splendor; / her robes are threaded with gold." (Ps 45:14, Revised Grail translation)

If you started this Bible journey on January 1, today should be Valentine's Day. Every year I'm delighted that this is the psalm for Valentine's Day, where the Lord gushes about your strength and your beauty, calls you glorious, and longs for you to enter his courts as his bride and worship him for all eternity. This Psalm speaks of the wedding feast between God and his people, describing the bridegroom Messiah in the same language of Revelation (19:11–16). This reminder of the all-consuming love each of us was made for is a perfect meditation on the day the world sets apart to revel in romantic love. But it's true whatever day you read it: He is captivated by you. You are loved beyond imagining by a God who died to know you. You are not your sin. You are not your abuse or addiction or abortion or adultery or disability or mental illness or resumé or clothing size or bank balance. You are a totally accepted, deeply loved child of God. That's who you are.

46 | *Romans 3–4*
Psalm 46
Matthew 22:1–14

"Be still and know that I am God!" (Ps 46:11)

How striking that the psalmist's refrain isn't about what God will do — just about who God is. The earth will shake, the mountains quake, but God is with us. He may be silent, but he is with us. He may not seem to act on our behalf, but he is with us. The solution in times of turmoil is to be still and know that he is God.

47 | *Romans 5–6*
Psalm 47
Matthew 22:15–33

"But God proves his love for us in that while we were still sinners Christ died for us." (Rom 5:8)

There are some great lines in this reading from Romans (5:3; 5:8; 5:20; 6:1; 6:11), but what I find most interesting is Paul's understanding of Christians and sin. He doesn't insist that we avoid sin in order to earn God's favor; instead, he points out how little sense sin makes for one who has been reborn in grace. "That's not who you are," he says of sin, as in Colossians 3:3: "For you have died, and your life is hidden with Christ in God." God doesn't ask us to live differently in order to earn his love but because our new identity has taken root and changed us. That's where true virtue comes from: a new identity in Christ, not servile fear. Fear may be a first step, but God doesn't want his children to live in fear. He wants us to delight in the freedom of sons and daughters.

48 | *Romans 7–8*
Psalm 48
Matthew 22:34–46

"He who did not spare his own Son … how will he not also give us everything else along with him?" (Rom 8:32)

This passage at the end of Romans 8 is one of the most comforting in all of Scripture: God is for you. Nothing can change that. If he gave his Son to die for you, there's nothing he won't do for you and nothing he won't endure from you. And he will make all the ugly things in your life work for your good. But note: Paul doesn't say *only* good things happen to Christians. He says God will make all things work for good (eventually) for those who have been conformed to the image of the crucified Christ. This is no glib declaration that only good things happen to Christians but the promise that if you cling to Jesus, all suffering will draw you deeper into his Sacred Heart and make you better able to love him and live in his joy.

49 | *Romans 9–10*
Psalm 49
Matthew 23

"You ... have neglected the weightier things of the law: judgment and mercy and fidelity." (Mt 23:23)

This excoriation in Matthew 23 is not meant to show us how to bring people down a notch, but to demand that we consider how we, too, are blind, how we are hypocrites. Though we like to think the Pharisees were all out-of-touch hypocritical legalists, by and large they were faithful Jews doing the right things. The ones Jesus was criticizing, though, had forgotten that the heart of the law — the whole purpose of the 613 commandments given in the Old Testament — is love of God and neighbor. Jesus didn't condemn their tassels or their tithing or their respect of the sacred, but he called them blind for missing the heart of it all. How are we the same? Do we congratulate ourselves for what we wear or how we pray or what we post or how we vote, while condemning the broken or feeding our hidden vices or holding the Father at arm's length? How have you neglected justice and mercy and fidelity? Having been convicted of your sin and hypocrisy, remember how Jesus ends this critique: with a heart bleeding for love of the lost.

50 | *Romans 11–12*
Psalm 50
Matthew 24:1–28

"Rejoice in hope, endure in affliction, persevere in prayer." (Rom 12:12)

We tend to read today's Gospel passage as a prediction about the end of the world, but most of this discourse was about the coming destruction of Jerusalem in AD 70, not the destruction of the whole world. Jesus foretold the horror of the temple's destruction, when "there will not be left here a stone upon another stone that will not be thrown down." Some of those stones weighed 500 *tons*. This was the level of devastation that was to come: unimaginable violence and the demolition of the temple, the center of the world. But Jesus didn't encourage his followers to fight back, to avenge themselves, or even to try to avert this coming violence. He insisted instead that his followers not fight the Romans, though their pacifism would surely get them branded traitors and cowards. They obeyed, and not a single Christian was reported killed in the fall of Jerusalem. It was through that tragedy that they were dispersed and the name of Jesus preached to the ends of the earth. What battles is the Lord calling you to run from right now?

51 | *Romans 13–14*
Psalm 51
Matthew 24:29–51

"Turn away your face from my sins; / blot out all my iniquities." (Ps 51:11)

This psalm, so heartrending and hopeful, expresses David's anguish when the Prophet Nathan made him confront the wickedness of his adultery, sexual assault, and murder. David was gutted by his guilt ("my sin is always before me," Ps 51:5) but certain that God could make him new. He prayed to be recreated, to be able to dance again (verse 10). Then — not in spite of his sin but (by God's incredible grace) because of it — he would call sinners to the Lord. Fallen humanity limps in pursuit of God. We fall behind or turn away, and suddenly we're back in the pit he pulled us from. Down he comes again, picks us up again, rejoices again. Our God never tires of pouring out his mercy — it's we who tire of seeking it. But if we knew the joy our homecoming brings him, we would never stop reaching out our arms for our Father to pick us up again. When he makes us new, our healing can be a gift to the world. Sin is not the end of our story. It might just be the beginning of a testimony that draws countless people to Jesus.

52 | *Romans 15–16* *Psalm 52* *Matthew 25:1–30*

"Well done, my good and faithful servant. … Come, share your master's joy." (Mt 25:23)

I want to hear the smile in his voice when he looks at me, poor and disheveled as I am, dragging all kinds of brokenness and baggage behind me. It won't matter that he did all the work, that he carried me and fought for me and saved me in spite of myself. It'll only matter that he's pleased. And that I'll hear him, not speaking in a still, small, wordless sense deep in my soul, but in real words, in a strong voice of jubilation. I want to look into his eyes, to see the smile lines that crease his weather-worn skin. I want to hear the voice of the one who made the woman at the well abandon her jar to speak about him to the people who hated her. I want to see what filled Mary's heart even on the darkest nights in Egypt, in Jerusalem, on Calvary. I want to look into the eyes that sent Mary Magdalene running to tell the others. I want to see the love that called Zacchaeus scrambling out of his tree. This is what it's all about: to hear him say "well done" and be welcomed into his joy.

53

Leviticus 1–3
Psalm 53
Matthew 25:31–46

"Whatever you did for one of these least brothers of mine, you did for me." (Mt 25:40)

Leviticus is infamous, a book that everybody knows will bore them to tears. But it is the word of God, not a useless, outdated book of rules, and the Lord is always working through his word. If you're deliberately looking for a takeaway every day, you'll usually find something. Watch for when God tells people to be holy. See if there are sacrifices that remind you of Calvary or the Eucharist. Look for words that are familiar from the New Testament. Take today's discussion of sheep and goats. Sheep aren't treated as better than goats. The only difference in the description of how to sacrifice them is that sheep have a fatty tail and goats don't. We think of goats as bad because of today's Gospel, but the point of Matthew 25 isn't that it's easy to tell the good from the wicked; it's that the good and the wicked often seem exactly the same. It's not by labels or allegiances that they're judged but by their deeds. What we see in Leviticus sheds light on the Gospel — because it's the word of God, of infinite value.

54 | *Leviticus 4–5*
Psalm 54
Matthew 26:1–25

"A woman came up to him with an alabaster jar of costly perfumed oil, and poured it on his head." (Mt 26:7)

These sacrifices in Leviticus seem excessive at first. Every time you inadvertently become unclean, you have to slaughter a sheep? But really, it was God's way of drawing his people back to him again and again. "You failed? Okay. Come visit me in the temple. You can't afford a goat? Okay, two pigeons. No? How about some flour?" That's a $300 sacrifice in today's terms — or 65 cents if that's all people could manage. God just wanted his people to know him, to offer themselves to him, however much they felt they had to give. Whether their gift was $5 in the collection plate or $30,000 of ointment like Mary's gift. What would it take for us to live like Mary here: a life that would make no sense if Jesus weren't God? A life of lavish love that even some disciples would view as irresponsible excess, saying, "What a waste"? How are you recklessly pouring yourself out for Jesus?

55 | *Leviticus 6–7*
Psalm 55
Matthew 26:26–56

"My Father, if it is possible, let this cup pass from me; yet, not as I will, but as you will." (Mt 26:39)

The Last Supper was the beginning of the passion, the Passover meal at which Jesus took the teaching of John 6 and made it reality, turning bread and wine into his Body and Blood. His sacrifice began when he handed himself over in that first Eucharist, and his suffering only increased from there. Jesus' divine nature could have suppressed his anguish in Gethsemane, but he chose to suffer in the fullness of his humanity. His prayer echoed the Our Father ("my Father," "not as I will but as you will"), modeling surrender for us. He continued to love the Father even as his prayer for deliverance went unanswered. And then he looked at Judas (whom he had referred to as a devil in John 6:70) and called his betrayer "friend." Handing himself over in sacrifice had evidently made it possible for him to love his enemy in a radical way. How does all this challenge you to live differently? Can you suffer with greater trust? Pray with greater surrender? Love with greater mercy?

56 | *Leviticus 8–10*
Psalm 56
Matthew 26:57–75

"I trust in God, I do not fear. / What can mere flesh do to me?" (Ps 56:5)

It can't just be Christians who find these passages in Leviticus repetitive, filled with seemingly arbitrary rules; many Israelites likely felt the same. But there was heroic obedience in their choosing to fulfill the command of the Lord when they didn't necessarily understand it. Similarly, there's heroic obedience in my choosing to pay attention to every word even when I can't see the point. After the Israelites' obedience, they saw the glory of the Lord revealed in Leviticus 9:23. When I read deliberately, there is room for the Lord to reveal himself. The high priest bearing the sins of his people was a type of Jesus our Great High Priest; we'll see in 12:6 and 21:10 that the high priest was forbidden to tear his robes, which is why Jesus' robe wasn't torn at Calvary. But in today's Gospel, the high priest did tear his robes, reminding us again that only Jesus fulfills the law perfectly. Today, God may show you some of the significance of Leviticus; if he chooses not to, that's okay, too. It's beautiful just to have given him the gift of your attention even if you don't get anything tangible out of it.

57 | *Leviticus 11–13*
Psalm 57
Matthew 27:1–26

"I, the Lord, am your God. You shall make and keep yourselves holy, because I am holy." (Lv 11:44)

The ritual laws of Leviticus were given for the spiritual good of Israel, inserting mindfulness of God into their eating and mourning and loving. They are about holiness, about belonging to God and becoming more like him. They remind us that today, too, holiness isn't just about great acts of heroism; it's a matter of every moment, even in the smallest of details. But they were also for Israel's physical good: quarantining the sick, keeping newborns out of crowds, requiring the destruction of contaminated food, forbidding the consumption of diseased livestock. This was all decreed so that they might be holy, but also so that they might live. Moral laws are similar: They're not arbitrary restrictions but explanations that sin hurts us. God's law is always for our good.

58 | *Leviticus 14–16*
Psalm 58
Matthew 27:27–66

"But Mary Magdalene and the other Mary remained sitting there, facing the tomb." (Mt 27:61)

Their powerlessness before his corpse must have broken what was still whole in their hearts. Joseph offered all he could, but providing a new tomb (though impossibly extravagant) was cold comfort in the face of a death that all his power and influence couldn't avert. The Gospel of John tells us (19:39) that Nicodemus brought a hundred pounds of myrrh and aloes — enough for a king's burial — but that didn't assuage his grief, either. Mary Magdalene and Mary Salome couldn't even bring themselves to leave when he was first buried, sitting there staring at the tomb, wondering who on earth they were now that he was gone. It's awfully encouraging to know that the great heroes of our faith have felt just as despondent as we do. And to remember that their desolation was short-lived. For all the anguish of Friday, Sunday was coming. And though our graveside vigils may be much longer — decades longer — it's true for us, too. The dead will rise. Our grief will be made joy. Sunday is coming.

59 | *2 John, 3 John* *Psalm 59* *Matthew 28*

"Let us love one another." (2 Jn 5)

I'm always amazed by the gentleness and love of Saint John at the end of his life — the same man who tried to call down fire on a town while he was standing beside Jesus (Lk 9:54). This "Son of Thunder" had become the world's gentlest pastor, a man whose only homily (according to tradition) was, "Little children, love one another." What a difference grace makes, leading him to write so tenderly in his epistles. But there's a hint of that thunder still about him (2 Jn 10), reminding us that God wants to purify our natures, not to destroy them. Sometimes God uses our fiery (or timid or weak) natures for his glory; other times, he heals the wounds that have made us that way and returns us to ourselves. Take a moment to invite the Lord into your brokenness, to heal your wounds and glorify the nature he gave you. Ask him to make you fully yourself, as he did with John. Ask him to show you how he delights in your idiosyncrasies and where he needs you to let him refine you.

60 | *Leviticus 17–18*
Psalm 60
Mark 1:1–13

"Prepare the way of the Lord, / make straight his paths." (Mk 1:3)

There are two major categories of rules in the Pentateuch: ritual and moral. The ritual laws (governing worship and ritual purity) dictated the way the Israelites were expected to behave in the Old Covenant. Moral laws (as in Lv 18) are universal, unchanged in the New Covenant and applicable to all people. This distinction is similar to the difference between changeable disciplines of the Church (e.g., Friday abstinence) as opposed to moral absolutes (e.g., the prohibition of murder). So while these laws governing sexuality stand alongside such ritual disciplines as the prohibition of shrimp or polyester, they aren't the same type of rule and can't be dismissed so easily. Distinctions between moral and ritual law aren't simple to make ("shall be unclean until evening" is a good indicator that it's a ritual law, but other ritual laws have much more severe consequences); mercifully, we have a Church that is led by the Spirit and given the authority to make these judgments.

61 | *Leviticus 19–20*
Psalm 61
Mark 1:14–31

"You shall love your neighbor as yourself."
(Lv 19:18)

Many of the laws of Leviticus are rooted in what we often assume to be a New Testament command: "You shall love your neighbor as yourself" (Lv 19:18). But Leviticus 20:23 gives us a key insight into why some seemingly arbitrary things were forbidden: They were the customs of pagan nations and thus might lead the Israelites into paganism. The problem wasn't tattoos or the trimming of sideburns; the problem was that these practices might be undertaken out of superstition or because one was dabbling in paganism. What are some things in your life that might not be wrong in themselves but could be pulling you in a dangerous direction?

62 | *Leviticus 21–23*
Psalm 62
Mark 1:32–45

"A man with leprosy came to him and begged him on his knees, 'If you are willing, you can make me clean.'" (Mk 1:40, NIV)

It's heartbreaking to read Leviticus' list of defects that disqualified a man from being a priest (or an animal from being a sacrifice). If we look at the blemishes of our souls, not one of us would be eligible. In the New Covenant, it's not quite that Jesus says the broken can serve as priests and be offered as sacrifices; rather, he who is perfect makes us perfect. The broken and the blemished and the unworthy — that is to say, all of us — are invited to be made worthy in him, to serve as priests by our baptism and to offer ourselves in sacrifice alongside him. Nobody is ineligible. Having read Leviticus, we have a much better sense of what's going on here in Mark. The leper (who was forbidden from approaching Jesus and threatening him with contamination) came to Jesus asking not to be healed but to be clean, to be restored to community. And Jesus, who calls even those the world finds most abhorrent, loved the man and made him new.

63 | *Leviticus 24–25*
Psalm 63
Mark 2:1–17

"My soul clings to you; / your right hand upholds me." (Ps 63:8, RSV2CE)

Try praying this psalm (particularly verses 1–9) as a plea: "O God, you are my God, I wish I sought you … I wish my soul were satisfied in you … I wish I believed that you were my help." Pause after each line to imagine what that could look like in your life or to remember a time when it was true. Recognize the parts that you can honestly pray as written and praise the Lord for that!

64 | *Leviticus 26–27*
Psalm 64
Mark 2:18–28

"Ever present in your midst,
I will be your God, and you
will be my people." (Lv 26:12)

Here, at the end of Leviticus, God told his people why he had given them all these rules: to protect them. If they sinned, there would be consequences — the natural consequences of sin as well as punishment from God (which is always for our rehabilitation). But even when they deliberately defied him, he would be with them. He would remember his covenant. He would not abandon them. God's rules are always for our good. And he is faithful even when we aren't.

65 | *1 Corinthians 1–3*
Psalm 65
Mark 3:1–19

"You still the roaring of the seas, / the roaring of their waves, / the tumult of the peoples." (Ps 65:8)

The Corinthians were a mess in just the same way we are. They were a society ravaged by sexual sin, split a thousand ways by a thousand divisions that put each of them in opposition to everyone else. They were obsessed with the *idea* of wisdom and thought very highly of their intelligence, but few of them had any real philosophical acumen, as the greatest intellectuals moved to Athens. They were deeply in need of the peace and wisdom of God. As we read this epistle, it's helpful to ask which of *our* society's evils Paul is speaking directly to. It may be a different specific situation from that of the Corinthians, but there's always some resonance with contemporary struggles — and usually with some sin in our own lives.

66 | *1 Corinthians 4–6*
Psalm 66
Mark 3:20–35

"You are not your own, for you have been purchased at a price." (1 Cor 6:19–20)

"You are not your own, for you have been purchased at a price." Paul was exhorting the Corinthians, calling them to holiness because they owed it to Jesus to live a life worthy of his sacrifice. What a gift these words are when they come to mind in the moment of temptation, when we're about to sin and then remember how our sin has hurt Jesus and what our redemption cost. But I find it even more powerful in the context of the shame that so often follows after repentance, the conviction that our sin has irrevocably corrupted us. To that lie of the devil Paul says, "You are not your sin. Your shame was purchased with the blood of Jesus and destroyed forever. You aren't your failure. You aren't your inadequacy. You are HIS. You were worth the cost."

67 | *1 Corinthians 7–9*
Psalm 67
Mark 4:1–25

"Some seed fell on rich soil and produced fruit." (Mk 4:8)

The beauty of the parables is that they contain layers of meaning well beyond the explanation that may be given by the text. Though we know that the seed is the word of God, God sows more than just his word in our hearts. Read it today as though the seed were heartbreak, allowed by God for our good. When heartbreak happens in a useful, self-sufficient, no-time-to-suffer-gotta-push-through life (the path), it gets brushed aside and bears no fruit. When it falls on a bitter, hardened heart (the rocky ground), it can't pierce the stoniness and bears no fruit. When it falls in a life that's constantly seeking distraction in wealth and pleasure (the thorns), the good things of this world may overshadow our suffering, leaving it little room to bear fruit. But when it falls on empty, broken soil, when it feels as if all there is in your life is heartbreak, when you surrender your broken heart to God, that's when the yield can be miraculous. What a gift that God uses our weakness and brokenness for his glory!

68 | *1 Corinthians 10–11*
Psalm 68
Mark 4:26–41

"Teacher, do you not care that we are perishing?" (Mk 4:38)

Oh, those poor, sweet apostles. "Don't you even care?" they asked, feeling abandoned even with Jesus right there beside them. "Don't you even care?" Martha asked in Luke 10. "Don't you even care?" we ask time and again when God's apparent silence or distance or refusal makes us certain that he's forgotten us. This time, maybe, he was silent because he was waiting for them to ask for help. Or maybe because he knew they would be fine. Or maybe (because he was human) he really was that tired. But the whole time, he was there. He was with them. How often do we interpret his silence as unconcern when he is right there with us, watching over us and holding us close even when we can't feel it? I spent a holy hour meditating on this story once, praying, "Do you not care? Do you not care?" Each time, my eyes landed on the crucifix or the tabernacle. He cared then. He cares now. Just because he's silent doesn't mean he's not right there with you.

69

1 Corinthians 12–13
Psalm 69
Mark 5:1–20

"Go home to your family and announce to them all that the Lord in his pity has done for you." (Mk 5:19)

This is the only time in Mark that Jesus directed someone to tell about his healing — and it was a Gentile who'd been possessed by demons. He doesn't seem like the most qualified candidate for the missions, but Jesus sent him as the first missionary to the Gentiles. And because he had a personal testimony of brokenness and healing, he was remarkably effective: When Jesus came back in Mark 7:31—8:9, the people flocked to him because of the witness of this man. We tend to want to conceal the ugliness of our backstories, but God can use them for his glory. Who needs to hear your testimony this week? Will you let God speak through you, even if it means being vulnerable?

70 | *1 Corinthians 14–16*
Psalm 70
Mark 5:21–43

"Daughter, your faith has saved you. Go in peace." (Mk 5:34)

We spend so much time meditating on the hemorrhaging woman and the dead child that we often miss the selflessness and faith and integrity of Jairus. He had the courage to approach Jesus though his peers were already opposing the Lord. Then, as they were rushing to his daughter, Jesus stopped. Not just to heal, but to chat. With a woman. Who was unclean. How long must their conversation have taken, as Jairus's daughter lay dying? How impatient must Jairus have been? How certain that God's gift to the hemorrhaging woman meant there was less for Jairus? (Have you been there, begrudging people their answered prayers?) And then Jesus called her "daughter" — the only time he did that in any recorded incident — to tell her that she had always been beloved. He spoke also to remind Jairus that this woman, too, was a beloved daughter, that Jairus's was not the only pain that mattered. So Jairus continued to trust, even after he was told his daughter had died. Even as people ridiculed Jesus, refusing to believe in his promise of resurrection. And what a reward there was for that faith.

71 | *Numbers 1–3*
Psalm 71
Mark 6:1–29

"O God, do not stay afar off; / O my God, make haste to help me!" (Ps 71:12, Revised Grail translation)

Though there are more stories in Numbers than in Leviticus, you might not find it an easier read, leaving you once again with the inclination to skim. I try to fight that by praying for the people named and their descendants as I read. Isn't it wild to think that one of these men might be an ancestor of yours? And to consider how precious these faceless men are in the eyes of a God who loves them eternally? It's got me thinking of the millions of unborn babies who go unmourned in this world but are wonderfully alive in the heart of God. And the millions of people who feel forgotten by God but absolutely aren't. Let these names stand as a reminder to you that no one is unseen or unloved.

72 | *Numbers 4–5*
Psalm 72
Mark 6:30–56

"When he disembarked and saw the vast crowd, his heart was moved with pity for them." (Mk 6:34)

It's remarkable to see the restrictions in Numbers that kept the people from direct contact with God, especially when we so casually receive him in his fullness whenever we want. But God was protecting them, unbaptized as they were, from the harm that comes when the sinful seize what is holy — the same way he warns us against receiving communion in a state of sin (1 Cor 11:27–28). At the same time, he was calling them to intimacy. Consider how similar the ordeal for an adulteress (Nm 5) was to the punishment meted out when Israel worshiped the golden calf (Ex 32). Their idolatry was an act of adultery against the God who had offered himself as their bridegroom. He had created them for relationship with him, and the rituals of the law were designed to draw them deeper into that relationship, but a world still marred by original sin couldn't handle the fullness of God's glory. What a gift to live in the New Covenant, where ritual draws us to the heart of God without the barrier of original sin, where this marital relationship with the Lord is fully realized through the sacrifice and resurrection of Jesus.

73

Numbers 6–7
Psalm 73
Mark 7:1–23

"What comes out of a person, that is what defiles." (Mk 7:20)

Having read Exodus and Leviticus, we have a better sense of what Jesus was talking about in Mark when he drew distinctions between God's (many) commandments and the (even more numerous) traditions of the Pharisees. The disciples still didn't realize that Jesus had such authority. That's why when he went a step further and declared all foods clean (ending the ritual demands of a Jewish diet), they thought it must have been a parable. Surely he couldn't have been denying the necessity of ritual purity! But the ritual purity laws had been established to draw the People of God toward the purity of heart Jesus was preaching. And now he made it clear that in calling the people to conversion, he wasn't just advocating a return to Sinai and its purity but inaugurating an entirely New Covenant. The moral laws would persist, but ritual laws would be fulfilled by his perfect sacrifice, and the Christian life wouldn't be governed by them as the life of Israel had been.

74 | *Numbers 8:1—10:10*
Psalm 74
Mark 7:24–37

"At the direction of the LORD they pitched camp, and at the LORD's direction they broke camp." (Nm 9:23)

Numbers 9:22–23 is so convicting, telling of the faithfulness with which the Israelites followed God during their trek through the desert. If only they could say that of us. The call of the Lord isn't always as clear for us as it was for them with the pillar of cloud or of fire, of course. Except when it is — when the Church tells us exactly what to do. Or when our state in life requires something of us. What are the pillars of fire and of cloud through which God is clearly speaking to you?

75 | *Numbers 10:11—12:16*
Psalm 75
Mark 8:1–26

"The people complained bitterly in the hearing of the Lord." (Nm 11:1)

Numbers 11 makes the hard work of reading the last ten chapters so worth it. Israel had been camped at Mount Sinai for nearly a year, learning what God was asking of them. Finally, they set out again, following the miraculous pillars of fire and cloud. And almost immediately they were complaining — complaining of having been rescued from slavery and genocide. Why? Because manna was boring. They were willing to sell their souls for cucumbers. They had miraculous bread from heaven (bread that, like the body of Jesus, had to be broken in order to save them, as we see in verse 8). But they hated it because though it filled their bellies, it didn't satisfy their appetites. How have we refused to let God satisfy us? How have we longed to sell our souls for cucumbers? And how have we regretted our pleas, like the Israelites (vv. 18–20), when God relented and gave us what we asked for?

76 | *Numbers 13–14*
Psalm 76
Mark 8:27–38

"Why are you disobeying the LORD's command? This will not succeed!"
(Nm 14:41, NIV)

Though they had just witnessed his earth-shattering love for them, the Israelites still didn't trust God. They refused to be obedient. When the scouts who had been sent to determine a strategy for conquering the land returned with warnings of doom instead, the people believed them. They said it would have been better for them to die in the desert than to take possession of the land that God was able to give them as surely as he had freed them from Egypt. So they got what they asked for: death in the desert. God had hoped to lead them straight to the promised land, but they weren't ready. He allowed them forty years in the wilderness to purify Israel of the evil they'd absorbed in Egypt. It seemed like revenge, but this wandering was for their good, to purify them (though it would have been so much easier if they had trusted and obeyed when first given the chance). You've likely seen the same thing in your life, when you've defied the Lord and he's still worked it for good (eventually). Praise God that he is faithful even when we aren't.

77

Numbers 15–16
Psalm 77
Mark 9:1–32

"It is good that we are here!" (Mk 9:5)

Tradition has it that the Gospel of Mark was written by Saint Peter's secretary, John Mark, possibly while Peter was in prison awaiting death (1 Pt 5:13). It explains Mark's sense of urgency (using the word "immediately" forty-one times), if Peter expected to be executed soon. It also makes sense of Mark's focus on action, given what we know of Peter. As you read Mark's Gospel, watch for little reminders that Mark was getting his story from Peter. "He hardly knew what to say, they were so terrified" is clearly Peter's sheepish recollection of the time he saw the two greatest men in Israel's history standing with God the Son, heard the voice of God the Father — and could only babble about tents. Though he likely suggested the tents because it was the Feast of Tabernacles (when the Jews lived in tents to remember their time in the desert), there was more to it. For all he was exhausted and confused and terrified, he knew it was good to be with Jesus. "I'm not going anywhere," he said, knees knocking. "I'm glad to be with you." Peter was never very smooth, but he was Christ's, which matters far more.

78 | *Numbers 17–18*
Psalm 78
Mark 9:33–50

"If anyone wishes to be first, he shall be the last of all and the servant of all." (Mk 9:35)

The word *way* is used seven times in Mark 8–10, indicating that Jesus and his disciples were on the way to Jerusalem for Jesus' sacrifice. Every time we see this word, we should think of the Way of the Cross, of Jesus who is the Way to heaven. This background of Calvary and eternity makes their squabbling here all the more disturbing: As they took up their crosses, they argued about whose was heavier, whose more impressive. They made discipleship a competition, even while walking behind Jesus to Calvary. And they made service (and their coming priesthood) about power, exactly the error Moses was fighting in our readings from Numbers for the last two days. How do we wield our crosses as weapons? How do we exploit our service for power? What needs to change for us to accompany Jesus more worthily to Calvary?

79 | *Numbers 19:1—22:1*
Psalm 79
Mark 10:1–31

"Help us, God our savior, / on account of the glory of your name." (Ps 79:9)

Moses' error in Numbers 20 seems minor until we see the gravity of the punishment. There must be something we're not seeing. Maybe it's Moses' implication that the water would come through *his* power (v. 10). Maybe it's that he was told to speak to the rock and instead he struck it (twice), turning a sign of God's gentle providence into an act of violence. Regardless, it's clear that Moses knew what he was doing, otherwise the punishment wouldn't have been so severe. In chapter 21, the Israelites grumbled again, with dire consequences. The Hebrew that's often translated as "the Lord sent snakes" might be better rendered "the Lord stopped holding back the snakes." God gave them a glimpse of what their time in the desert would have looked like without his protection. When he instructed his people to look upon the bronze serpent for healing, he was saying, "Turn your eyes toward heaven and remember what you would suffer were it not for my loving mercy." This points to the passion, telling us to look upon Jesus crucified and come to him who died the death we deserved (Jn 3:14–15).

80 | *Numbers 22:2—24:25*
Psalm 80
Mark 10:32–53

"I could not of my own accord do anything, good or evil, contrary to the command of the Lord." (Nm 24:13)

God warned Balaam not to be swayed by Balak's offer of riches, but eventually allowed him to go prophesy to Balak (likely risking his life). Balaam had insisted that no amount of treasure could induce him to do anything contrary to God's command — great or small, *good* or evil — but as he went, Balaam seems to have been tempted, either by greed or fear. To protect his master from the avenging angel of the Lord, Balaam's donkey balked, leaving his master furious at the obstacle that was truly his salvation. How often do we fail to see our thwarted plans as an act of God's providence? Here, God's hand was clearly at work. The donkey served to purify Balaam's intention so that he was strong enough to speak only the truth to Balak, no matter how many times Balak awkwardly suggested that perhaps the truth would change if Balaam prayed on a different mountain. Because of his (ultimate) faithfulness, Balaam was given a word of prophecy that foretold the Nativity from afar (Nm 24:17). God, make us obedient like Balaam (even if you have to send a talking donkey to make it happen).

81 | *Numbers 25–26* *Psalm 81* *Mark 11:1–14*

"Hosanna! Blessed is he who comes in the name of the Lord!" (Mk 11:9)

There is so much that we miss on Palm Sunday if we're not steeped in the Old Testament. The palms remind us of the Jews greeting their conquering hero (1 Mc 13:51) and celebrating the purification of the temple (2 Mc 10:7). The cloaks strewn on the path serve to acclaim Jesus as king (2 Kgs 9:13), while the colt is reminiscent of David designating Solomon as his heir by sending him to ride through the streets of Jerusalem on David's mule (1 Kgs 1:33). Jesus also came into the city from the Mount of Olives, as the Messiah was expected to (Zec 14:4–9). Let this be a word of encouragement if you've been struggling with the Old Testament. It's the word of God through which the Spirit speaks to our hearts, but it's also the only way we can ever understand the New Testament.

82 | *Numbers 27–28*
Psalm 82
Mark 11:15–33

"I shall ask you one question. Answer me." (Mk 11:29)

Jesus said, "Answer me, and I will tell you," not, "Answer *correctly* and I will tell you." He was asking so little of them: "You don't have to get this right. You just have to be willing to listen, willing to engage." But they weren't interested in an answer, just in furthering their agenda. So they refused to reply, and he told them he wasn't going to play their game (though he went on to answer their question in the parable that follows). How often do we demand answers from God without being willing to listen? How often do we lament dryness in prayer when we treat him not as a person to be known but a problem to be solved? What other questions might the Lord ask that you would be unwilling to answer? Can you be honest with him today?

83 | *Numbers 29–30*
Psalm 83
Mark 12:1–27

"Repay to Caesar what belongs to Caesar and to God what belongs to God." (Mk 12:17)

Those who quote this verse are usually focused on the first half of the axiom — on what is due the state. But Jesus was calling them to more, telling them to give to Caesar what had Caesar's image and to God what had God's image. We who are made in the image and likeness of God, then, owe him our whole selves. That's a far bigger challenge than paying our taxes.

84 | *Numbers 31–32*
Psalm 84
Mark 12:28–44

"My heart and flesh cry out / for the living God." (Ps 84:3)

There is a lot of slaughter coming up in our reading of the Old Testament. And there are lots of different ways of understanding it. Maybe dying at that moment, in that way, was the only way some people would be saved eternally. Maybe the command to kill everybody was a deterrent, since the Israelites wouldn't want to go out conquering the whole world if it meant that much bloodshed. Certainly, Israel's only shot at resisting the allure of paganism was by remaining separated from the nations. But it's also okay to look at this and say, "I don't know what's going on here. I find it really upsetting. But I trust that God is good even when I don't understand what he's doing, both in my life and in salvation history. And I believe that it will be made clear when I see him face to face."

85 | *Numbers 33–34*
Psalm 85
Mark 13:1–23

"Justice will march before him, / and make a way for his footsteps." (Ps 85:14)

All the geographical details of this section of Numbers can make for tedious reading, but one thing God is telling us here is that he sees us. He knows where we are, physically and emotionally and spiritually. He's with us in all the little details. He doesn't abandon us, even when he seems distant. He's leading, even when we can't see him.

86 | *Numbers 35–36*
Psalm 86
Mark 13:24–37

"On the day of my distress
I call to you, / for you will
answer me." *(Ps 86:7)*

Take a look at the trajectory of Psalm 86. It begins with anguished pleading, then moves into praise, then a longing to do God's will, then thanksgiving, and finally more pleading. I imagine the psalmist catching himself wallowing in self-pity (however legitimate) and trying to shake himself out of it by refocusing on the goodness of God and his desire to do God's will. Remembering eternity and trying to praise in suffering are good things — but it's also good to pour out your brokenness to God. Can you pray according to this schema, with praise and surrender and thanksgiving mixed in with the cries of pain? Try it today.

87

2 Corinthians 1–3
Psalm 87
Mark 14:1–21

"As Christ's sufferings overflow to us, so through Christ does our encouragement also overflow." (2 Cor 1:5)

I find Paul's description of his anxiety in 2 Corinthians 1:8 so encouraging. He was "utterly weighed down," despairing of his life. But in the midst of that soul-shaking anxiety, Paul fixed his eyes on Jesus. He who had made his home in the Lord (Ps 87:7, NAB) was able to find peace even in the face of what seemed to be certain death. It was in the wake of this unexpected rescue that he wrote 2 Corinthians 1:3–7, as close as Saint Paul ever gets to gushing. He who had been encouraged (or "comforted") in his suffering was now so filled with confidence in God that he sang of the way that his suffering had become a gift to strengthen and encourage other Christians. Can you see any of your suffering (past or present) as a gift to others? How does that change your approach to pain while you're enduring it?

88 | *2 Corinthians 4–6*
Psalm 88
Mark 14:22–52

"This momentary light affliction is producing for us an eternal weight of glory." (2 Cor 4:17)

Paul suffered but still trusted. Afflicted, perplexed, persecuted, struck down, but refusing to despair, he trusted that he was not abandoned. And then he tells us he was not discouraged (though we'll find out in chapter 11 that his sufferings included beatings, imprisonments, scourgings, shipwrecks, starvation, and more). For all that he'd endured, he called it a "momentary light affliction" and saw the "eternal weight of glory" wrought by all his suffering. God, give me perspective like that in suffering!

89 | *2 Corinthians 7–9*
Psalm 89
Mark 14:53–72

"God … encourages the downcast." (2 Cor 7:6)

Compare the talk of encouragement in 2 Corinthians 7:6–7 with what Paul says in 1:3–7. It is "God who encourages the downcast," but he often does it through others. He provides for us, but he often does it through others. He calls us to conversion, but he often does it through others. It's a gift to receive that encouragement, provision, or conversion. It's also a gift to be the one through whom God supplies it.

90 | *2 Corinthians 10–11*
Psalm 90
Mark 15:1–20

"Make us glad for the days you have afflicted us, / for the years when we saw evil." (Ps 90:15, NAB)

While most translations indicate that the text of Psalm 90:15 means "give us joy for as many days as you afflicted us," I've always used the NAB and read this verse as "make us thankful for the days when you afflicted us." Teach us through this affliction, Lord. Let us so trust in you that we can be grateful even during the hardship. Help us, one day, to see just what you were doing in our loneliness and anxiety and exhaustion and suffering and grief. But if not, let us still be grateful because we know you are good, even when we don't know what you're doing. The God who calls the ugliest day in history "Good Friday" can make you grateful for the suffering in your past — or the good he's brought out of it — as well. It might not happen on this side of eternity, but it's worth taking to prayer, trying to trust that it's possible even when you're not there yet.

91 *2 Corinthians 12–13*
Psalm 91
Mark 15:21–47

"Because he clings to me I will deliver him." (Ps 91:14)

This is one psalm that most English-speaking Catholics are quite familiar with because of its use in the hymn "On Eagle's Wings." In the Orthodox Church, similarly, this is the opening psalm of the funeral liturgy. Because you probably associate it with funerals, you likely understand intuitively that this promise of prosperity must be read as a promise of eternity, not an assertion (to a people constantly beset by attempted genocide and agonizing loss) that nothing bad would ever happen to them (as the false prophets claimed in Jeremiah 5:12). The psalmist insists that those who cling to the Lord will be delivered, but God's deliverance sometimes comes only after death. Certainly, Jesus was clinging to the Lord during his passion. Onlookers believed that he had been abandoned, but Jesus knew (even in his anguish and desolation) that the Father was with him. There are times when we haven't yet been delivered, but we're still able to sense God's tender care. What does that look like in your life?

92 | *Deuteronomy 1–3*
Psalm 92
Mark 16

"The Lord, your God, carried you, as one carries his own child." (Dt 1:31)

Think of the Book of Deuteronomy as Moses' last time standing before the Israelites, reminding them of all they'd come through together and all that God had done for them. There's a real fondness in Moses here that we don't see elsewhere, and the tenderness of God is much more evident than in the rest of the Pentateuch. There's a summary of the past and some modifications to the law because of the hardness of Israel's heart, but there's also just lots of pleading from a father to his children to live as he taught them and be saved. In 1:31, Moses reminds the people that though they had been exhausted in their decades of wandering, feeling lost and abandoned, God was carrying them all the while. Imagine Moses' voice breaking as he speaks to the nation he has so loved, the nation he soon won't be able to guide anymore.

93 | *Deuteronomy 4–5*
Psalm 93
Luke 1:1–38

"You shall finally return to the LORD, your God, and listen to his voice." (Dt 4:30)

What a consoling passage in Deuteronomy, as God tells us that everything that happens (our redemption, our punishment, the law) is because of his love. He will even use our separation from him to draw us near again. How comforting this must have been to the Jews who read it during the Babylonian captivity. How much the more striking when the angel declared unto Mary, and she realized that the God who asks us to seek him is always the one running after us, even to the point of coming into our world, becoming one of us to bring us back to himself. What kind of God is born in a stable and laid in a feed trough? What kind of king chooses to become a refugee? What kind of Messiah lives in poverty and dies in agony? The same God whose backward, messed-up reasoning turned the darkness of that Friday into the glory of the empty tomb. The same God who pours out upon us his reckless, fierce, tender, consuming, unconditional, life-changing, sacrificial love, from Genesis even till today.

94 | *Deuteronomy 6–8*
Psalm 94
Luke 1:39–80

"Blessed be the Lord, the God of Israel. / He has come to his people and set them free." (Lk 1:68, ICEL)

After decades of praying for a child, Zechariah had lost hope. When Gabriel promised him an answer to his prayer, Zechariah demanded proof and was struck dumb. This punishment was intended to rehabilitate him, to give him space for silence and prayer, and it surely also humbled him, as he was pushed out of his role in the community. It seems (from the way they interacted with him about John's name) that Zechariah's sudden disability had convinced his neighbors that he'd lost his hearing or his mind. Zechariah must have been counting down the days till he got his voice (and his life) back. Then John was born, and Zechariah was still mute. Perhaps his voice would never return. It may well have seemed that God had forsaken him. Would he still trust God? He could disobey the Lord and name the child after himself. Or he could trust that God was still good, even if he felt distant. He could cling to hope. Zechariah was faithful, his voice was returned, and he erupted in praise of God who had already come (in the womb of Mary) to set his people free.

95

Deuteronomy 9–11
Psalm 95
Luke 2:1–21

"The Lord ... chose you ... from all the peoples." (Dt 10:15)

Our lives are much like the promised land: It's all gift. It's all grace. We earn nothing, but still God pours out in generosity. Because of his great love for Israel, God led them into a land where everything was given them. Which sounds wonderful, but it also meant that they had to rely on Providence, recognizing that no matter how hard they worked, everything they received — pleasant or unpleasant — was a gift. Often it's harder to receive than to earn. Certainly it takes far more trust. But living from gratitude changes everything. If we recognize that everything is gift, we not only trust that good things will come, we also begin to trust in the will of the giver, in his choice of gift and in his timing. If everything is earned or deserved, we become impatient and demanding, easily devastated by unrealized hopes. True hope isn't expectation but trust in God who works all things for good. And we only learn to trust when we exercise gratitude, perhaps even as a discipline. What would intentional gratitude look like in your life?

96 | *Deuteronomy 12–14*
Psalm 96
Luke 2:22–52

"Now, Master, you may let your servant go in peace." (Lk 2:29)

Imagine the longing of Simeon that erupted in such joy when he recognized Jesus at last, after a lifetime of waiting, after his people had endured four hundred years of silence from heaven, after all of human history separated from the Lord. Taking Jesus in his arms, he exulted. A lifetime of unanswered prayers had prepared him to receive the longed-for Messiah. The desired of all nations was before him, the only joy of every human heart. "Now, Master, you may let your servant go in peace," he said. Having seen Jesus, all his suffering and loneliness and longing was worth it. Having seen Jesus, he could die happy. That was all he wanted.

97 | *Deuteronomy 15–17*
Psalm 97
Luke 3:1–22

"You are my beloved son, with you I am well pleased." (Lk 3:22)

The baptism of Jesus forces us to confront the scandal of the sinless God-man being bathed in the same waters that were symbolically washing away the people's sins. Perhaps this is why Luke's Gospel seems to skim past it. But he couldn't fail to mention the Spirit who descended upon Jesus to anoint him as Messiah and Lord. He couldn't help but speak of this manifestation of the Trinity, nor leave out the beautiful words that came down from the Father: "You are my beloved Son; with you I am well pleased." Each time we hear these words, we must pause and ask the Father to speak this truth over us as well, as he did on the day of our baptism. "You are my beloved son, my beloved daughter. With you I am well pleased." By our baptism, this has become true. Jesus has delivered us from the anguish of unknowing, from the futility of a life of sin, from the guilt and despair of life without Christ. We are no longer orphans but sons and daughters of the Father, who is so terribly pleased with us.

98 | *Deuteronomy 18–20* *Psalm 98* *Luke 3:23–38*

"He has remembered his mercy and faithfulness." (Ps 98:3)

Deuteronomy 18:15 is central to the Jewish understanding of the Messiah: He would be a prophet like Moses to whom the people would listen. This is what people in the Gospel meant when they wondered if John the Baptist might be "the Prophet" (Jn 1:21) — not just *a* prophet but the foretold Mosaic Messiah. And when the Father spoke from the heavens at the Transfiguration and said, "Listen to him" (Lk 9:35), he verified that Jesus was the Prophet, the one God's people must listen to. For nearly 1,500 years, the People of God awaited the fulfillment of this passage. But God was laying the groundwork, preparing the way for one who was not just a prophet like Moses but far more than anything they could have asked for or imagined. When Jesus came, God's people were seeking freedom from the Roman oppressor; never did they dream of freedom from sin and death. They were longing for bodily healing but had no idea they could ask for their broken hearts to be made new. They mourned the dead without ever hoping they would be restored to life. But the Messiah was coming. And when he came, everything would change.

99 | *Deuteronomy 21–23*
Psalm 99
Luke 4:1–13

"You shall not put the Lord, your God, to the test." (Lk 4:12)

Satan was trying to be so clever, quoting Scripture at the Son of God. Here he quotes Psalm 91:11–12, which might have been rather compelling had Jesus not known the context so well. Look up Psalm 91:13. The very verses the Serpent was quoting were followed by a promise that God's faithful ones would trample upon snakes and dragons. When we are steeped in Scripture, we're able to see the ways people take it out of context to distort God's word.

100 | *Deuteronomy 24–26*
Psalm 100
Luke 4:14–44

"He has anointed me to bring glad tidings to the poor." (Lk 4:18)

I cannot even imagine the electric feeling in the air when Jesus proclaimed this Scripture in the synagogue. And after reading this messianic passage, he just sat down (which was a posture of authority) and said, in effect, "This is what I'm going to do." He had come to bring glad tidings to the poor, to proclaim liberty and forgiveness to captives and those in exile, to set the oppressed free and bring a jubilee of mercy and rebirth. But they insisted that he be the Messiah *they* wanted, that he serve them and demand nothing. And when he refused, they tried to murder him. Today, contemplate how you use the Lord and reject him, how you claim him as Lord while refusing to be set free from bondage to sin and shame and selfishness. Can you let him be Lord of everything?

101 | *Deuteronomy 27–28*
Psalm 101
Luke 5:1–26

"Because you did not serve the Lord your God with joyfulness and gladness of heart … therefore you shall serve your enemies." (Dt 28:47–48, RSV2CE)

Though Deuteronomy 28 seems to be a series of threats, God wasn't threatening punishment so much as describing what happens when we turn from him. There may not be immediate material suffering, but there is always deep suffering in a life that isn't sustained by the hope and joy and love of the Lord. Deuteronomy 28:47–48 speaks clearly about this: We can't be masters. The question is not will we serve but whom will we serve? Or, rather, whom will we worship? In Hebrew, those are the same word. When we worship money and pleasure and success, we end up becoming slaves of money and pleasure and success. When we worship God, we start as slaves or servants but become sons through the blood of Christ. But even those who reject the law and are placed under a curse (Dt 27:26) will find mercy (as promised in chapter 30) when Jesus takes on our sin and our curse (Gal 3:13) and wins our salvation instead. We can't be masters. The question is not will you serve but whom.

102 | *Deuteronomy 29–30*
Psalm 102
Luke 5:27–39

"Even from there will the Lord, your God, gather you; even from there will he bring you back." (Dt 30:4)

What a perfect group of readings for those of us who are longing for Christ to come again, who feel like exiles in this valley of tears. Luke speaks of the bridegroom who will be taken away, while Deuteronomy promises the end of the exile: "Though you may have been dispersed to the farthest corner of the heavens, even from there will the Lord, your God, gather you; even from there will he bring you back" (Dt 30:4). Psalm 102, meanwhile, expresses so perfectly the anguish we so often feel in this life. May our suffering always teach us to long for the Lord, and may he come again soon.

103 | *Deuteronomy 31–32*
Psalm 103
Luke 6:1–26

"As a father has compassion on his children, / so the Lord has compassion on those who fear him." (Ps 103:13)

Try reading Deuteronomy 32 as though it's an interaction between a father and his child — his deeply loved but petulant teenager who got caught doing something terrible and is grounded as a result. "My dad used to love me so much," Israel seems to say, "and he took such good care of me, and he was so sweet and so kind. And I admit it. I messed up. Bad. But then he totally overreacted, and he ruined my whole life and took away everything I care about and I'm never going to be happy again! The only reason he didn't throw me out on the street is that he's trying to impress his stupid friends!" These wrathful tirades fit so much better with what we know of God's tender mercy if we read them as Israel's perspective (or God speaking in language Israel will understand) and not as his actual loathing for the people he keeps calling his darling (Dt 32:15; 33:5; 33:15).

104 | *Deuteronomy 33–34*
Psalm 104
Luke 6:27–49

"May the glory of the LORD endure forever, / may the LORD rejoice in his works."
(Ps 104:31, RSV2CE)

Listening to the creation story at the Easter Vigil one year, I tried imagining the Trinity delighting in the millennia-long process of creation, being entranced by the beauty of the world he had made and rejoicing in the things he knew would bring us joy. Trace the creation story in Psalm 104 as it moves through each of the seven days of creation and rejoices in all God has done. I wonder what our planet would look like if Christians treated the world as something that brought joy to the heart of God because it is good itself, not *only* because it would be a blessing to us. How can we learn to see the world around us as something delighted in by God? And what difference would that make in the way we choose to live?

105 | *Galatians 1–3*
Psalm 105
Luke 7:1–28

"Blessed is the one who takes no offense at me." (Lk 7:23)

It must have been incredible to watch Jesus raise the dead like this. It must also have been devastating for the grieving members of that crowd when they watched Jesus raise someone else's loved one while theirs stayed dead. But they followed him anyway. Every person who followed Jesus had lost somebody. But they managed to love him even when their dead stayed dead. John the Baptist must have felt this when his disciples came back to him. John was languishing in prison, and his cousin sent word that he was going to work all kinds of miracles for all kinds of people but not liberation for John. Jesus, who had promised at his first public appearance that he would bring liberation to the captives (Lk 4:16), was listing so many other messianic miracles foretold by Isaiah. But he left off the one John needed so desperately. He asked John to trust him even unto death. Can you continue to love God if everybody else's prayers are answered and yours aren't — if none of your dead are raised, none of your hopes fulfilled, none of your relationships healed?

106

Galatians 4–6
Psalm 106
Luke 7:29–50

"Her many sins have been forgiven; hence, she has shown great love." (Lk 7:47)

"Her many sins have been forgiven; *hence,* she has shown great love" is sometimes translated "*because* she has shown great love." The latter makes us more comfortable. We prefer the idea that we've been forgiven because we earned it, because we're good people. But it doesn't fit with the parable. Jesus wasn't saying we can earn mercy or that only really wonderful people are Christians. He was saying that his love is so good, it can even turn our ugliest sin into an avenue for grace. *Because* she had been such a sinner, she loved God all the more. Which doesn't mean we should sin more to get extra grace, of course (Rom 6:1), but that we should praise God who can bring good out of all things (Rom 8:28). We mustn't become discouraged when we fall or write off other people because of their pasts. Instead, let us wonder at a God who is always making all things new, who can turn our greatest shame into glory.

107 | *Joshua 1–3*
Psalm 107
Luke 8:1–25

"They cried to the Lord *in their tribulation: / and he delivered them out of their distresses." (Ps 107:6, DRA)*

Psalm 107 is so beautiful, especially when you examine its structure. Each section talks about a way that God's people suffered (hunger, captivity, illness, natural disaster). Then each section says that they called on the Lord and he rescued them. Then we're told of their rescue and the praise and thanksgiving that followed. This psalm is a perfect prayer in suffering as we remember God's marvels of the past and seek to trust in his coming rescue. And how providential that Psalm 107:23–32 (especially verse 29) is paired with Luke 8:22–25 today. It really helps us see the messianic notes of the psalm, after which we notice the harrowing of hell (vv. 14, 16), the healing power of the word (20), the allusion to the Messiah foretold in Isaiah (33–35), and the divine reversals proclaimed in the Magnificat (40–41). Read this as poetry, with its repeated sins and suffering, the cry to God, the rescue, the thanksgiving. How have you seen this pattern in your life? Which section resonates the most strongly with you?

108 | *Joshua 4–6*
Psalm 108
Luke 8:26–56

"That Your beloved may be delivered, / save with Your right hand, and hear me." (Ps 108:6, NKJV)

It's amazing to hear, as we did yesterday in Joshua 2, of how the people of Canaan were in awe of Israel because of what the Lord had done forty years earlier. But while all of Canaan believed in God's power, only Rahab had responded with trust and not fear. She staked her life on God's power but also on his goodness. And then as the rest of the people were hiding for fear of the power of God, the Jews were asked to do something ridiculous. Rather than attack with military power (and the immense power of God's reputation), they were told to march in silence in a circle around the city. How often does God ask us to do something that seems utterly ridiculous? So often we refuse and realize later what he was trying to do. Whether or not the Israelites understood it, their greatest weapon was the worship of God. This is where all their power came from, and this is what made it possible for Rahab to be brought into Israel and become part of the lineage of Jesus: not just acknowledging the power of God, but trusting him and following.

109 | *Joshua 7–9*
Psalm 109
Luke 9:1–27

"In your great mercy rescue me. / For I am poor and needy." (Ps 109:21–22)

This story from Joshua 7–8 is such a powerful witness of God's ability to turn even our sinfulness to good. Obviously, it would have been ideal if Achan hadn't defied God's command (in a sin whose language — "saw," "greed"/"covetousness," "took" — is so reminiscent of the Fall). But when Achan sinned, God was able to use the consequences of that sin to bring about Israel's victory after they had rooted out the sin (Jos 8:6). Look at how God can use our flaws and failures for our rescue and his glory if only we turn back to him. Do you have moments like this in your life, where you messed up and suffered the consequences but somehow Providence brought good out of that?

110 | *Joshua 10–12*
Psalm 110
Luke 9:28–50

"And all were astonished by the majesty of God." (Lk 9:43)

Can I be very honest with you? I hate all this killing. And I think that's okay. I think it should upset me. While I can give answers about what God was doing in allowing (or even commanding) all this slaughter, it still leaves me profoundly disturbed. And I think it should. I just have to keep trusting that God loved every one of those people just as much as he loved the Israelites. He loves them far more than I could ever imagine. And so, somehow, this was for their good, too. The Bible is a really hard book to read. I'm grateful for a Church that helps us to understand it better. I'm grateful for the knowledge that God is love. I'm grateful that I don't need to have all the answers.

111

Joshua 13–16
Psalm 111
Luke 9:51–62

"He has shown his people the power of his works, / giving them the lands of other nations." (Ps 111:6, NIV)

Though it's not easy to remain focused as you read today's selection from Joshua, pay attention to the sections that tell stories. Focus on Caleb's faithfulness being rewarded, on his daughter's remarkable self-advocacy. And as you plow through the rest, remember that God cared about these very exact boundaries, and he cares about every tiny thing in your life. And pray for the people who live in this land today, for peace and for every heart to be handed over to the Lord.

112

Joshua 17–19
Psalm 112
Luke 10:1–24

"Nothing will harm you." (Lk 10:19)

It's not unreasonable that we usually view Jesus' advice here as being limited to the apostles. But if it's in Scripture, it has value for everyone. What can each of these admonitions mean in our lives? What does it mean to carry no money bag? What does it mean not to move from one house (community or friend group) to another? What does it mean to eat and drink what is offered to us? How can we proclaim the kingdom of God? There's so much more here than just directives from a particular mission two thousand years ago. Notice also what he said to the seventy-two when they returned. "Nothing will harm you," he said, to men who would be tortured and martyred, who would lose everything, who would be rejected by everyone they loved. He wasn't lying. In the end, none of that would be able to harm them. But all that can be miserable when it isn't yet the end. When this is hard to believe, ask the Lord to keep your eyes fixed on the kingdom in the midst of an ugly, awful, miserable world.

113

Joshua 20–22
Psalm 113
Luke 10:25–42

"You are anxious and worried about many things." (Lk 10:41)

Once when I was haunted by the feeling that God doesn't care, haunted by comparison and loneliness and loss, I read this Gospel passage as though I were Martha. I thought about the disciples on the Sea of Galilee, terrified in a storm when Jesus was asleep in the stern. "Teacher, do you not care?" And I felt it, that abandonment even when he's *right there,* that longing for the God who loves you to show it, to do what you think you need. And I saw him look at me, with sorrow and love (and some amusement), and speak to me. "Dear heart, you are anxious and worried about many things. You have chosen the better part." I already chose him. I already handed my life over to him. I already gave him control, gave up all worry and anxiety (at least in theory). Today, let him take your hand, speak your name, smile, and say (with no judgment, only compassion for your anxiety), "I get it. You are anxious and worried about many things. But you chose me. Because I chose you first. So remember that I'm here. Remember that you're mine. I care. I promise you I care."

114 | *Joshua 23–24*
Psalm 114
Luke 11:1–28

"Not one of all the promises the Lord, your God, made concerning you has failed. Every one has come true for you." (Jos 23:14)

Joshua's speech reminding the Israelites of all of the promises that God has fulfilled for them is so beautiful, especially because it took so long for the promises to be fulfilled. It had been some eighty years since they left Egypt, and they were only now seeing the fulfillment of all that God had promised to Moses. But this was more than his promise to Moses. He was fulfilling his promise to Abraham from hundreds of years before (Gn 13:14–15). These people had gotten used to unanswered prayers and promises as yet unfulfilled, but God was working that whole time. What promises in your life can you see that God has fulfilled? Which ones are you still waiting for? And can you trust him in the waiting?

115 | *Ephesians 1–3* *Psalm 115* *Luke 11:29–54*

"Not to us, LORD, not to us / but to your name give glory / because of your mercy and faithfulness." (Ps 115:1)

Evidence suggests that Jesus and his apostles would have been singing Psalms 115 to 118 after the Last Supper. The first verse of Psalm 115 feels very different when you imagine it being sung on the way to the agony in the garden. John gives us an insight into Jesus' disposition on Holy Thursday when Jesus prays, "I am troubled now. Yet what should I say? 'Father save me from this hour?' But it was for this purpose that I came to this hour. Father, glorify your name" (Jn 12:27–28). This pleading with the Lord to glorify his name, then, is not just an act of humility on the part of one who is seeking to glorify God by his life, but an act of sacrifice, a surrendering of the self to whatever God wills for the glory of his name. Paul says to the Ephesians that we were chosen "so that we might exist for the praise of his glory," which means that all our lives need to be this self-sacrifice in humility, this embracing of whatever comes for the glory of God's name.

116 | *Ephesians 4–6*
Psalm 116–117
Luke 12:1–34

"Do not be afraid any longer, little flock, for your Father is pleased to give you the kingdom." (Lk 12:32)

If Jesus was singing this psalm on the way to the agony in the garden, he was crying out victory, knowing he was on his way to defeat. Consider Psalm 116:15, where Jesus sang about how precious his death would be to the Father, or the following verse where he sang about his mother, or the verse after where he promised a sacrifice of thanksgiving (which is "Eucharist" in Greek). What confidence he had! The same confidence is exhorted in today's Gospel, so perfect in our uncertain world. Speak to Jesus today of your ruined plans. Listen to his words insisting that we can't allow worry to control our lives. Verse 32 in particular is so consoling: "Do not be afraid any longer, little flock, for your Father is pleased to give you the kingdom." Not necessarily healing or the life you want or bills you can easily pay, but the kingdom. That he has promised, and his promise never fails.

117 | *Judges 1–3*
Psalm 118
Luke 12:35–59

"It is better to take refuge in the LORD / than to trust in man." (Ps 118:8, Revised Grail translation)

If Psalm 118 was a Passover hymn, that means that the men who arrested Jesus had been singing it only a few hours before. Singing Hosanna, which is what verse 25 says. Singing "Blessed is he who comes in the name of the LORD!" (Ps 118:26). Singing about processions with leafy boughs. They were singing about their last encounter with Jesus, of the joy of Palm Sunday, as they were going to take him to his death. Maybe not one of those men had shouted Hosanna on Palm Sunday, but I bet some of them saw the connection. And I bet most of them knew that this whole situation was very wrong. But powerful men had told them what to do, so they did it. Where have you played the same kind of role?

118 | *Judges 4–6*
Psalm 119:1–48
Luke 13:1–17

"I delight in your commandments, / which I dearly love." (Ps 119:47)

It's very easy for Christians to get a warped sense of the law of Moses. Many of us have been told our whole lives that the problem with the Pharisees was their focus on the law. But the problem with the *bad* Pharisees was not their love of the law but that they viewed the law as something to accomplish, to congratulate themselves for, and to restrict others with, not something to lead them to God. They became so obsessed with restrictions that they created more and more and more, making an idol of the law itself (and their additions to it). But that wasn't true of all the Pharisees. Many of them likely loved the law because it drew them to God, as the psalmist does here. The law given at Sinai is what made Israel God's bride, what made it possible for them to do God's will. Even before the coming of Christ, before the effusive love of God became man, back when all he did was gush about his love for us rather than proving it in his body and blood, even then the law wasn't about rules for their own sake. Every rule has always existed for the sake of love.

119

Judges 7–9
Psalm 119:49–88
Luke 13:18–35

"It was good for me to be afflicted, /in order to learn your statutes." (Ps 119:71)

You've likely begun to see the pattern of the Book of Judges: Israel ignored God, so he allowed them to be subject to Kingdom A. They begged him to save them, and he delivered them through one of the Judges. Then everything was okay for a bit until they ignored God, and he allowed them to be subjected to Kingdom B. They begged him to save them, and he delivered them through one of the Judges. Then everything was okay for a bit until … This continues for the entirety of the book, really hammering home the point that our actions have consequences and that a life in defiance of God's law will always be full of chaos and suffering. If you underline every different nation who ruled over Israel, you'll see just how tumultuous the time of the Judges was, as they were conquered by one nation after another. But their many defeats weren't a sign that God was no longer with them (Jgs 6:13); rather, God allowed them to suffer so that he might draw them back to himself.

120 | *Judges 10–12*
Psalm 119:89–136
Luke 14

"Your word is a lamp for my feet, / a light for my path." (Ps 119:105)

It's possible that the incident of Jephthah's daughter is less upsetting than it seems. One translation of the Hebrew suggests that in verse 11 he said he would *either* offer the person to the Lord *or*, if it were an animal, offer him up as a holocaust. If that's the case, his distress at seeing that it was his daughter wasn't that he had to kill her but that she had to be consecrated to the Lord and was thus unable to continue the family line that this son of a concubine had finally vindicated through his leadership of Israel. If his only daughter were unable to carry on the family name, all his work would have been for nothing. This theory is supported by the daughter's calm consent to his plan, as well as by verse 37 where she mourns her virginity, not her life. Though this isn't a common reading of the text, it is a plausible one. If Jephthah did kill his daughter, it was evil, not heroic; the Bible is clear that human sacrifice is an abomination. I often wonder how frequently I find something in Scripture disturbing because I haven't yet found the right translation or commentary to make it all clear.

121 | *Judges 13–16*
Psalm 119:137–176
Luke 15:1–10

"I have wandered like a lost sheep; / seek out your servant." (Ps 119:176)

Samson is an excellent reminder that just because someone is a hero in your children's Bible doesn't mean he was wise or holy. The people Samson kept rampaging against were the oppressors of Israel, not innocent bystanders; but his impetuous rage and his lust were anything but virtuous. Still, God was able to use him. And while it would have been better for Samson to have become holy, his faults didn't disqualify him as an instrument in God's plan of salvation. The same goes for you. (And for those who are put off by this particular element of the supernatural, Samson's hair wasn't magic. It was a symbol of his obedience to the Lord. When — through lust — he became disobedient to God's command to be set apart by his uncut hair, he lost the strength given him by God. The hair's regrowth symbolizes his repentance and renewed obedience.)

122 | *Judges 17–19*
Psalm 120–121
Luke 15:11–32

"I lift up my eyes to the hills. / From where does my help come?" (Ps 121:1, RSV2CE)

Today in Judges we watch the People of God spiral out of control after turning their backs on him again. Theft and idolatry and false priestly consecrations precede intertribal conflict that ignored the fact that all the tribes were equally the People of God. After that we're introduced to a Levite so vile the text refuses to name him, who (for revenge on his concubine) sent her out to be assaulted, slept through her suffering, then callously ignored what had happened to her until he decided to make use of her once more to begin a civil war. The only sympathetic person in this whole passage (other than the concubine) is her father, who tried so hard to protect his daughter by distracting her husband and trying to keep him there long enough to calm down. It hopefully isn't necessary to point out that the Levite is not a hero, and the Bible isn't saying he treated this woman right. But the story reminds us just how bad things can get — how bad we can become — when God isn't at the center of our lives.

123 | *Judges 20–21*
Psalm 122
Luke 16:1–15

"In those days there was no king in Israel, and every man did as he pleased." (Jgs 21:25, Jerusalem Bible)

Judges continues to show us what happens when we turn from God: warring between the tribes, killing members of their own nation by the thousands, kidnapping women. But there are other interesting lessons in here as well. Notice that they were told that Judah should attack first but not that Judah would succeed; it seems that God willed their failure not once but twice, but then brought about victory because of their previous failure. I imagine we've all been there. And then after they'd murdered all their relatives, they blamed God for it (21:3). Their complaint against God for something that was their fault is the most human of reactions. And then, because they did something horrific, they felt they had to do even more terrible things to fix it, all the while complaining that God had allowed it to happen. The last verse sums up the brokenness of Israel at the time of the judges: "Every man did as he pleased." It feels like a final sigh of defeat from the author, a last reminder that we were made for more than the chaos and violence of the period of the Judges.

124 | *Ruth*
Psalm 123
Luke 16:16–31

"Like the eyes of a maid / on the hand of her mistress, / So our eyes are on the LORD *our God." (Ps 123:2)*

In marrying Ruth, Boaz became not only an ancestor of Christ but also a foreshadowing of Christ. Just as Christ was bridegroom Messiah for Gentiles as well as Jews, Boaz married the poor, foreign Ruth. He was the next of kin or kinsman-redeemer, a blood relative who was free and willing to redeem. That redemption could require saving the relative from slavery (Lv 25:47–49), marrying her (Ru 3:13), buying back her land (Lv 25:25), or avenging her death (Nm 35:21). Boaz would play the role of redeemer by marrying Ruth, but Christ would fulfill all four roles of the redeemer. Ruth, likewise, is a type of the People of God, who turn to him in the midst of uncertainty and find themselves redeemed and espoused, becoming fruitful for their bridegroom.

125 | *1 Samuel 1–3*
Psalm 124
Luke 17:1–19

"In her bitterness she prayed to the Lord, weeping freely." (1 Sm 1:10)

It may seem odd that Hannah's story is interrupted by the story decrying Eli's sons, but the author is making a point in juxtaposing these characters: It was the lowly, barren woman who was faithful, not the priests. I love her raw and broken prayer. I love her absolute trust that God will answer it. I love her surrender in giving Samuel back to God and the fact that she rejoices in that sacrifice even as she's leaving her toddler behind with no promise that her empty arms will ever hold another child. And I love that she ends up with all those children, not as replacements for the child she gave to the Lord but as individuals to be delighted in, reminding her to wonder at God's goodness even as she misses Samuel. Hannah gave the Lord the thing she spent years longing for, and then she worshiped him and declared her sacrifice a victory, in words that the Mother of God herself echoed in her great Magnificat. Lord, make me more like Hannah.

126 | *1 Samuel 4–7*
Psalm 125
Luke 17:20–37

"The LORD surrounds his people / both now and forever." (Ps 125:2)

The Philistines understood the power of the God of Israel, feared the havoc they knew he would wreak on their gods, and knew that he was truly God. To our minds, it's baffling that they didn't convert. But that's not how things worked then. With rare exception, people didn't pick the best god; they worshiped the god of their people. This is part of what's so remarkable about Jesus, who came to bring Gentiles into communion with the God of Israel. God had promised from the time of Abraham that the Gentiles would be blessed through him (Gn 12:3), but the idea that they would *belong* to Abraham's God was revolutionary. We see this in the aversion many Jews felt when Jesus invited Gentiles in and spoke favorably about them. It's hard for us to understand a religion that doesn't seek to convert others. But while we may know that the Gospel is offered to everyone, many of us could identify people we really don't think the mercy of God is for. That's not the message of Scripture — Old Testament or New. When we find ourselves denying people access to God's mercy, we're the ones truly in need of repentance.

127 | *1 Samuel 8–10*
Psalm 126
Luke 18:1–14

"Deliver us, O Lord, /
from our bondage as
streams in dry land."
(Ps 126:4, The Grail)

This is a psalm of returned exiles, praising God for the end of their captivity and begging him to restore them completely. It begins with awestruck wonder at God's goodness in bringing back the exiles from Babylon — a land from which they'd surely felt they'd never return. But when they returned, it was to a land left untended. Their fields had gone to seed, their roofs fallen in, and brigands patrolled their highways. They faced a lifetime of toil as they sought restoration. But despite the toil that lay before them, the people were certain of their victory. They knew that God would restore them, that he would strengthen and protect them. So the psalmist begged for the healing he was confident of, asking for blessings that would thunder through his life like a flash flood in a desert. Finally, he declared in faith that God would bring joy even into their sorrow. This is a perfect psalm for a time of suffering when hope seems impossible. Take some time today to write a psalm like this for your life, a prayer that wonders at the good things God has done, leads into entreaty, and ends in hope.

128 | *1 Samuel 11–12*
Psalm 127
Luke 18:15–43

"You have indeed committed all this evil! Yet do not turn from the Lord, but serve him with your whole heart." (1 Sm 12:20)

The Book of Judges repeatedly declared that the reason the people were so sinful was that they didn't have a king, so it's not unreasonable to be confused that they're now in trouble for asking for a king. Had they been asking for a king to help guide them out of moral anarchy (as seen in the time of the Judges), there would have been no problem. But they weren't asking for a king to help them be holy. They were asking for a king because they wanted to be like everyone else. Because they thought a king could help them be victorious. Because God wasn't enough for them. The problem wasn't with having a king; the problem was with the reason they wanted one. What is it that you seek because God isn't enough for you?

129 | *1 Samuel 13–14*
Psalm 128
Luke 19:1–27

"The Lord has sought out a man after his own heart." (1 Sm 13:14)

Saul is an intriguingly mercurial character. Sometimes he was only concerned with the people's opinion and his reputation, as when he offered a sacrifice he had no business offering (1 Sm13:8–13). Sometimes he was trying to make up for it by calling down a curse on people and offering to kill even his son in order to fulfill it (14:24–27, 44). Ultimately, I think this is the difference between David and Saul: David was a man who sought after the Lord but failed sometimes — even horrifically. Saul, on the other hand, was a man who only ever cared about himself and sought the Lord only insofar as it benefited him. Like his daughter Michal (2 Sm 6:20–23), he was driven by vanity and a need for others' good opinion. Ultimately, the only thing he was willing to fight for was his reputation. Are you more a David (wholehearted, though you often fail) or a Saul (going through the motions for what you get out of it)?

130 | *1 Samuel 15–16*
Psalm 129
Luke 19:28–48

"Obedience is better than sacrifice." (1 Sm 15:22)

Saul's insistence that his disobedience was acceptable because he did it for love of God is far too relevant to Catholics today. But we can't disobey God for love of God, because "obedience is better than sacrifice." Saul continued to swing back and forth between obsession with people's opinion and obsession with impressing God, but it was always rooted in self-obsession. It becomes clear at the end of this passage that there was mental illness involved, but not all of Saul's decisions proceeded from that illness or he wouldn't have been punished for them. He freely chose himself over obedience and had to bear the consequences. Meanwhile, in the Gospel, we see a man for whom "The Master has need of it" is answer enough. How can we become the kind of people who can say, "Yes, Lord" in all circumstances?

131 | *1 Samuel 17*
Psalm 130
Luke 20:1–19

"You come against me with sword and spear and scimitar, but I come against you in the name of the Lord *of hosts." (1 Sm 17:45)*

There's a certain courage and wisdom demonstrated here by Saul and all the Israelites. If David lost, it wouldn't just have been David who lost. All of them would have been enslaved to the Philistines. But they had seen God do more with less, so they trusted him to go and fight. Saul tried to form David in his own image, as people so often do, but David insisted that his strength would be hindered by his attempt to be like Saul. David's success came from God, yes, but it was through David's own strengths. He knew how to fight, knew how to sling a stone. And God used a warrior who seemed like a scrawny kid (so pathetic that Goliath hadn't even bothered to draw his sword) to show not only that God's power can work through anyone, but that strength can often be hidden and that people are at their best when not attempting to fit themselves into somebody else's mold.

132 | *1 Samuel 18–20*
Psalm 131
Luke 20:20–47

"They kissed each other and wept aloud together." (1 Sm 20:41)

I love Jonathan so much. I love his heart, his loyalty to his friend. I love his humility and selflessness. He knew that in loving David he was losing the crown that was coming to him, but he didn't care. He knew David would make a better king. And even if that hadn't been the case, Jonathan wouldn't have harmed David even to win a kingdom. I especially love the end of this passage. They'd worked out a code so that Jonathan could get a message to David without risking exposure, but he was too heartbroken at the coming separation from his friend to follow the plan. After giving the message, he sent away his servant so that he could hug his friend goodbye. I wonder what our world would look like if we encouraged this kind of intimate, vulnerable friendship between men.

133

1 Samuel 21–23
Psalm 132
Luke 21:1–19

"She, from her poverty, has offered her whole livelihood." (Lk 21:4)

It turns out Saul *was* willing to put a city under the ban, just not in obedience to God. He *was* willing to alienate the people, but not in order to be faithful to God. Only for himself, for revenge. How many things in our lives are we willing to endure for worldly reasons but not for God? We have time for Netflix every evening, but not for prayer. We'll lose face to defend our preferred politicians, but not to fight racism. We'll turn down a promotion that requires us to work on Thanksgiving but not bat an eye at a schedule that makes Sunday Mass impossible. What sacrifices are you willing to make for this world but not for the next? But hold this in tension with the widow in today's Gospel. Her story directly follows a condemnation of the scribes who "devour the houses of widows." She wasn't just generous; she was wrung dry by their demands. That's not what God calls us to. Gospel generosity shouldn't destroy us — or our families. It shouldn't make us scrupulous, constantly exhausted, or haunted by guilt. What can healthy generosity look like for you?

134 | *1 Samuel 24–25*
Psalm 133
Luke 21:20–38

"Beware that your hearts do not become drowsy from carousing and drunkenness and the anxieties of daily life." (Lk 21:34)

It's intriguing that Jesus lists the anxieties of daily life along with carousing and drunkenness — not that dealing with the necessities of this world is sinful but that it can become all-consuming, numbing us to heavenly realities because we're so focused on the here and now. How often do we become so absorbed in our stress that we forget all that God has done, forget who he is? What a gift it is, in those moments, to step back and remind ourselves of the good things God has done; to see his power, the tender care he takes for his creation, the truth that nothing comes from nothing; to know that this world has been designed. The God whom we serve is already taking care of us. How can we allow the anxieties of daily life to drive us to a deeper trust in Providence and a stronger longing for heaven?

135 | *1 Samuel 26–28*
Psalm 134
Luke 22:1–38

"Were you in need of anything?"
"No, nothing." (Lk 22:35)

It's encouraging to hear Jesus give the apostles instructions contrary to the ones he'd given them previously about not taking a money bag or an extra pair of sandals (Lk 9:3; 10:4) — not because it lets us off the hook, but because it shows us that God asks different things of us in different seasons. Earlier he'd been showing them that he could provide for them, but here he was telling them that in general they needed to be prudent, making wise decisions to take care of themselves rather than always expecting miraculous provision. Each follower of Jesus is given a different call, and that call changes according to our needs and the needs of our families, our communities, and our Church. These disparate instructions to the apostles remind us that following the Lord requires regular time in silent prayer so that we can hear what he's asking of us right now. Praise God for the liturgical year that calls us continuously to return to him and ask him what new thing he's inviting us to.

136

1 Samuel 29–31
Psalm 135
Luke 22:39–71

"And the Lord turned and looked at Peter; and Peter remembered." (Lk 22:61)

Luke 22:61 feels like a punch to the stomach. Imagine Jesus, as he was being beaten and interrogated and ridiculed and spat upon, knowing that Peter was there. Knowing that Peter would deny him. Knowing that Peter had insisted he didn't need any grace, insisted that he wouldn't fall. Hearing Peter's denial, then again. And then the third time, and the cock-crow, and Jesus looked over at Peter. Looked him in the eye. I wonder what his face looked like. I imagine sorrow and pain and love and mercy and an appeal to Peter not to let this be the end of his story. Not to be another Judas. Not to give up without seeking mercy. I expect that Peter only saw judgment and spent some time feeling ashamed and abandoned and unworthy. Until Jesus made all things new by that second charcoal fire (Jn 21:9), and Peter realized that the moment that had felt like condemnation was really love.

137 | *2 Samuel 1–3*
Psalm 136
Luke 23:1–32

"Give thanks to the Lord, for he is good. / His love endures forever." (Ps 136:1, NIV)

This psalm depicts all of salvation history as a product of God's loving mercy. It's a striking litany, especially when you look at the distressing elements — every bit of history is the result of God's love, even when it's hard to see how he was present in that ugliness. Throughout Scripture, we see the wonders of God revisited over and again, the people finding their hope in remembering God's wonders of old (Ps 77:11). Remembering the things God has done reminds us who he is — that he is good, that he is for us. And if that was true in the past, it must be true now. I like to take Psalm 136 as an invitation to sit back and look at my life, moment by moment, and recognize all that God has done. Then I try to trust that our God, who can work all things for good, is redeeming the suffering he allowed. We may not yet be able to thank God for the ugliness of our past, but we can try to trust that he was with us in our suffering and that he is working it for good, to draw us deeper into his Sacred Heart.

138

2 Samuel 4–6
Psalm 137
Luke 23:33–56

"I will be lowly in your eyes, but in the eyes of the slave girls you spoke of I will be somebody." (2 Sm 6:22)

Like her father, Michal was obsessed with other people's opinions — so much so that it destroyed her already fraught marriage and left her unable to bear fruit. (To be clear: She wasn't *punished* with infertility as a curse of God. The rift in her marriage made bearing children impossible.) How often do I become so consumed with what other people think that I, too, am unable to bear fruit? I don't speak truth, or I speak only tentatively, or I'm overcome with anxiety and unable to receive what the Lord is offering me. The sin of human respect (an excessive concern with others' opinions) sterilizes us, but living for God alone means we will bear much fruit. And as we live in exile, plagued by failure even when our lives are handed over to the Lord, we can meditate on Psalm 137. Unlike the exiled Jews, we can sing even in this our exile because heaven is promised to us in a way that a return from exile wasn't promised to any individual Jew. And we have a foretaste of heaven here in the Eucharist, which makes joy possible even in the midst of anguish and seeming futility.

139 | *2 Samuel 7–10*
Psalm 138
Luke 24:1–35

"Then beginning with Moses and all the prophets, he interpreted to them what referred to him in all the scriptures." (Lk 24:27)

The promise God makes here in 2 Samuel is about the House of David, his dynasty that would reign over Judah. But it's also pointing ahead to the true son of David, the Messiah who would build the house (or kingdom) of God, who would rule forever, who would be the Son of God. The language earlier in Luke's Gospel at the Annunciation is reminiscent of what we read here. Gabriel said Mary's son would be the son of the Most High, ruling on the throne of David his father forever, with a kingdom that would not end. Obviously, the verses about God chastising him when he sins pointed to Solomon and Rehoboam and their ilk, not to Jesus. But this covenant made with David spoke on two levels: of the kingdom of Israel and of the coming Messiah. And the whole thing came in response to David's desire to build a temple for God. From the beginning, the Jerusalem temple existed to point to the Messiah whose body would be the new Temple struck down and rebuilt in three days. What a perfect passage to read alongside Luke's allusion to Jesus' exhaustive Bible study of Messianic prophecies!

140 | *2 Samuel 11–12*
Psalm 139
Luke 24:36–53

"Rising from the ground, David … went to the house of the Lord and worshiped." (2 Sm 12:20)

David's sin began with pride that caused him to attack the Ammonites, then laziness that kept him napping at home while his army did his dirty work. This was followed by lust and sexual assault, abuse of power, deceit, and murder. It's incredible that the Israelites would include such flaws in the story of their most heroic king, but they understood that God was the one who truly reigned over them; they had no need to cling to any pretense of immaculate monarchs. Sinful as he was, though, David was not his sin. He was a man who sought God's own heart (1 Sm 3:14), though he constantly failed. How can we tell that he truly sought the Lord? When Nathan corrected him, David repented, pleading for his child's life. When his prayer went unanswered and the child died, David worshiped. For all his brokenness and sin, he trusted in God, even in the midst of unanswered prayers. And, perhaps most significantly, David and Bathsheba later named their son after Nathan (1 Chr 3:5). David was that repentant, and they were that grateful that Nathan had had the courage to correct his king. That shows real integrity.

141 | *2 Samuel 13–14*
Psalm 140
John 1:1–18

"Lord, guard me from the hands of the wicked; / from the violent keep me safe." (Ps 140:5, Revised New Jerusalem Bible)

Tamar experienced a horrific assault and responded with courageous protest. By the standards of the culture, she ought to have kept quiet and hoped nobody found out. She could have been punished. She knew that Amnon wouldn't be. But she refused to let it pass. She grieved and mourned and accused. Still, she was ignored by the powers-that-be (her *father*) and patronized by the brother she trusted. And then her assault became the catalyst for a civil war. Imagine if David had punished Amnon the way he deserved. Imagine if we as a Church had learned from this Scripture and sought to expose and discipline sexual abusers. If David had done so, he could have prevented not only the continued suffering of his daughter but also a civil war and the death of his son. If the Church had done so, think how many more people would know the love of God. If you're a survivor, I believe that Tamar stands with you, weeping and consoling. I pray that the Lord will bring you healing. If you're not a survivor, spend some time today aching for and loving and interceding for all who've been violated like this. Sometimes the best response to Scripture is lament.

142 | *2 Samuel 15–17*
Psalm 141
John 1:19–51

"I am ready; let him do to me as he sees fit." (2 Sm 15:26)

Throughout the Old Testament, we see types (prefigurements or foreshadowings) of Christ, of the Church, of the Blessed Mother. David is obviously a type of Christ, but not simply because he was a king of Israel. In this reading from 2 Samuel, David's struggle points forward to the events of Holy Thursday. David, having been betrayed, went to the Mount of Olives. He prayed, and then his prayer was answered not by immediate victory but by strength to fight the battle (through Hushai's service). Ahithophel, on the other hand, is a type of Judas, a close adviser to the king who wanted to go after him at night when he was weary and discouraged, causing all those with him to flee so that the death of only one man (Jn 11:50) could be accomplished for the salvation of the people. When his plan failed, Ahithophel (God rest his soul) despaired and took his life. David, meanwhile, trusted in the Lord in his suffering and betrayal and was ultimately victorious.

143 | *2 Samuel 18–20*
Psalm 142
John 2:1–12

"My son, my son Absalom! If only I had died instead of you, Absalom, my son, my son!" (2 Sm 19:1)

There is a lot about David that's not okay (most notably, the way he interacted with women). But there is so much of Davidic masculinity that our world is hungry for. The way he loved other men fiercely, without fear or pretense. The way he wept, unafraid of his emotions. His artistry, and his mercy toward those he loved — not just Absalom but Amasa (David's nephew who deserted him to become Absalom's general). One reason David stands as such a powerful type of Christ is that in many ways he points forward to Jesus' integrated masculinity, his loyalty and mercy and self-emptying love and willingness to feel deeply. David's most Christlike moment came here, as he wept over the well-deserved death of his beloved, wishing that he could have died in Absalom's place. We can hear in his voice the grief of God over his fallen people and his willingness to die in our place. To ransom a slave, he gave away his son.

144 | *2 Samuel 21–22*
Psalm 143
John 2:13–25

"He rescued me because he delighted in me." (2 Sm 22:20, NIV)

David's song in 2 Samuel (also found in Psalm 18) is no typical hymn of praise in the wake of a storm. No, this psalm sings of David's deliverance not *from* the storm but *through* the storm, through the anguish of the many struggles we've read of in 1 and 2 Samuel. As he crouched in terror, God routed the enemy with lightning and blasted them with the wind of his wrath. Then he seized David and snatched him away. God's rescue isn't always gentle, but it is always good. And when he rescues us, he gives us strength to follow him. Now safe from his enemies, the beleaguered king sings of the joy and confidence that come from following a God who brightens the darkness, who strengthens his people to break through any barrier and scale any wall (see the Grail translation of Ps 18). What storms in your life weren't an obstacle to your safety but the cause of your safety? Seeing how God has saved you through your suffering in the past, can you trust that he will do it again in the future — or even in the storms you're currently weathering?

145 | *2 Samuel 23–24* *Psalm 144* *John 3:1–21*

"Blessed the people whose God is the LORD.*" (Ps 144:15)*

There are some interesting moments here at the end of 2 Samuel to help us understand how different the ancient Near Eastern worldview was from ours. David's elite warriors were called the Thirty, even though there were admittedly thirty-seven of them. It's clear that numbers had a symbolic value as well as a literal value, and the authors were comfortable moving from one to the other. Immediately after that, we're told that God was angry at Israel, and so he incited David to sin.* That's totally foreign to our understanding of who God is, but it helps us to understand what's going on in the portrayal of God as the one who acts in all things (hardening Pharaoh's heart, etc.). A careful reading here, as elsewhere, helps us to see that God was allowing sin, not inspiring it in people's hearts. Here, Israel's sin influenced David, just as David's faithlessness manifested in Israel's growing distant from God.

---

* David's sin in ordering the census was that it was forbidden in Exodus 30:11–16 to count the Israelites without first offering a sacrifice as a reminder that the people belong to God, not to the king.

146

Colossians 1–2
Psalm 145
John 3:22–36

"He must increase; I must decrease." (Jn 3:30)

It's likely that Jesus and John the Baptist knew each other growing up, since both families would have visited Jerusalem for pilgrim feasts. So when John said, "I did not know him" (Jn 1:31, 33), it seems he meant that he'd had no idea just who his cousin was. Nor had he known what to expect of the Messiah. But John had always known there was somebody better coming — and spoken about it. As the first prophet in four hundred years, he would have found it easy to exploit the people's adulation. But he was always pointing beyond himself. And here, he spoke of Jesus as his best friend, the bridegroom Messiah, the one who brought joy to John as well as to the rest of the world. And because John loved him so much, and because he was so humble, he was happy to step out of the spotlight. Can you play the same role as John, the best man? Can you be thrilled by other people's drawing near to Jesus, even when you don't experience intimacy and consolation? Can you be excited to get out of the way?

147 | *Colossians 3–4*
Psalm 146
John 4:1–42

"Sir, give me this water, that I may not thirst."
(Jn 4:15, DRA)

I used to find this Gospel passage frustrating because it felt so disjointed. The woman's change in attitude and Jesus' preaching just didn't make any sense to me. But then I realized that you can't just read this Gospel story; you have to meditate on it. You have to imagine the awkwardness of Jesus' request and the woman's frustration. You have to see him asking something she wasn't ready to give, and wonder at the love there must have been in his eyes to change her rebellion to longing. You have to feel her shame in having the circumstances of her life cast before her, then her relief in realizing that Jesus wasn't there to condemn her. You have to realize that she changed the subject out of a desire to keep him at arm's length, but that he didn't let her off that easily. You have to understand what overwhelming grace it must have taken for her to go back to the people who'd made her life miserable and offer them the good news of Jesus. And you have to recognize that when God made her uncomfortable, she didn't walk away. She pushed back, but she stayed. And that made all the difference.

148 | *1 Kings 1–2*
Psalm 147
John 4:43–54

"A throne was provided for the king's mother, who sat at his right." (1 Kgs 2:19)

We read the Old Testament first and foremost because it is the word of God, through which the Holy Spirit speaks to us to draw us deeper into his heart and further along the path to holiness. But it's also such a gift that we see the New foreshadowed in the Old. Here in Solomon's proclamation as king through his ride through Jerusalem on David's mule, we see Jesus acclaimed as king as he rides a donkey into Jerusalem. We see Bathsheba's intercession, powerful because she was the mother of the king, the queen mother whose presence throughout the Old Testament promised that the Mother of God would be an intercessor to whom honor is paid. There is an enormous difference between Bathsheba in 1 Kings 1 and 1 Kings 2: Bathsheba as queen consort versus queen mother. She paid homage to David but was honored by Solomon, seated on a throne at his right hand. The queen mother was an office in Israel, not just an honorific. So, too, for the Blessed Mother, who is hard at work for us in the kingdom of her son.

149 | *1 Kings 3–5*
Psalm 148
John 5:1–30

"Do you want to be well?" (Jn 5:6)

"Do you want to be well?" always struck me as a silly question. Of course he did! Who wouldn't want to be well? But so much would change if he were healed. He'd been sick for thirty-eight years, begging for thirty-eight years, part of a crew of outcasts for thirty-eight years. If he were healed, who would he be? How would he make money? Being healed was going to be hard, even if the healing itself took place in the blink of an eye. I think it's a question Jesus is asking many of us. Is there an area of your life about which you complain a great deal but that you don't actually want healed? Are you willing to do the work that healing requires? Are you willing to deal with the shame and regret of realizing who you've been, with snide remarks and broken friendships when others see you change? Is justice worth it? Is peace worth it? Is holiness worth it?

150 | *1 Kings 6-8*
Psalm 149
John 5:31–47

"May he draw our hearts to himself, that we may walk in his ways." (1 Kgs 8:58)

Some years ago, I finally realized why God spends chapter after chapter describing the temple in minute detail. Every bit of God's temple was intentional, glorious, made exactly as he wanted it to give honor to his name. In 1 Corinthians 6:19–20, we read, "Your body is a temple." So now, as I read about how precious the temple was, how beautiful, how worthy of praise, I remember that God is also trying to tell me how deeply loved I am, how perfectly I was made, to house the very presence of God. Dear heart, you are not an accident. There is no part of you that is not willed — deeply, desperately desired — by the God of the universe. You are his temple, every bit of you covered in glory as the inside of the temple was covered in gold. You are marvelous, a wonder, a sight to behold. This is truth. Written in the word of God. He made you — just as you are — on purpose. He thinks you're stunning. Stop telling him he's wrong.

151

1 Kings 9–11
Psalm 150
John 6:1–21

"His heart turned away from the LORD, the God of Israel, who had appeared to him twice." (1 Kgs 11:9)

In Deuteronomy 17, God warned the king not to accumulate weapons (horses), wives, or wealth. These are (essentially) the temptations condemned in 1 John 2:16: lust, greed, and pride. Solomon was crowned and immediately set about accumulating all three, as we see in 1 Kings 10. These things blinded him to his need for God and tempted him to the idolatry that led to the downfall of the kingdom. David had been many things, but he was never an idolater. And for all his flaws, he knew how to repent. That's what makes a man after God's own heart. That's what makes a saint. But within one generation Israel began its slide into destruction. And all because Solomon wanted to be safe and comfortable and distracted. His sin wasn't adultery or murder, just the ordinary sin of turning to everything but God for comfort and security. His strength led him to forget God, which led him to idolatry, which was his downfall. Despite all God had done for him, he placed his trust in the things of this world and destroyed the kingdom of God in the process.

152 | *1 Kings 12–14*
Proverbs 1
John 6:22–59

"And so Israel has been in rebellion against the house of David to this day." (1 Kgs 12:19)

Flip back to the end of this book to study the timeline of the Old Testament. Today's reading takes place at the spot where the tree forks under Solomon, leaving us with two separate kingdoms. Though he was forty-one years old, Rehoboam acted with all the desperate posturing of the most immature adolescent, and the kingdom of God was divided forever. Jeroboam led the northern ten tribes into secession and then idolatry with a golden calf, and the kingdoms of Israel and Judah were basically at war until the destruction of Israel (often called the Northern Kingdom). From now on, Judah was no longer one tribe of Israel but a separate kingdom, the one that remained (somewhat) faithful to God and became the Jewish people. Israel, meanwhile, turned to idolatry, built its capital in Samaria, and would eventually become the Samaritans. From here on, "Israel" will generally refer to this separated Northern Kingdom, while "Judah" is the kingdom still ruled by the Davidic dynasty established by God. Neither kingdom would remain entirely faithful, but while some kings of Judah would try to follow the Lord, the Northern Kingdom began in rebellion and false worship and would never return to the Lord.

153 | *1 Kings 15–16*
Proverbs 2
John 6:60–71

"The fear of the Lord is the beginning of wisdom."
(Prv 1:7, DRA)

Proverbs can be difficult to read, especially a whole chapter at a time. It can feel rather like drinking from a firehose. You might consider trying to split it up over the course of your day so that you don't just feel thirty verses of wisdom washing over you and ignore them. Or you could look for one verse each day that you need to learn from, then use it as an examination of conscience at the end of the day. Proverbs is nothing if not practical, and if we don't apply these aphorisms to our lives, they can easily begin to seem like irrelevant clichés.

154 | *1 Kings 17–18*
Proverbs 3
John 7:1–13

"How long will you straddle the issue? If the Lord is God, follow him; if Baal, follow him." (1 Kgs 18:21)

I used to read this as a triumph. "Elijah taunted the prophets of Baal, exposed their lies, and then slaughtered them, showing the power of God! We win!" And then I realized that nothing changed after this. The people didn't come back to God. Elijah had demonstrated the power of God, but not his love. Though the people cried out that the Lord was God, it was an acknowledgment of a fact they had seen, not evidence of the conversion of their hearts. What could have been a moment that pulled God's people back to him became instead another in a long litany of Israel's failures. After his ugliness and violence, Elijah was still alone and on the run, because he wrapped the truth in cruelty instead of mercy. How often do we forget to speak to hearts, demanding instead that people bow before our superior arguments? How have we slaughtered the prophets and lost the souls of their followers? I know that when I get overexcited about truth, I often forget that I'm talking to a broken, suffering soul and not merely a mind. I have much to repent of here, and so much need for growth.

155 | *1 Kings 19*
Proverbs 4
John 7:14–36

"Enough, LORD! Take my life, for I am no better than my ancestors." (1 Kgs 19:4)

We have a very short first reading today so that we can really take the time to sit with it and be still. Elijah was coming off a great failure caused by his own sinfulness, and he was consumed by self-pity, devastated and despairing. So God called him away to take some time in stillness, seeking God instead of just working for him. He strengthened his servant with food and rest, then called him away for a while. Elijah must have expected God to speak in triumph and victory. But God was speaking in Elijah's life through opposition and suffering, which he showed Elijah by his unexpected presence not in the fire and earthquake of Sinai (Ex 19), but in the still, small voice that we all know is the most powerful way the Lord draws our hearts. In what unexpected way is God trying to speak to you right now? How can you retreat a little to hear him better?

156 | *1 Kings 20–22*
Proverbs 5
John 7:37–52

"The evil deeds of the wicked ensnare them."
(Prv 5:22, NIV)

It can be upsetting to read Scripture's warnings against adulterous women because it sounds as though women are seductresses and men are helpless victims. Remember, though, that this is speaking to good men, men who are fighting against sin, to warn them away from near occasions. It's not saying that all women are bad or only women are bad. If lust and adultery aren't temptations for you, consider reading this chapter in the light of another sin. Pray about the way that gossip seduces you, the way that laziness wraps its arms around you, the way that judgment stokes a comfortable fire in your belly. What sin do you find seductive, and what do you need to avoid in order to protect yourself from it?

157 | *1 Thessalonians 1–3*
Proverbs 6
John 7:53—8:11

"What thanksgiving, then, can we render to God for you, for all the joy we feel on your account before our God?" (1 Thes 3:9)

Paul's humanity in 1 Thessalonians is so encouraging. We see how deeply he loved the Thessalonians, how hard he tried to be gentle with them even though he was rather inclined to intensity. But he also took some time to defend himself, wanting to make sure that his people understood just how hard he worked for them. It's not pride, really. There's something in it of a father trying to make his children understand how deeply he loves them. And it makes sense that he started this way, before going on in chapter 4 to call them to holiness. That call to holiness feels very different when it's from somebody who you trust loves you. I wonder how many Thessalonian souls were ultimately saved because Paul loved them so deeply. Do you love people so well that they come to know Jesus?

158 | *1 Thessalonians 4–5*
Proverbs 7
John 8:12–30

"I am the light of the world. Whoever follows me will not walk in darkness, but will have the light of life." (Jn 8:12)

Context matters. This passage in John takes place during the Feast of Booths. This feast celebrated the water from the rock and the pillar of fire and cloud that led the Israelites through the desert; the festival, then, featured water and light imagery to recall the power of the God who cared for them. In the previous chapter, Jesus called himself the source of living water — at a festival celebrating the water God miraculously gave his people. Here Jesus said he was the light of the world — at a feast that celebrated the pillar of fire leading them through the darkness of the desert. When we understand that, we can see all the more clearly that these are brazen, earth-shattering claims of divinity. (And if he seems rather harsh in speaking to the crowds, remember that he just watched some among them drag a woman into public shame out of cruel hypocrisy. It seems they needed him to be a bit curt.)

159

2 Kings 1–2
Proverbs 8
John 8:31–59

"You will know the truth, and the truth will set you free." (Jn 8:32)

I was always uncomfortable with the story in 2 Kings 2:23–24, where God's prophet cursed a group of children, and God murdered dozens of them in a gruesome way. Until I finally stopped and paid attention. It's easy to read rather too much into the text while understanding too little. Those "small boys" might well have been young men — the Hebrew certainly allows that reading. There was a mob of them in Bethel, the center of false worship erected by King Jeroboam of Israel (1 Kgs 12:28–30), and they were assembled to mock a prophet of the Lord, almost certainly *because* he was a prophet of the Lord. This isn't childish jeering, then, but organized sacrilege. This makes sense of Elisha's cursing of them, but how can we worship a God who sent the she-bears? The text doesn't say he did. It's not unreasonable to assume causation, but that's not what Scripture says. The implication is that these men got what they deserved but not that God caused their anguish. What Scripture passages make you uncomfortable? Pick one this week and do some research in an attempt to make sense of it.

160 | *2 Kings 3–4*
Proverbs 9
John 9

"Did I not beg you not to deceive me?" (2 Kgs 4:28, NAB)

What a gift it would be to sit with the Shunammite woman from 2 Kings 4, to see the hope she could barely hold onto, her fear that good things would be taken from her, her anguish and sense of betrayal when her fears were realized. I want to honor her as a warrior, riding out to Elisha to save her son. I want to ache with her as she cries out, "Did I not beg you not to deceive me?" (NAB) I want to fight with her, as she refuses to leave without Elisha. I'm not sure I'm ready yet to rejoice with her, to fall at Elisha's feet in gratitude. Today, I just want to sit with her in the sorrow and the despair and the betrayal and the anguish. I want to learn to fight alongside her and alongside everyone whose "too good to be true" turned out to be just that.

161 | *2 Kings 5–6*
Proverbs 10
John 10:1–21

"Hatred stirs up disputes, / but love covers all offenses." (Prv 10:12)

There's so much in the story of Naaman that's amazing: the little girl's generosity in offering a cure to her master; Naaman's humility in seeking a cure in Israel and then in being willing to be dunked in the muddy waters of the Jordan (submerged seven times in a sign of covenant with the God of Israel); Elisha's understanding when Naaman says he doesn't have it in him to renounce the gods of Aram entirely; and Gehazi's deception and greed. But perhaps what we need more than anything is the reminder that comes in 2 Kings 5:13, where God reminds us that so often radical change and deep holiness come through ordinary, everyday work.

162 | *2 Kings 7–8*
Proverbs 11
John 10:22–42

"When pride comes, disgrace comes; / but with the humble is wisdom." (Prv 11:2)

How remarkable to consider that the Shunammite woman was a friend of Elisha's. Her husband is just a footnote to the story; Elisha's relationship was with her, a woman and a foreigner. I wonder what that looked like. I wonder whether their friendship drew her to know the Lord. And I wonder whether she was a mother to Elisha, a mentor, a woman who had permission to correct him. There certainly does seem to be that familiarity, especially at the death of her son when he listened to her grievance and submitted humbly to her demand for resurrection. It can be fruitful to meditate on these human connections, the relationships and personality traits not just of people in the Gospels, but throughout the Scriptures, so that we can really try to enter in. Much of it is speculation, but the Spirit can speak strongly through just such imaginative prayer.

163 | *2 Kings 9–10*
Proverbs 12
John 11:1–54

"I have come to believe that you are the Messiah, the Son of God, the one who is coming into the world." (Jn 11:27)

Jesus stayed away *because* he loved them. That doesn't feel like love to us, as it doesn't feel like love when God seems distant. But Jesus' distance was intentional, leaving space for them to mourn and learn to trust. And how Martha trusted, transformed from her attitude in Luke 10. Her brokenness sent her to sit at Jesus' feet. Earlier she'd rebuked him for not micromanaging the division of labor in their home, but now she trusted him in the death of her brother. Her attitude was of hard-won resignation, choosing Jesus over control. Still, she ran out to meet him. Still, she had much to say. Still, she was giving advice even at the entrance to the tomb. After all, Martha had no need to be more like Mary; the two had different gifts and calls and were at their best when not trying to ape each other. Active, busy Martha was entirely herself, finally at peace because she'd handed herself over to the Lord who grieved alongside her. Jesus knew he was about to raise Lazarus. Still, he wept because it hurt him to see their suffering. What a gift to know that he weeps with us.

164

2 Kings 11–13
Proverbs 13
John 11:55—12:36

"Whoever loves discipline loves knowledge, / but whoever hates reproof is stupid." (Prv 12:1)

I'm always Mary when I pray through this passage. But recently, as I tried to enter into that intimacy of anointing the Lord, I found myself Martha, healed through Jesus' gentle rebuke in Luke 10. I was bustling about in the kitchen and came into the doorway to see if I could get Mary's attention and ask her to help me. And when I saw her there, anointing Jesus, surrounded by judging and confused apostles, I wasn't bitter that she had left me to do the serving. I was so grateful that my work had made space for her to have this encounter. I heard him commend her for the gift she had given, and I knew that my willingness to work behind the scenes had made her gift possible. I knew he was grateful to me, too. And I wasn't bitter the way I had been the last time, because I knew that my work was good and her work was good and neither of us was lazy or taken advantage of. We were both his. What spirit of envy and competition do you need the Lord to heal in your life?

165 | *2 Kings 14–15*
Proverbs 14
John 12:37–50

"The house of the wicked will be destroyed."
(Prv 14:11)

Today's reading from 2 Kings led us through half a dozen different kings of the Northern Kingdom of Israel, including five in only six years. Israel was rocked by one coup after another during this time, a period of extreme instability. Because of all this unrest, the Northern Kingdom was vulnerable to the kingdom of Assyria, which would result in the Assyrian Exile (2 Kgs 17) — the deportation that destroyed the Northern Kingdom forever in 722 BC. But the cause of all this political instability wasn't purely politics; it was sin. Almost every king of Israel is introduced with a sentence like this one (2 Kgs 15:9): "He did what was evil in the LORD's sight, as his ancestors had done, and did not desist from the sins that Jeroboam, son of Nebat, had caused Israel to commit." God was so patient, correcting Israel again and again as one generation after another refused to seek him. But in the end, they collapsed under the weight of their sin.

166 | *2 Kings 16–17*
Hosea 1
John 13:1–20

"They worshiped the
LORD, but they also
served their own gods."
(2 Kgs 17:33, NIV)

The capital of the rebellious, schismatic Northern Kingdom was in Samaria. The Israelites had split from the Davidic kings of Judah and from worship at the one temple in Jerusalem, setting up golden calves (1 Kgs 12:28) and warring with Judah off and on for two hundred years. They believed themselves to be followers of the God of Israel, but they worshiped him through idols and worshiped other gods as well. They refused to follow the Lord as he'd asked. All that might have made them more rivals of the Jews than eternal enemies, but it got worse. Here we see the Israelites deported and pagans brought into the land. They intermarried with those who were left in the land of Israel and combined their purely pagan worship with the Israelites' pseudo-pagan worship, resulting in the Samaritan people who would spend the next seven centuries as enemies of the Jews, particularly over the question of right worship. This is a family squabble that turned into centuries of loathing. That's why Jesus' love for Samaritans was so shocking and why it ought to inform our attitude toward neo-Nazis, abortion providers, Democrats, Republicans, in-laws, bullies — everyone.

167 | *2 Kings 18–19*
Hosea 2
John 13:21–38

"I will lead her into the wilderness / and speak tenderly to her."
(Hos 2:14, NIV)

We're taking a break from Proverbs right now to read Hosea because the Prophet Hosea was speaking during this time in the history of Israel and Judah. God told the prophet to marry a prostitute and continue to love her no matter how she might turn away. This is, of course, an image of God's love for his people. He speaks of leading her into the wilderness to speak to her heart, allowing her to endure suffering and captivity so that he can win her for himself eternally. And then God proclaims his never-ending love for her (for us) in 2:21–22, verses that have been such a balm to my soul in seasons of loneliness and perceived abandonment. He has espoused me to himself forever. He's led me into many a desert so that he could speak to my heart. I hated some of those deserts, but every one has been worth it. Looking back on your life, when did God lead you into a wilderness (or allow you to wander there yourself) so that he could draw you deeper into his love?

168 | *2 Kings 20–21*
Hosea 3
John 14

"I will not leave you orphans; I will come to you." (Jn 14:18)

This chapter of John feels like a much-needed hug. Jesus, who had just told Peter how tragically Peter was going to fail, told the apostles not to let their hearts be troubled. He told them that the ugly things they were about to endure would happen so that he could bring them to himself. He promised to bring them to the Father. He promised the Holy Spirit. He promised that he would not leave them orphans — that he would come to them. Then again, he offered them peace and told them not to be troubled or afraid. And I expect that the disciples became more and more apprehensive as this soliloquy went on, wondering what exactly he was preparing them for that he had to shore them up with so much encouragement. But when they were running scared, standing at the foot of the cross, hiding in the upper room, I'm sure these words consoled them. What moments of encouragement and intimacy with the Lord have you experienced in your life that can console you when all hope seems lost?

169 | *2 Kings 22–23*
Hosea 4
John 15:1–10

"Before him there was no king like him, who turned to the LORD *... nor did any like him arise after him." (2 Kgs 23:25, RSV2CE)*

King Josiah of Judah could be the patron saint of trying so hard and being so good and doing all the right things and suffering anyway because of the consequences of somebody else's actions. It is deeply consoling that the greatest king in the history of Judah couldn't overcome the mess of his nation. The Second Book of Kings makes it clear that Judah had no other king to compare with Josiah (23:25), but within twenty-five years of his death, the kingdom had been destroyed. Not only that — he didn't even become a footnote in the New Testament. Because however amazing we may be, virtue doesn't always lead to success, and goodness doesn't always lead to greatness. God can do just as much through the stumbling attempts of broken sinners as he can through the most astonishing of saints.

170 | *2 Kings 24–25*
Hosea 5:1–14
John 15:11–17

"Thus was Judah exiled from her land."
(2 Kgs 25:21, NAB)

"Thus was Judah exiled from her land." This is heartbreaking. The destruction of the temple, of a people. The separation of Judah from God. So much of the Old Testament is written during and about this suffering or the attempt to recover from it. Stop for a moment and consider the agony of the Babylonian captivity, when the people were far from their homes, their land, their families, when all temple worship had ceased and there was no way to be reconciled with God when they became impure. Then consider that every mortal sin wreaks just as much destruction. Mercifully, we don't have to wait decades to be brought home again. Praise God for the Sacrament of Confession.

171 | *2 Thessalonians*
Hosea 5:15—7:2
John 15:18—16:4a

"It is he who has torn, but he will heal us; / he has struck down, but he will bind our wounds." (Hos 6:1)

The active voice in Hosea 6:1 is very discomfiting for us moderns, who tend to think more of God allowing us to be wounded, but the sentiment remains: By allowing us to suffer, God is laying the groundwork for far deeper healing. Hosea was certain that God would return, that he would heal. He knew that God had allowed the suffering of Israel in exile not because he didn't care for them, but because he longed to heal them, to bind their wounds and raise them up. Their suffering had a purpose: their ultimate healing and wholeness (though in this situation, it was only individuals who would be restored, never the whole Northern Kingdom of Israel). This passage becomes all the more clear in light of the Resurrection, as Hosea 6:3 foretells. We know that the Father was not far from Jesus in his suffering, however it may have felt. No, he was bringing meaning out of this suffering, not just bringing it to an end. The Resurrection teaches us that the cross has meaning. God's promise is not just that he will fix things in the end, but that the suffering we experience in the meantime is working for good.

172 | *Amos 1–3*
Hosea 7:3–12
John 16:4b–15

"You only have I chosen / of all the families of the earth; / therefore I will punish you / for all your sins." (Am 3:2, NIV)

Amos was a disdained shepherd writing in very simple Hebrew to elites in Israel at a time of great national prosperity — a few decades before they were deported and their nation destroyed. He started by condemning the ancestral enemies of Israel, which must have had his audience nodding their heads. But then he began to rebuke Israel itself, at which point we can imagine the grumbling started, only increasing as he went on and on in warning of the suffering to come. Amos was trying to avert their impending doom, but the complacent people of Israel were too wrapped up in their comfort to see the threat. Amos 3:2 tells us that the purpose of the coming punishment wasn't vengeance but rehabilitation — it's because God loved them so deeply that he chastised them. Sometimes what feels like God abandoning us or mistreating us is really a great mercy. Perhaps always. But sometimes we get to see it.

173 | *Amos 4–6* *Hosea 7:13—8:14* *John 16:16–33*

"Yet you did not return to me." (Am 4:6)

Amos 4 is so moving, where God makes it so clear that all the suffering Israel had experienced was intended to bring them back to him. Over and again he describes their struggle and says, "Yet you did not return to me." What would our lives look like if we viewed suffering as an invitation to draw deeper into the heart of God? And if we recognized (as 5:24 reminds us) that true worship must be rooted in justice? That we can't consider ourselves faithful if we ignore the cries of the marginalized, no matter how many rosaries we recite and how many Masses we attend? In order to offer God holocausts, we must let justice surge. Woe to us who are complacent (6:1).

174 | *Amos 7–9*
Hosea 9
John 17

"You loved them even as you loved me." (Jn 17:23)

So much in Amos 8 points to the passion — buying the lowly man for silver (v. 6), the land trembling (8), the sun setting at midday (9), the people mourning as for an only son (10). All this we read in the midst of Amos's warnings and condemnation, inviting us to pause and remember that while the passion is a good thing inasmuch as it won our salvation, it's a horrific, wicked thing that ought to make us tremble with dread at the thought that we are responsible for it. We who can see this connection to the passion must hear the warning of the Holy Spirit that if we keep exploiting and oppressing the poor and the outcast, we will be crucifying God. But after this warning, Amos can't help but speak of resurrection (9:11) and then of the heavenly banquet (9:13–15) awaiting even those whose injustice nailed Jesus to the cross. Even threats of divine justice exist only to draw our hearts to him so that we can dwell with the Father in eternity, the Father who loves us even as he loves the Son.

175 | *Micah 1–3*
Hosea 10
John 18:1–27

"Who eat the flesh of my people, / flay their skin off them." (Mi 3:3, NRSV)

Did Micah 3:3 stand out to you, its language so reminiscent of John 6? "They have devoured the flesh of my people," the Lord says, and it's clearly a metaphor. But when eating someone's flesh is used metaphorically (as in Isaiah 9:18 and Psalm 27:2), it's symbolic of attacking and destroying that person. So if Jesus was speaking metaphorically in John 6, he was saying that everyone who attacks and destroys him will live forever; since that's nonsensical, our logical conclusion must be that he was speaking literally. Unlike the leaders here condemned by Micah for eating the flesh of God's people, the leader who will be announced in Micah 5:1 would give his flesh to his people as true food.

176 | *Micah 4–5*
Hosea 11
John 18:28–40

"When Israel was a child I loved him, / out of Egypt I called my son." (Hos 11:1)

I feel so embraced by Hosea 11:1. And then I hear the Lord remind me of how I've strayed from him, how he's always called me back though I didn't realize that every good thing in my life was from him. He calls out in anguish, proclaiming how he loves me even when I least deserve it. And then he says he will bring his children back from Egypt (where much of Judah would flee 150 years later) and Assyria (where Israel was even then being sent into exile). Which means he longs to bring all his children home, home from the sin of Egypt and home from the loneliness and sorrow of exile. How much he loves us, and how little we notice.

177 | *Micah 6–7*
Hosea 12:1—13:1
John 19:1–30

"My people, what have I done to you? / how have I wearied you? Answer me!" (Mi 6:3)

Micah 6:3 is the inspiration for the Good Friday laments, in which the voice of Jesus cries out from the cross, begging his beloved to let him love us but willing to bear our abuse instead. As we read this verse, we can hear Jesus' voice call out from the past. But can we hear him today? Can we hear the cry of the oppressed and condemned and rejected, the body of Christ crying out? Can we hear God in the enslaved and the unborn and the refugee and the disdained and the forgotten, crying out, "My people, what have I done to you? How have I wearied you? Answer me!" Lord, teach us to see you in the least of these.

178 | *1 Timothy 1–3*
Hosea 13:2—14:1
John 19:31–42

"Nicodemus, the one who had first come to him at night, also came." (Jn 19:39)

Nicodemus must have felt such shame that he hadn't been willing to stand for Jesus. He'd only sought him in secret (Jn 3), and when he'd spoken up for Jesus, it was in a general way that Nicodemus knew would bring him no condemnation (Jn 7:50–51). When the Sanhedrin had convened, he hadn't used his privilege, but had cowered, refusing to risk anything for the one he secretly loved so much. He finally found the courage after Jesus' death to declare himself, but it must have seemed too little too late. But the myrrh he brought was worthy of a king, poured over Jesus' corpse in an unimaginable quantity. And he anointed Jesus' body and sat with his corpse and it was good. It wasn't too little too late. He was a gift, just exactly when he showed up. If you're late to this party — to the Church as a whole or to pro-life ministry or anti-racist activism or daily Scripture reading or Friday abstinence — it is good that you are here. Don't be bound by shame over what you've missed. Just give what you can and know that it is good that you are here.

179 | *1 Timothy 4–6*
Hosea 14:2–10
John 20:1–18

"Jesus said to her, 'Mary!'" (Jn 20:16)

I wonder if there has ever been a word so tenderly spoken as that "Mary." The man who had wept over the death of Lazarus looked on his heartbroken beloved, grieved her suffering, rejoiced at their reunion, and offered her hope. Mary Magdalene had fixed her whole life on Jesus. She had nothing else. So if Jesus was gone, she would stay weeping at his tomb until she was gone, too. And her heart so fixed on him, so shattered by his death, led her to be the very first to see the risen Christ. It made her the apostle to the apostles, but most importantly it meant she heard him call her name with all the love the world has ever known. I meditate often on what it will be like to hear him say my name the same way. When I have hard choices to make, I try to let this longing to hear him drive my decisions. And when this world seems too ugly, I remember: I am his. I am awaited with breathless anticipation. One day, I will be home. And this valley of tears doesn't seem so unbearable. Because it will end in glory.

180 | *1 Chronicles 1–3*
Proverbs 15
John 20:19–31

"Blessed are those who have not seen and have believed." (Jn 20:29)

The two books of Chronicles are a retelling of the history of Israel and Judah from Judah's perspective. As before, the genealogies can be difficult to read, but try keeping an eye out for phrases that don't match the pattern. In this passage, I particularly noticed how very many women are named. I noticed that Caleb's life was something of a soap opera. I saw that Joab and Amasa were cousins (and nephews of David). I saw that David named a son Nathan *after* the Prophet Nathan rebuked him for his sin with Bathsheba. Reading in conjunction with Jesus' words to Thomas, I saw the many names of faithful men and women whose stories we won't know until heaven but whose lives were a model of believing in what they had not seen, in following the Lord even when they had no particular evidence of his goodness and his love. As we go on, look for something worth underlining or commenting on every day, especially people you recognize from round one of Judah's history (1 and 2 Kings). The more you're looking for something of note, the easier it will be not to feel weighed down by Chronicles.

181 | *1 Chronicles 4–6*
Proverbs 16
John 21:1–14

"When Simon Peter heard that it was the Lord, he tucked in his garment, for he was lightly clad, and jumped into the sea." (Jn 21:7)

Sweet Peter was feeling so useless. He'd seen Thomas's reconciliation with Jesus, but nobody had yet said a word about Peter's denial. So he gave up and went back to what he knew: fishing. Imagine his frustration when he discovered that he was terrible at that, too. Imagine him feeling more and more miserable all night until he finally heard Jesus asking if they'd caught anything. It pulled him right back into the first wasted night, the first call, the first miraculous catch (Lk 5:1–11). He didn't need John to tell him that it was Jesus, but John's voice snapped him out of his stupor and sent him diving into the water, so desperate to be with Jesus that he'd forgotten the boat was more efficient, so eager that he dragged a net with 153 fish in it all by himself. (Imagine loving Jesus so much that this was your reaction when told where to find him!) He pulled right up to that charcoal fire that smelled like his denial (Jn 18:18), and God began to make him new.

182 | *1 Chronicles 7:1—9:34*
Proverbs 17
John 21:15–25

"What concern is it of yours? You follow me." (Jn 21:22)

It's utterly baffling and so very human to see Peter go from this moment of intimacy and reconciliation right into comparing himself to John. Jesus responded so simply, with the rebuke that every one of us needs when we're envying or judging: "What concern is it of yours? You follow me." It's totally natural to turn from the Lord to see what other people are up to and how we compare, but it's not the call of Christ. He calls us to fix our eyes on him and let him worry about the rest.

183 | *1 Chronicles 9:35—11:47*
Proverbs 18
Matthew 1:1–17

"The name of the LORD is a strong tower; / the just run to it and are safe." (Prv 18:10)

Proverbs 18:10 tells us that the name of God is a strong tower where we can be safe. For most of us, though, it's a casual interjection, a way of expressing shock or annoyance. How would our language (or our reaction to other people's language) change if we began to pray using different names and titles for God as expressions of intimacy? Which names for God draw you deeper into his heart? Are there certain ways you address God in times of need and other ways when expressing praise? Do you have flippant ways that you use God's name as well, or is it sacred to you?

184 | *1 Chronicles 12–14*
Proverbs 19
Matthew 1:18–25

"Who am I, Lord God, and what is my family, that you have brought me this far?" (1 Chr 17:16, NIV)

Chronicles is largely a summary of what we've read in Samuel and Kings, but it was written after the Babylonian captivity when the Jews had returned to their land and were struggling to remember who they were as a people. So it's very focused on David as the idealized king, rather than showing as many of his flaws as earlier books did. It also stresses the glories of Judah and the beauty of temple worship. At one level, the Chronicler was reminding the Jews who they were. At another level, he was living in a time when despair would be so easy; in writing about their glory, he was working to give the Jewish people hope that such a world might be possible again. If you're getting frustrated by the repetition in 1 Chronicles, try to see this as God viewing the goodness of his fallen people — viewing your goodness even in the midst of your fallenness.

185 | *1 Chronicles 15–17*
Proverbs 20
Matthew 2:1–12

"A man's steps are ordered by the LORD; / how then can man understand his way?" (Prv 20:24, RSV2CE)

There is in the joy of the Nativity the suffering foretold by the myrrh of the Magi, the anguish of the Innocents slaughtered as Jesus was spirited away. The wood of the manger is the wood of the cross, and this child raised by a carpenter would hear daily the echo of the nails that would bind him to his death. But there's more to myrrh than the anointing of a corpse and more to the Christ child than just one born to die. In the Old Testament, myrrh also anointed the tabernacle (Ex 30:22–26), the priest (Ex 30:30), and the royal bridegroom (Sg 3:6). That last is the only other verse where frankincense and myrrh appear together, as Solomon, the son of David, was anointed for his bride. Whether they knew it or not, the magi were declaring Jesus to be king, priest, presence of God, and bridegroom Messiah. They called him king of the Jews, the same title that would be nailed to the cross with him. The first Gentiles to be drawn to Jesus followed God's call even when they didn't entirely understand it. Because they abandoned themselves to follow God, they proclaimed the Gospel from the cradle to the cross.

186 | *1 Chronicles 18–20*
Proverbs 21
Matthew 2:13–23

"A voice was heard … / Rachel weeping for her children, / Refusing to be comforted, / Because they are no more." (Mt 2:18, NKJV)

God repeatedly told his people not to go to Egypt (Gn 26:2; Jer 42:15–16; Is 31:1; Dt 17:16). But he willingly sent his Son there, embracing our sin and captivity so that he could bring us out. And Matthew 2:15 makes it clear that his suffering had a purpose — as does ours. Still, my eyes are on Mary here, watching her cling to Baby Jesus and trusting that I can do the same when I, too, am haunted by trauma. Maybe you need her red-rimmed eyes and hoarse voice on the evening of Good Friday after she cried herself sick at the foot of the cross. Maybe you need her sparkling eyes, her head thrown back in laughter as she played with Jesus the toddler. Maybe you need her staring into space, her lips white as she remembered the lost little boys of Bethlehem. Maybe you need her looking daggers at your enemy — the Enemy — at your shame, at the lies that convince you that you're unloved. Maybe you need her to draw you to the empty tomb when you're wallowing in the misery of the crucifixion. Praise God for our powerful, suffering, protective, gentle, demanding, doting, immaculate Mother who is always, always bringing us to her Son.

187 | *1 Chronicles 21–22*
Proverbs 22
Matthew 3

"Devote your hearts and souls to seeking the LORD your God." (1 Chr 22:19)

It's interesting that the Chronicler ignored the Bathsheba incident entirely but still allowed us to see David's fallenness in the issue of the census. In featuring the census, the Chronicler tells us why the temple stands where it does. He also places the emphasis on David's call to virtue as a ruler, the one who stands at the head of Israel. David's sin against Bathsheba and Uriah was a personal sin, but in taking a census without an offering as commanded (Ex 30:12), he was treating the people as though they were his and not God's. He was abusing his power and forgetting that he ruled only as a steward of the Lord. We would do well to examine not just the obvious carnal sins that we struggle with but also the areas where we have usurped God's power in our lives.

188 | *1 Chronicles 23–25*
Proverbs 23
Matthew 4:1–17

"On those dwelling in a land overshadowed by death light has arisen." (Mt 4:16)

Notice that after Jesus used Scripture to respond to the devil's temptation, the devil quoted the Bible as well, adjusting his temptation to the one he was tempting. He began to use the word of God to try to pull Jesus from the will of the Father. He does the same to us, using good concepts like unity and meekness to keep us from fighting for justice or speaking truth boldly. Or he convinces us to fight evil through cruelty and ridicule — again, a distortion of a good. Jesus resisted the attack of the devil because he was so secure in the Father's love that he had nothing to prove, no uncertainty about his identity. The same will be true for us if we remain steeped in Scripture and the sacraments, seeking the voice of God in silence and seeking counsel from the wise.

189 | *1 Chronicles 26–27*
Proverbs 24
Matthew 4:18–25

"Immediately they left their boat and their father and followed him." (Mt 4:22)

It's dizzying to take a step back from what we know of Jesus and really pay attention to what's going on in Matthew 4:18–25. Here's a man nobody had heard of except for one time two months earlier when something odd had happened at the Jordan. But this stranger walked up to Peter and said, "Follow me." And he did! And James and John left behind their boat *with their father in it* and followed even though Jesus hadn't (in Matthew's account) worked any miracles yet. And then suddenly he was teaching in synagogues and proclaiming the Gospel, healing the sick and casting out demons. People were coming in droves, carrying their beloved sick and paralyzed and possessed. Crowds were coming from Galilee and Judea and even from Gentile lands. Imagine people getting on planes from New York City and quitting their jobs in Tokyo to hear a guy from small-town Mississippi preach and to follow him around. And it all happened in just a matter of weeks. He was either the greatest charlatan the world has ever known or his charisma came from the fact that he knew every inch of them and loved them just the same.

190 | *1 Chronicles 28–29*
Proverbs 25
Matthew 5:1–12

"Like an open city with no defenses / is the man with no check on his feelings."
(Prv 25:28, NAB)

As a person with very, very big feelings, I've found it fruitful to pray with Proverbs 25:28. If you're anything like me, having no check on your feelings makes you easily devastated. But it doesn't help me to repress them or attempt to ignore them; I have to bring them to Jesus. I have to take time every day to sit in his presence and feel my feelings with him (or sometimes *at* him). When I look at them in the light of his love and his cross, that perspective is just the check that I need. It doesn't always mean I feel okay afterward, but I feel much less controlled by my angst and anger and despair and much more certain that God alone matters.

191

2 Timothy
Proverbs 26
Matthew 5:13–26

"I have competed well; I have finished the race; I have kept the faith." (2 Tm 4:7)

Timothy was one of Paul's dearest friends, a young man the great apostle had mentored and then ordained (2 Tm 1:6). That's why there's a tenderness here (and yesterday in 1 Timothy) that we don't always see in Paul's letters. He wasn't just writing to a large community he loved; he was writing to his spiritual son, speaking from the depths of his heart. His description of his weariness in 4:6–8 shows us the hope that supported him and the longing that drove him on. It was this longing for Jesus that won Paul a crown. This is what it takes to compete well, to finish the race, to keep the faith. Not miracles and mysticism, but longing to be with Jesus — even when that longing isn't a feeling but a decision to live as though one desired him.

192 | *2 Chronicles 1–2*
Proverbs 27
Matthew 5:27–37

"Give me, therefore, wisdom and knowledge to govern this people." (2 Chr 1:10)

We all know that Solomon asked for wisdom, and we know to be impressed that he didn't seek money or power. But wisdom in the secular sense can be just as dangerous and self-serving. God was pleased with Solomon's prayer because Solomon sought wisdom not for himself but so that he might rule the people well. So that he might serve. The beauty of Solomon's request was that he was asking something of God only so that he could give it back to God. When we pray, how many of our petitions are intended to help us serve and love better? What intentions might we be better off setting aside?

193 | *2 Chronicles 3–5* *Proverbs 28* *Matthew 5:38–48*

"Love your enemies, and pray for those who persecute you." (Mt 5:44)

Revolutionaries gathered crowds and gave speeches on mountains. When the Sermon on the Mount began, Jesus' disciples were expecting a revolution, but not this kind. We can't read this as platitudes, familiar though it may be. It ought to spark a revolution of holiness in us. Today's selection calls us to radical generosity, to a meekness that seems painfully similar to weakness. But Jesus modeled this behavior for us in his passion. He let his enemies hit him, let them take his clothes, let them force him to carry a burden, loved his enemies, and prayed for those persecuting him. He showed us that what the world calls weakness is world-shaking strength. The Sermon on the Mount is fulfilled in (and only possible because of) the passion. When we look to Calvary as an image of love, we begin to see how such selflessness might be possible in our lives as well.

194 | *2 Chronicles 6–7*
Proverbs 29
Matthew 6:1–18

"Your will be done, on earth as in heaven." (Mt 6:10)

The Chronicler describes the glory cloud (called the *shekinah* by later rabbis) overshadowing the temple in 2 Chronicles 5 and 7. But Chronicles was written after the departure of God's presence from the temple, after the temple's destruction. The Chronicler was writing with longing of a time when God was so close to his people. He must have been trying to trust that God would dwell with them again someday. Think of a time when God felt distant, perhaps when you were separated from the sacraments for a time. Did you let your longing form your whole life, as the Chronicler did? Were you able to trust that God was with you even when he felt so distant? Or did you let your longing make you bitter? Maybe reading these lengthy descriptions of worship spaces and liturgies can teach us to long in a life-giving way for the presence of the Lord.

195 | *2 Chronicles 8–9*
Proverbs 30
Matthew 6:19–34

"Do not worry about tomorrow; tomorrow will take care of itself. Sufficient for a day is its own evil." (Mt 6:34)

Sit for a time with this Gospel passage today, trying to soak in it and trust in it and believe it. It's natural for us to read these examples as difficult decisions to make, or cares and distractions of worldly life. But for the people Jesus was talking to, on any given day they really might not have had anything to eat or drink or wear. He wasn't talking to them about the modesty debate or figuring out which clothes they could ethically buy or discerning how they were going to fast or what restaurants they were going to patronize. He was talking to people whose lives were utterly precarious, who had no real security. And to them he said, "Don't worry." They listened. Can we?

196 | *2 Chronicles 10–12*
Proverbs 31
Matthew 7

"She is clothed with strength and dignity." (Prv 31:25)

Many women cringe when they see Proverbs 31 because it's so often been misused to convince them of their inadequacy when compared to this domestic goddess. But I don't see Proverbs 31 as a list of the many accomplishments a woman has to have to be good enough. I see it as a wild and wonderful description of the possibilities of holy femininity, a description that includes courage and virtue and industry and entrepreneurship and leadership and wisdom and humor and trust and prudence. It's worth noting that these are the words of a woman, the advice the queen mother gave to the king. Jewish legend identifies Lemuel as King Solomon, which would make these the thoughts of Bathsheba, the wronged wife of Uriah who was made to marry King David and later won the throne for her son. This is a woman whose thoughts on femininity are far more complex than the boxes people have tried to force women into. Biblical femininity — like biblical masculinity, like biblical marriage, like biblical parenting or leadership or hospitality — is far more about letting God use you *as you are* than about conforming to the expectations of even the most well-meaning of people.

197 | *2 Chronicles 13–15*
Isaiah 1
Matthew 8:1–17

"Do you think you are a match for the kingdom of the Lord ... simply because you are a huge multitude?" (2 Chr 13:8)

The king of Judah looked in astonishment on a superior force not because he was cowed by their numbers, but because he was baffled that they truly thought their numbers mattered when they were coming against the Lord. "Do you think you are a match for the kingdom of the Lord led by the descendants of David, simply because you are a huge multitude?" Of course they did! They had power and false gods and every reason to expect that they would triumph. But they didn't triumph because they weren't serving the Lord. Remember this when you feel as though you're facing down a horde of soldiers armed to the teeth, when it seems as if everything you care about is opposed by all the powers of the world, when all you want to do is run and hide. Can you learn to have the confidence that Abijah had? Can you trust that the Lord is fighting for you, that you have only to be still? What seemingly overpowering forces are you currently cowering before when God is happy to brush them aside?

198 | *2 Chronicles 16–18*
Isaiah 2
Matthew 8:18–34

"He said to them, 'Why are you terrified, O you of little faith?'" (Mt 8:26)

There is a poem by Saint Thérèse of Lisieux in which she says that to live from love means that when Jesus is sleeping on stormy waves you tell him, "Do not fear, Lord, that I will wake you. I wait in peace for the shores of heaven." It's sometimes paraphrased, "You may sleep in my boat, Lord. I will not wake you." That is not my inclination. When the storm is raging, I don't want to cling in trust to Jesus. I don't even want to bail water frantically. I want to rage along with the storm, to complain loudly in the hopes that the people responsible will overhear and fix what they've screwed up. I am choked by fury against the waves and the ship and the ones trying to get us to shore and most especially against the one who told me to get on the boat, the one sleeping in the hull. I won't even shake him awake because I'm too mad that he isn't waking up on his own. With Thérèse's image in mind, I'm trying instead to place myself in his arms. I'm trying to trust.

199 | *2 Chronicles 19–21*
Isaiah 3
Matthew 9:1–17

"We ourselves do not know what to do, so our eyes are turned toward you." (2 Chr 20:12)

The Second Book of Chronicles is such an accusation of the ones praying it: "We ourselves do not know what to do, so our eyes are turned toward you" (20:12). Perhaps they wouldn't be in this mess if God weren't their last resort. For a moment the People of God turned to him, as King Jehoshaphat of Judah exhorted the people to trust in God and led them in praising and thanking God before he answered their prayer. It almost seems like a real, lasting conversion this time. But we see in verse 33 that they hadn't truly fixed their hearts on the God of their fathers, and the ascension of King Jehoram to the throne of Judah made matters even worse. I wonder how often we turn to God first, before erupting in rage or crumbling in worry or pulling out our phones to start googling solutions. I wonder how often we praise him and thank him before he has answered our prayer, trusting that whatever his answer is, it will be for our good. May we learn to praise God beforehand, knowing that whether he answers our prayers or not, it's all because of his love.

200 | *2 Chronicles 22–23*
Isaiah 4
Matthew 9:18–38

"For over all, his glory will be shelter and protection." (Is 4:6)

Isaiah was prophesying to a relatively prosperous Judah that had a decent king at this point. He was speaking of the trouble that was to come, as so many prophets do, but his prophecies of woe kept leading to the promise of the Messiah. We saw this when chapter 2 foretold the Messianic banquet for all nations, and again here when he tells us that the devastation and depopulation of war will be the opportunity the Lord takes to clean and heal and lead his people in a new Exodus. Isaiah 4:5 uses the language of the Spirit's presence among the wandering people of Israel in the desert to speak of God's presence in the temple. At this point the temple still housed the Ark of the Covenant (the presence of God), but Isaiah was telling them that on the other side of suffering would be an even more profound and tangible experience of God's presence. Lasting joy is only found on the other side of suffering. It was true of the passion, death, and resurrection of Jesus, and it's true of all suffering that we hand over to the Lord.

201

2 Chronicles 24–25
Isaiah 5
Matthew 10:1–15

"Woe to those who are wise in their own eyes / and clever in their own sight." (Is 5:21, NIV)

Look at the dramatic decline of King Amaziah of Judah. Here was a man who had been willing to alienate an entire nation of allies in order to be faithful to God, based only on the word of a single unnamed prophet (2 Chr 25:7–10). Then suddenly he was worshiping false gods, immediately after the Lord gave him victory over the false gods' devotees. What could have happened to him? He seemed such a hero, such a man of wisdom and courage. He was willing to follow the Lord at great risk, then suddenly he was bowing before idols? Scripture doesn't explain why, but it shows these two events in such proximity to remind us that there but for the grace of God go we. Our years of faithful service to the Lord are absolutely no guarantee that we won't fall and fall hard. Lord, keep us in your grace! Never let us betray you.

202 | *2 Chronicles 26–27*
Isaiah 6
Matthew 10:16–33

"Even all the hairs of your head are counted. So do not be afraid." (Mt 10:30–31)

These words of Jesus in Matthew 10:29–31 are words to hide in your heart, to memorize and recite when the devil's lies begin to overwhelm you. I imagine Jesus speaking them to a heartbroken street urchin as he wipes the tears from her cheek: "Sweet girl, look how God takes care of the sparrows. He knows each of them by name, sees where they go and what they do. He cares when they fall and when they go hungry. And those are just birds! How can you believe he doesn't care about you, see you, love you? He knows every hair on your head, every tear you cry, every smile, every half-dreamed dream. He knows your hunger and your fear and your joy and your anger and he loves you all the same. Don't be afraid, little one. Your Father will take care of you." Imagine Jesus speaking these words to your broken, fearful, weary heart, wiping the tears from your eyes. Imagine the love in his voice, the strength with which he forbids you to fear. It's enough to give you the strength to go on. You are seen in your suffering. You are loved.

203 | *2 Chronicles 28–29*
Isaiah 7
Matthew 10:34—11:1

"I will not ask! I will not tempt the LORD!" (Is 7:12)

We are very familiar with the prophecy in Isaiah 7:14, but reading this chapter of Isaiah alongside 2 Chronicles 28 helps us see what kind of man King Ahaz of Judah was. He seems in Isaiah 7:12 to have been humbling himself before God, but 2 Chronicles clearly shows that he was not a humble man. Perhaps he refused to ask the Lord for a sign because he wanted to seek the power of other gods, dismissing the God who asks so much of his followers. Perhaps he trusted in Assyria to save him and had no need of the God of Israel. Either way, God was offering Ahaz a purely unmerited gift, but Ahaz preferred to fend for himself. Saint Francis de Sales said of this passage, "When God wants to favor us, it's pride to refuse." What grace is the Lord offering you that you're too proud to accept?

204 | *2 Chronicles 30–31*
Isaiah 8
Matthew 11:2–19

"I will trust in the LORD, who is hiding his face from the house of Jacob; yes, I will wait for him." (Is 8:17)

How beautiful is the heart of King Hezekiah of Judah? Most of Israel had been in exile in Assyria for several years, but Hezekiah didn't exult in the desolation of his rivals. He went out looking for them. He sent couriers throughout the land, calling people to come back to the Lord, to celebrate the Passover and believe that the God who'd saved them once would save them again. Today we read this alongside Isaiah 8:17, where Isaiah (speaking around the same time) says, "I will trust in the Lord, who is hiding his face from the house of Jacob; yes, I will wait for him." Isaiah was trying to trust in a God who seemed awfully far. Hezekiah was offering hope to a people he had every reason to scorn and ignore. May we, too, trust in God when he seems to be hiding his face. May we, too, proclaim good news to our enemies. May we offer this prayer of trust: I will trust in God when he is silent. I will trust in God when he denies my prayers. I will trust in God when he seems to have forsaken me. I will trust in God.

205 | *2 Chronicles 32–33*
Isaiah 9
Matthew 11:20–30

"Take my yoke upon you and learn from me, for I am meek and humble of heart; and you will find rest for yourselves." (Mt 11:29)

I've always loved this Gospel passage, with its comfort and gentleness and promise of rest for my weary soul. But years ago, I realized that the promise of rest isn't about a life without work; this rest comes from bearing the yoke alongside Jesus. Rest is the fruit of work done according to our calling and ability. And very specifically, the work he is calling us to here is the work of becoming meek and humble of heart. To be meek doesn't mean to be a pushover, but to submit one's power to control: the control of the one who bears the yoke alongside you. At first, this seemed to me just to be a demand: "If you're good, I'll give you rest." But over the years, I've come to realize how much meekness and humility themselves give rest. Pride is exhausting, as I so well know. Uncontrolled rage and selfishness drain us. But genuine meekness and humility are restful and life-giving; they empower us to be his and to rest in his Sacred Heart without the tension of all our passions trying to pull us out of that peace.

206 | *2 Chronicles 34–36*
Isaiah 10
Matthew 12:1–14

"Early and often the LORD ... sent his messengers to them, for he had compassion on his people." (2 Chr 36:15)

The conclusion of 2 Chronicles offers us much-needed perspective, especially verses 15 and 16, where the author explains how desperately the Lord tried to convert his people. Every punishment he sent was an attempt to heal them and draw them back to him. But even after sweet seventeen-year-old King Josiah of Judah finally destroyed the pagan cult they had nurtured for hundreds of years, the people weren't willing to turn to God. They wouldn't abandon their pagan worship. They wouldn't keep the Sabbath or honor sabbatical years. As a last-ditch effort to save the nation, Jeremiah 34:8–11 tells us, they were told to set free the slaves whose liberty hadn't been granted during the many sabbatical years the people of Judah had refused to observe (Ex 21:2). But after freeing their slaves, the corrupt people enslaved them again. God finally withdrew his protection entirely. Jerusalem was overrun. The temple was destroyed. The people were deported to Babylon. And the kingdom of Judah was no more.

207 | *Zephaniah*
Isaiah 11
Matthew 12:15–37

"The Lord, your God, is in your midst, a mighty savior. … / Who will sing joyfully because of you." (Zep 3:17)

The people listening to these words of the Prophet Zephaniah had no idea what joy was coming. They had no idea that when the Lord was in their midst as savior — dancing with joy over them — he would be a man they could see and touch and consume in the Eucharist. They had no idea how he would delight in each lost lamb set upon his shoulders. They had no idea that he would set them free not just from exile and oppression but from sin and from hell and from the slow, agonizing soul-death of being unloved. Today, ask the Lord to show you how he rejoices over you, how he sings joyfully because of you. Imagine Jesus singing this canticle of Zephaniah at a festival in Jerusalem, thinking of you.

208 | *Titus*
Isaiah 12
Matthew 12:38–50

"God's grace has been revealed, and it has made salvation possible for the whole human race." (Ti 2:11, Jerusalem Bible)

It's easy to assume that Jesus was just using Jonah and Solomon as examples because both were effective in converting people. But there are more layers to the typology. Jonah went to the Gentiles to draw them miraculously to the Lord, as did Jesus. Solomon, whose wisdom was immeasurable, was the son of David, as is Jesus, who is wisdom itself. It's also worth noting that Jonah is the only Scripture Jesus ever referenced about the Resurrection. Jonah is the anti-Jesus in many ways, particularly because he ran from God's will and refused to offer God's mercy. But there's no denying that Jonah's time in the belly of the whale pointed forward to Jesus' time in the tomb, nor that the very mention of the story would remind his listeners of the dangers of lamenting the conversion of the Gentiles (as they themselves were so apt to do). How often do we refuse to follow or trust God without signs when the only sign we need is the Resurrection?

209 | *Nahum*
Isaiah 13
Matthew 13:1–30

"The LORD is good, / a stronghold in the day of trouble; / he knows those who take refuge in him." (Na 1:7, RSV2CE)

The violence and doom of Nahum can be disturbing, but context helps. Nahum was prophesying against the city that had destroyed the Northern Kingdom of Israel, the same city that had repented at the preaching of Jonah but whose conversion lasted no more than a few decades. The destruction that Nahum prophesied was so complete that after it fell, Nineveh wasn't seen again until it was discovered in 1847 — 2,454 years later. But while this is speaking to a moment in history, it also speaks of God's plans to destroy our enemies. Forget for a moment that Assyria was a nation of people and just read the allegory. God will destroy your enemy — your sin, your shame, your pain, your brokenness, even death and the devil himself — so thoroughly that it will be as though none of it ever existed. Our God will fight for us against all the spiritual enemies that oppress us. And in the midst of the promised victory and the violence that surrounds it, Nahum 1:7 speaks hope. Not just hope to us who cling to the Lord, but hope to those Assyrians who might hear this prophecy and repent before it was too late.

210 | *Philemon*
Isaiah 14
Matthew 13:31–53

"If he has done you any injustice or owes you anything, charge it to me." (Phlm 18)

Saint Paul's Letter to Philemon has been misused over the centuries to tell enslaved people who've escaped that God wants them to go back to their captors, or to tell people in slavery that they can't seek freedom. That is not what it's saying. It's talking about Onesimus, one specific man who was given a specific call (in the context of ancient slavery, which is very different from chattel slavery). With that caveat, consider Paul's trust in Philemon, certain that one who had been ransomed from slavery to sin would respect the freedom of Onesimus, whose debt Paul had taken on in imitation of Jesus (18). And look at Onesimus's amazing act of courage. He went back freely, not out of shame but in trust that conversion had so changed Philemon that Onesimus would truly be received as a brother. He was living in freedom but went back to a man who had the power to imprison him, trusting in the power of grace to change people radically. Are we living lives that give evidence of that grace? Do people look at us and believe that Christians are prodigally merciful, kind, and selfless?

211 | *Habakkuk*
Isaiah 15
Matthew 13:54—14:21

"Yet I will rejoice in the LORD / and exult in my saving God." (Hb 3:18)

I've always loved Habakkuk 3:17–19 as a cry of hope in the midst of suffering, but it was only recently that I realized that the specific suffering is a lack of fruit. This is Habakkuk rejoicing in God's goodness even when he's a failure, even when his work is bearing no fruit. In my desolation. In my futility. In my feelings of abandonment. He is still good. I will praise him.

212

James 1–3
Isaiah 16
Matthew 14:22–36

"With it we bless the Lord and Father, and with it we curse human beings who are made in the likeness of God." (Jas 3:9)

James's discussion of the tongue in chapter 3 is so convicting. With it we bless and curse. With it we receive the Body of Christ, and with it we revile members of his body. But the tongue (representing both the spoken and the written word) isn't just a fire; it's also a lamp. Which means you can't just extinguish it, you have to learn how to steward it, when to let the light blaze and when to dial it back. The beginning of chapter 2 sheds a great deal of light on this when talking about partiality. Online especially, it's so easy to shout things that will meet with resounding agreement from our followers. But we need to be more concerned with the hearts of the wounded and alienated and marginalized and oppressed than we are with the egos of the powerful — even when they're powerful only in our circles. It's even easier to bow before those people without realizing our fault; may God give us the grace to cling instead to what is true, however much it might cost us.

213 | *James 4–5*
Isaiah 17
Matthew 15:1–20

"Therefore, confess your sins to one another and pray for one another, that you may be healed." (Jas 5:16)

Everybody's got something to repent of in these chapters of James: pride, materialism, envy, gossip, judgment, presumption, greed, impatience, a complaining spirit. Take some time to pray about which of these condemnations you really need to be convicted of. But then take heart: James speaks to us also of the Sacrament of Reconciliation and (at the very end) a promise that even in our sinfulness we can be instruments by which God draws a soul back to himself. What a tremendous gift that he allows us to help in his work of redemption.

214 | *Jeremiah 1–2*
Isaiah 18
Matthew 15:21–39

"Lord, help me." (Mt 15:25)

This Gospel passage about the Canaanite woman is awfully upsetting. At first glance, Jesus seems callous, even cruel. But we know who he is. We know he can't be cruel. We also know that God is able to work for good for all people simultaneously, even seemingly opposing goods. What if he were proving a point to the disciples about their prejudice and selfishness while simultaneously encouraging the woman to pray earnestly? By his silence, he exposed their belief that she was a burden, then he treated her as they asked, knowing that her desire (and her understanding of him) would be purified by his resistance. It seems harsh, but he knew her heart — knew what she needed. In the end, he left her with praise and a prayer answered. And then (in answer, it seems, to her prayer) continued his healing among the Gentiles and multiplied loaves for them, too. She was never abandoned, never unloved. May the Canaanite woman, patroness of prayers long unanswered, pray for us. May our unanswered prayers always draw us to the side of Jesus.

215 | *Jeremiah 3–4*
Isaiah 19
Matthew 16:1–12

"Blessed be my people Egypt, and the work of my hands Assyria, and my heritage, Israel." (Is 19:25)

This passage in Isaiah always makes me so glad that I mark up my Bible. It's easy to skim these oracles against all sorts of nations we don't recognize, but every year I have to pause and remember why I underlined 19:21–22, 25. Egypt represents all that is sinful. Egypt was the ancestral enemy of Israel, the vile oppressor who forced them into slavery and slaughtered their children. And Assyria was the terrifying enemy that was about to destroy the Northern Kingdom of Israel. But here, God promised the salvation of Egypt and set Egypt and Assyria up as the People of God alongside Israel. This is like a promise in 1942 Poland that Adolf Hitler would be converted and ultimately canonized, or a prediction to enslaved people that their kidnappers would become wildly, radically holy. It's horrifying and baffling and so beautiful that God's mercy reaches out even to oppressors and turns the wicked into saints. Who is this God of ours who turns his enemies into his children? What a gift to us who were Egypt and Assyria and have become his own.

216

Jeremiah 5–6
Isaiah 20
Matthew 16:13–28

"They have treated lightly / the injury to my people: / 'Peace, peace!' they say, / though there is no peace." (Jer 6:14)

Jeremiah was warning the people of Judah of their impending deportation to Babylon, begging them to repent before their nation was destroyed. As the Book of Jeremiah goes on, we'll see him opposing false prophets who offered the people a false sense of security rather than calling them to repentance and preparing them for the Babylonian captivity. His condemnation in 6:14 is so important — especially in our day, so prone to division. We become inclined to silence outcries in order to "keep the peace," but we forget that there is no peace without justice. When we refuse to listen to those who are suffering, we side with the oppressors. It's a difficult balance to strike, as we seek to speak truth with compassion and gentleness and charity, to be bold without being ugly or disdainful. But our insistence on being "nice" to loud or powerful people whose words and actions hurt the marginalized is no response. Our silence harms the suffering, whatever our intentions. We must honor people's woundedness, listen to their pain, and stand beside them seeking justice if we ever want peace.

217 | *Jeremiah 7–8*
Isaiah 21
Matthew 17

"I am broken by the injury of the daughter of my people." (Jer 8:21)

In Jeremiah 8:18–23, we see just how painful it is to love sinners well, to grieve over their suffering even when it's the direct result of their bad choices. What would our lives look like if we truly loved sinners like this? If we were heartbroken over their suffering, disconsolate because of their pain as well as lamenting their mistakes? Even those whose lives haven't fallen apart, who aren't reaping what they've sown? How would we live if we hated injustice enough to be willing to weep with those who weep, even the perpetrators? What if leaders in the Church lamented people's suffering like this? Even their self-inflicted suffering? Jeremiah called out, "Is there no balm in Gilead?" There is none. None but the blood of Jesus. Chapter 9 will begin with God's cry of hatred against sin, but it's always, always rooted in his love of sinners.

218 | *Jeremiah 9–10*
Isaiah 22
Matthew 18:1–20

"Treat him as you would a Gentile or a tax collector." (Mt 18:17)

It's easy to assume that treating someone as a Gentile or a tax collector means counting him as one of the damned and cutting him out of your life. I expect that's what most of the apostles thought he meant at first. But not Matthew, the tax collector who was the only one to have recorded this saying of Jesus. He knew just how Jesus treated Gentiles and tax collectors. The Good Shepherd loves his sheep with a stern-as-death, burn-away-your-sins, wild, rejoicing love that heals broken hearts and pulls addicts from the miry pit. But somehow we look at a God with bleeding hands and think he won't have mercy. We hear the witness of a filthy, smelly, ornery sheep whose shepherd came rappelling down the side of a ravine to save him and still think that some people are too much trouble. They are worth loving. You are worth loving. Have boundaries, of course. Don't make yourself available for people's abuse or ignore their persistent sin just so things stay pleasant. But our response to unrepentant sinners must always, always be love.

219

Jeremiah 11–12
Isaiah 23
Matthew 18:21–35

"A man who owed him ten thousand bags of gold was brought to him." (Mt 18:24, NIV)

Some rabbis at the time of Jesus said that a righteous man had to forgive a sinner three times. Peter clearly thought he was being tremendously merciful when he offered to forgive seven times. He knew that Jesus' mercy exceeded the rabbis', but he didn't realize that it was on a completely different scale. Jesus made it clear why he expected such radical mercy in the parable that follows. The "huge amount" the man owed was 10,000 talents. One talent was worth about 6,000 days' wages for a laborer, or half a lifetime's work; this man owed a debt of 164,000 years of work. We are obviously this man, owing God such a debt not only for our sin but also for the million unmerited graces he's given us. But he forgives us this debt. And then we act like the man in the parable, encountering someone who owes us 1/600,000 of what we owe. We're so caught up in our own need, so fixated on what we deserve, that we forget all that we've been given. Our whole lives are the product of overflowing mercy; may we learn to offer mercy in the measure in which we've received it.

220 | *Jeremiah 13–14*
Isaiah 24
Matthew 19:1–15

"Let my eyes stream with tears / night and day, without rest." (Jer 14:17)

Here at the end of Jeremiah 14, God sent Jeremiah to Jerusalem not, in this moment, to tell them what to do, but only to weep over them. We see how deeply he longs to be united to his people, closer to them than they are to their underwear. But here, Jeremiah's job wasn't directly to draw Judah back to God. There were certainly times when he was exhorting them, but in this moment his prophetic action was weeping over the suffering of the broken. That was his mission as much as it was Mary's mission at the foot of the cross. Perhaps right now, our mission is to weep over a terrorist attack or an act of racist violence, over mass incarceration or abortion, over the plight of refugees or the plague of loneliness in our world. Like Jeremiah, we also have to act. We also have to cry out what is true. We also have to orient our lives toward bringing God's justice into this world. But sometimes, it is prophetic merely to weep and mourn.

221 | *Jeremiah 15–16*
Isaiah 25
Matthew 19:16–30

"On this mountain he will destroy / the veil that veils all peoples." (Is 25:7)

Isaiah really is an astonishing book. He spends chapter after chapter foretelling doom and judgment, then suddenly stops to promise the good things that are to come. I think verse 1 must just have been a sudden gasp of wonder at the Lord's goodness when God revealed the coming Messianic Kingdom. This feast that Isaiah describes is an invitation to all peoples, even the ones that Israel and Judah may have wanted to exclude. It foretells the Eucharistic feast, which is itself a foretaste of the eternal wedding feast of the Lamb, when the veil that separates us from God will be removed, completing its rending that began at the crucifixion (Mt 27:51). The people there will recognize the God who saved them. Remember that Jesus means "God saves." Remember the people united in feasting on a hilltop as at the multiplication of loaves and fishes. Remember the veil torn in two at the crucifixion, and delight in our God who has planned everything so well for our salvation.

222 | *Jeremiah 17–18*
Isaiah 26
Matthew 20:1–16

"Are you envious because I am generous?" (Mt 20:15)

I cannot tell you how much I love this parable. I love the image of the Father going back for his people again and again. I love the humiliated workers waiting all day, worrying that they would go home empty-handed but never giving up. I love the bitter workers who couldn't see that their day in the vineyard was a gift, that their hard work was easier than the hopelessness outside. I love the master's generosity and the discomfort I feel when I sympathize with the workers. Obviously, Jesus is telling us about the gift of salvation offered to people who haven't "earned it" (as though any of us could). But this parable is equally applicable when we begrudge people a living wage or supportive parents or a debt-free life just because we don't have them. How often do we envy people their good fortune, even when it takes nothing from us? By God's grace, may we learn to rejoice at his generosity rather than incessantly demanding an accounting.

223 | *Jeremiah 19–20*
Isaiah 27
Matthew 20:17–34

"You duped me, O Lord, and I let myself be duped." (Jer 20:7, NAB)

Poor Jeremiah. He was so young and so alone and trying so hard to be faithful while being attacked on every side. It's easy to understand his anger and pain in chapter 20, to think back to times in our lives when we, too, felt that we had been duped by the Lord, seduced by the promise of love and joy and peace and left with a life that demands far more than we feel we can give. Even in Jeremiah's suffering and frustration, though, God's glory and mercy are too great not to proclaim. He serves God not merely because of an external obligation but because the praise of God erupts from within him and he can't help but proclaim it. There's a healing that comes here, a conversion through prayer to trust and confidence in God, but in verses 14 to 18 he sinks back from praise into self-pity. It's tremendously relatable and so encouraging to see that one of the great prophets of God also felt abandoned and conflicted and discouraged and yet continued speak of God's love and mercy and judgment, whatever the cost.

224 | *Jeremiah 21–22*
Isaiah 28
Matthew 21:1–17

"Behold, your king comes to you, meek and riding on an ass." (Mt 21:5)

I imagine that some in the crowd that day were very confused by the conflicting imagery they were seeing. Jesus entered the city in triumph, but riding a lowly and humble animal. He was hailed as the conquering hero, but he was going into battle meek. The imagery was so profoundly Messianic as to leave the whole city shaken, especially when he went straight to the temple and brought the sacrifices to a halt. But then he left the city again, going to Bethany to stay with his friends. There's nothing predictable about our God — not in the way he worked then and not in the way he works now. And there's nothing predictable about the call he's going to place on your heart. Some of us are naturally timid and will be asked to stand up and be counted. Some of us were born with both feet in our mouths and will be asked to be silent and humble. Most of us will be asked to do some of both, and we'll only know which one if we're rooted in prayer.

225 | *Jeremiah 23–24* *Isaiah 29* *Matthew 21:18–32*

"How long shall there be lies in the heart of the prophets ... who prophecy the deceit of their own heart?" (Jer 23:26, RSV2CE)

Every time we encounter Scripture as an accusation against our enemies, we need to stop and let it accuse us first. When I read Jeremiah's excoriations of wicked or worthless shepherds, of people who prophesy in God's name without being sent by him, all I can think of is everybody else. I think of priests and bishops who refuse to root out sex offenders; racist clerics or anyone who is complicit in racism; bishops who refuse to speak boldly against abortion; people who claim that God has sent a particular political candidate or that Catholics must vote a certain way or be damned. All of these people need a prophet like Jeremiah to talk sense into them — but so do I. There are times when all of us are the faithless shepherd, when we mislead our children or abandon our seeking coworkers. There are times when we use the name of the Lord in vain, claiming to speak on behalf of God when we've been given no word of prophecy. If Jeremiah's denunciations of the prophets make you feel triumphant, take a step back and ask what they're condemning in you.

226 | *Jeremiah 25–26*
Isaiah 30
Matthew 21:33–46

"By waiting and by calm you shall be saved, / in quiet and in trust shall be your strength." (Is 30:15)

Isaiah was speaking to a people desperately searching for their salvation anywhere but God. They were so panicked that they went to their worst enemy to seek help. But Isaiah promised them that waiting, calm, quiet, and trust would be their only path to salvation. The Lord, he said, was waiting, longing to show them favor, to heal them and wipe away their tears. How would he do this? He would offer them bread and (living) water. He would come as their teacher whom they would see with their own eyes. He would break them of their idolatry so that he could bind up their wounds. You may be tempted to turn to other gods to save you — the gods of politics or ideology or pleasure or self-actualization or whatever. But Isaiah reminds us that only in the love of Jesus can we find healing. And that love is found when we turn to him in silent prayer and give him space to speak his peace to our hearts.

227

Jeremiah 27–29
Isaiah 31
Matthew 22:1–14

"For I know the plans I have for you … to prosper you and not to harm you, plans to give you hope." (Jer 29:11, NIV)

Jeremiah was unpopular because he didn't tell the people to fight or run away or organize resistance movements. He told them to stay put and submit, to persevere through misery because salvation was coming, though a long way off. Jeremiah 29:11 is a promise of hope to those who were persevering in unimaginable difficulty. But the promise would only be fulfilled after seventy years of exile — when nearly all those listening had died. God was asking them to trust in his love when there was no hope for freedom, to trust that he was with them even when none of them would visit the temple again. We often find ourselves in situations like this: in a miserable (but not abusive) marriage, a dead-end job, a parish we'd gladly leave. Sometimes God is calling us to a change. But sometimes he's just calling us to persevere, to be holy in circumstances that aren't ideal. It's often easier to give up on what's hard and go after something radical or new or impressive. But more often than not, holiness is more a matter of persevering in difficulty and drudgery than it is wild adventures.

228 | *Jeremiah 30–31*
Isaiah 32
Matthew 22:15–33

"I have loved you with an everlasting love; / I have drawn you with unfailing kindness." (Jer 31:3, NIV)

With age-old, everlasting love he has loved you. What a thing to say! And then he calls Israel "virgin Israel." This is the Israel who had so often been accused of adultery for her unfaithfulness to the Lord — the Israel now destroyed for her sin. This kingdom was a wasteland, left in utter devastation a century earlier. But when God looked at Israel, he didn't see sin; he only saw his beloved. When God looks at you, he doesn't see your sin; he only sees his beloved, the one he has loved with an everlasting love. He will lead you back to himself, though the road may be steep and rocky, and you may feel abandoned and alone on your journey. He will turn your mourning into joy and console you after your sorrow. He will be your God, and you will be his beloved. That is the promise of Jeremiah, fulfilled in Jesus and offered to each of us. God can make our brokenness radiant in this life and heal it perfectly in the next. He can restore us to innocence and make our scars as glorious as Christ's wounds, transformed by the grace that makes us new.

229 | *Jeremiah 32–33*
Isaiah 33
Matthew 22:34–46

"I am the LORD, the God of all the living! Is anything too difficult for me?" (Jer 32:27)

When God told Jeremiah to perform the seemingly idiotic task of buying a piece of land in a country that was being destroyed, Jeremiah didn't ask why. He did it. Only after obeying did he ask God why. But first he listed all the amazing things he knew about the Lord, as though trying to convince himself that God is trustworthy even when his commands seem nonsensical. Only then, having declared that he trusted in the Lord and would continue to obey, did he question. His witness is so important to us. First, because he obeyed immediately without demanding that God explain himself. Second, because he really seems to have needed to remind himself to trust God. Third, because he did question God. He obeyed, but then he wrestled and struggled and didn't hide his doubts and fears but brought them before the Lord. And finally, because he was content with a less-than-ideal answer. The answer was that good things would come again eventually, though not necessarily to Jeremiah. And that was enough for him.

230 | *Jeremiah 34–35*
Isaiah 34
Matthew 23

"So I now proclaim 'freedom' for you, declares the Lord — 'freedom' to fall by the sword, plague and famine." (Jer 34:17, NIV)

After all their idolatry and hypocrisy and even the sacrificing of their children, this was the final straw. They had refused to free their slaves as God had commanded they do every seven years. Then they tried to trick him into blessing them by freeing their slaves and then re-enslaving them the very same day. This finally violated the covenant beyond repair, calling down upon them the punishment alluded to in Genesis 15 when Abram cut the sacrifices in half. Still, God was faithful. Though they violated the covenant and called this punishment down upon themselves, God came himself to be destroyed in their place, offered for their salvation — for our salvation. Sometimes Jeremiah speaks words of consolation, other times words of doom and woe, but it's all part of the same message of God's wild love. He loves us exactly as we are, but loves us too much to leave us that way. The condemnation of sin is a gift because it calls us to healing and transformation and eternal life.

231

Jeremiah 36–37
Isaiah 35
Matthew 24:1–28

"Say to the fearful of heart: / Be strong, do not fear! / Here is your God." (Is 35:4)

This chapter of Isaiah is obviously foretelling the deliverance of God's people, first when they return from exile and again when the Messiah comes and sets us all free. But it's a beautiful canticle of hope to pray at any time, trusting that God will bring healing and joy and fruitfulness and strength, even if only in eternity. Sit with this chapter today and ask for the grace to believe that it's true.

232 | *Jeremiah 38–39*
Isaiah 36
Matthew 24:29–51

"Please obey to the voice of the LORD and do as I tell you." (Jer 38:20, NAB)

There's a seductive voice that tells us to hedge our bets, to put up safety nets and secure our comfort rather than trust in the Lord. Sometimes it's insidious, as with the commander of Sennacherib's army, when he insisted that Judah's reliance on the Lord was actually failure to trust in God. But it can be difficult to discern what is prudence and what is faithlessness, what is trust and what is recklessness. Here in Isaiah, trust in God meant resisting the enemy. In Jeremiah, it meant surrendering to the enemy. There is always a degree of uncertainty when it comes to doing God's will in anything other than moral absolutes; he rarely sends angels with detailed plans. But we become more attuned to God's voice when we spend time with Scripture and make time for silent prayer every day, asking him to form our heart to desire what he desires. May we listen to the voice of God and live in his will, whatever it might be.

233

Jeremiah 40–42
Isaiah 37
Matthew 25:1–30

"Whether it is pleasant or difficult, we will obey the command of the Lord.*" (Jer 42:6, NAB)*

I wonder whether Jeremiah was optimistic, if he managed to convince himself that the Judahites truly had been humbled and would finally be obedient. You would think that after all this suffering, a people would finally decide to rely on God. But that's not necessarily how things go. For all they insisted that they would obey, they weren't in the habit of following the Lord in small things, so they were unlikely to be faithful in this large one. Jeremiah seems almost to have been begging them not to go to Egypt, not just because it would be disobedient, but also because of the fate awaiting them there. But by the time he finished giving God's message, it was clear to Jeremiah that the people would not obey. It is a heartbreaking thing to beg someone you love not to do something that will hurt them, only to watch helplessly as they refuse to listen and end up devastated. I can only imagine how it must break the Sacred Heart of Jesus, given how much more he knows about all we will suffer.

234 | *Jeremiah 43–44*
Isaiah 38
Matthew 25:31–46

"We will not listen to what you say. ... Rather we will continue doing what we had proposed." (Jer 44:16–17, NAB)

Only two chapters ago the people had promised Jeremiah that they would obey the command of the Lord no matter what. Now they were outright saying that they would not listen to God but would continue doing whatever they wanted. It seems ridiculous because it's so overt, but it's something we all do. Sometimes it's falling into patterns of sin we've repented of but not fully; sometimes it's outright hypocrisy; sometimes it's an insistent fidelity to Rome that only lasts as long as the right person holds the See of Peter; sometimes it's cruelty or cattiness allegedly for the sake of the Gospel. I'm not talking here about those times when we try and fail, the sins we resist but are genuinely addicted to. I'm talking about apparent penitence and faithfulness that cloak our own pride and self-will. Are there areas where this false piety and half-hearted obedience are the attitudes you take toward God?

235 | *Jeremiah 45–47*
Isaiah 39
Matthew 26:1–25

"At least there will be peace and truth in my days." (Is 39:8, NKJV)

King Hezekiah of Judah was profoundly relieved that Assyria had left him alone and that he'd recovered from his mortal illness. So when the Babylonian messengers came, he cheerfully showed them all the wealth of Judah. Those of us who know that Judah would be destroyed by Babylon a century later read this with shock and dread. Then, when the almost comically ignorant Hezekiah learned what would be the consequences of his action, his response was calm acceptance. He actually said that this was a favorable prophecy! And all because there would be peace during his lifetime. While it's reasonable not to expect a country to continue in peace for all time, Hezekiah could have pretended to be upset that the People of God were going to be destroyed. But he couldn't see beyond himself to the suffering of his descendants. It's not uncommon to be so relieved at our own safety and protection that we ignore the suffering of others, but this is unchristian. Whose suffering is the Lord asking you to recognize? Is there anything you can do to relieve it?

236 | *Jeremiah 48–49* *Lamentations 1* *Matthew 26:26–56*

"This is why I weep / and my eyes overflow with tears. / No one is near to comfort me." (Lam 1:16, NIV)

The Book of Lamentations is a series of poems traditionally attributed to Jeremiah as he lamented the destruction of Jerusalem when the Jews were taken into captivity in 587 BC. Many of us can identify with these prayers on a visceral level, having seen the destruction of so much we love while the rest all seems to hang precariously, waiting for the next natural disaster or outbreak of war or announcement of plague. But it's good to read mournful Scriptures even when we're feeling joyful, to sit in that mess and remember the times of suffering the Lord has brought us through, but also to pray in solidarity with those who are suffering right now and who have suffered in the past. Think of the millions of Jews who still long for the rebuilding of the temple, the many millions who have mourned the loss of Jerusalem over the centuries, and pray in solidarity with them. Whose suffering does this passage call to mind for you? How can you bring comfort to those who suffer today?

237 | *Jeremiah 50–51*
Lamentations 2
Matthew 26:57–75

"I will forgive the remnant I preserve." (Jer 50:20)

Jeremiah's prophecies about the fall of Babylon are awfully disturbing to most who read them today. But think what hope he was offering to the exiled people of Judah as they waited for the defeat of their enemies, the triumph of their God, the restoration of their homes, and freedom from oppression. Still, though Jeremiah may have prophesied of this at the beginning of the captivity, almost nobody who heard his prophecy would have seen it fulfilled. It took seventy years, long enough for even the babies who left Jerusalem to have largely died out. What does it look like to live in hope of a day you will never see? How do we continue to trust that God will turn all things to good when healing and answered prayers seem impossible in this world? Can we love him enough that even our anguish and loneliness and fear and dissatisfaction praise him? Perhaps only because of the Cross.

238 | *Jeremiah 52* *Lamentations 3* *Matthew 27:1–26*

"But this I call to mind, / and therefore I have hope: / The steadfast love of the LORD never ceases." (Lam 3:21–22, RSC2VE)

This chapter of Lamentations has brought me through some extraordinarily hard times. It comes in the middle of a book so mournful that it was given the name Lamentations. Jeremiah is so desolate that he says he has forgotten what happiness is and is incapable even of praying. Many of us have been there, trapped in a feeling of misery so oppressive we can't even penetrate it to throw up a prayer. Jeremiah reminds himself that even in our suffering, God is still good. He continues to love us, continues to work miracles, continues to be ours. He is good in our suffering, and any suffering that he allows is for our good. Though he may seem to wrap himself in a cloud that prayer cannot pierce (3:8), he is still good. This passage is so real and raw and painful and hopeful that it always takes my breath away. It strikes me not as a declaration of truth spoken through gritted teeth, but a sudden realization, a fleeting moment of joy in the Lord. Jeremiah follows it by exhorting his people to follow the God who seems so distant, then (God love him) falls back into his suffering.

239 | *Baruch 1:1—3:8*
Lamentations 4
Matthew 27:27–66

"Lord Almighty, God of Israel, the anguished soul, the dismayed spirit cries out to you." (Bar 3:1)

Baruch (Jeremiah's secretary) was speaking into the same anguish and hopelessness of the Babylonian captivity as Lamentations. How striking that in 2:27 Baruch leads the exiles in thanking God for his mercy in allowing them to go into exile, declaring his trust (in verse 30) that this exile would bring about a change of heart for the people so that they would be converted by their suffering. Can you pray this about your anguish? Perhaps all that God has allowed really will work for the transformation and healing of souls. As we wait and hope, take time today to pray Baruch 3:1–6 over our world. Pray for those in danger of political upheaval and natural disasters and those recovering from them, for those living in fear and those living from selfishness, for those who are grieving and those who are sick and those who are drowning in the uncertainty and the misery of it all. "Hear, Lord, and have mercy, for you are a merciful God" (Bar 3:2).

240 | *Baruch 3:9—5:9*
Lamentations 5
Matthew 28

"With mourning and lament I sent you away, but God will give you back to me with gladness and joy forever." (Bar 4:23)

A friend who placed her son in an adoptive home once told me that Baruch 4:22–23 is her favorite Bible passage because she prays it for her son. I always think of her when I read this, trying to join in her longing and her trust that everything will be healed in heaven. I think of all who've lost loved ones, whether to family separation or death or addiction or immigration or ideological divisions or any of the thousand things that separate people. I pray that we would all learn to live in the hope Baruch speaks of and that one day we would receive the healing he promises.

241 | *Baruch 6*
Isaiah 40
Mark 1:1–13

"The LORD is the everlasting God, / the Creator of the ends of the earth. / He does not faint or grow weary." (Is 40:28, RSV2CE)

I'm always excited when I reach this portion of my Bible schedule. I love Isaiah 40–66 (known as "the book of consolation") more than almost any other part of Scripture. In this chapter we read the prophecy that points to John the Baptist calling out in the desert, speaking of the Messiah who would bring comfort, cry out the good news (Gospel), and reward his people by coming himself and holding them to his heart. This God before whom all the nations are as nothing is satisfied by your heart. He does not faint or grow weary but shares his strength with those who follow him. There's a beautiful line in the Liturgy of the Hours that strikes me every week: "Oh Lord our God, unwearied is your love for us." Remembering that his love is unwearied sends a thrill through this sinner's heart. No matter what I do or how far I run, he is still longing to love me. His love is unwearied. So is his providence. His wisdom is unwearied, even when I can't see what he's doing. His power is unwearied, despite his apparent failure to act.

242 | *Tobit 1–3*
Isaiah 41
Mark 1:14–31

"You are righteous, Lord, / and all your deeds are just." (Tb 3:2)

Tobit tells the story of an Israelite family living in Assyria during the Exile — the only glimpse we get of the exiles' life. Tobit's family was among the few who remained faithful in Israel (and then Assyria) during centuries of false worship. Tobit 3 speaks so powerfully to those of us who feel abandoned by God. Both Tobit and Sarah were despondent. They could see no hope in their lives. Both prayed for death but began by praising God even in their anguish. And God heard their prayers. Providence drew out these beautiful, wretched prayers at the same time, then answered them with the same story, though they were hundreds of miles apart. They saw no change in the immediate aftermath, but God was working in a way they could never have foreseen. It took time. It took Tobit through even greater pain. But God was working, answering their prayers. He was faithful — even when they couldn't see it. I wonder for what prayers of mine for which he's setting answers in motion.

243 | *Tobit 4–6*
Isaiah 42
Mark 1:32–45

"A bruised reed he will not break, / and a dimly burning wick he will not quench." (Is 42:3)

The Book of Isaiah is often called the fifth gospel, brimming with allusions to the Messiah. In Isaiah 42:1–4, we see the first of the songs of the Suffering Servant (also found in 49:1–7; 50:4–11; and 52:13—53:12). Verse 1 reminds us of the language of the Father at the baptism of Jesus and at the Transfiguration, the tender voice of love spoken over his gentle servant who would cast out demons and slay death but break no reeds and quench no wicks. Verse 6 tells us that the Messiah would be a light to the nations, reminding us of the Canticle of Simeon (Lk 2:29–32). Verse 7 points to Jesus' healing of the blind and the liberation he brings to all, but in a particular way to the dead he would draw out of the tomb. Isaiah's merciful Messiah is the same God from Numbers and Judges, the same God whose commands might have made us cringe on occasion. This is the truth that undergirds all we understand about the God of the Bible: his never-ceasing tenderness.

244 | *Tobit 7–11*
Isaiah 43
Mark 2:1–17

"May the Lord of heaven grant you joy in place of your grief! Courage, my daughter!" (Tb 7:17)

It's striking how much energy the characters in Tobit spent agonizing over hypothetical suffering that the reader knows had already been averted. Edna wept over her daughter's past pain but also over the seemingly inevitable death of a bridegroom who had already been supernaturally equipped to liberate Sarah. Raguel had a grave dug for a man who was sleeping peacefully. Tobit and Anna were devastated over the loss of a son who was returning in triumph with a beloved bride. We read and smile, knowing how wasted their worry is. But we serve the same God who made everybody's worries look ridiculous in the light of his Providence, who brought sudden and impossible redemption to a hopeless situation. How much energy do we waste mourning over suffering that will never come, simply because we've forgotten how to hope? Spend some time today meditating on the wild and unexpected joy Sarah must have felt the morning after her wedding. Can you hand over your worry to God and trust that he offers you such joy?

245 | *Tobit 12–14*
Isaiah 44
Mark 2:18–28

"This one shall write on his hand, 'The Lord's.'" (Is 44:5)

There was a custom in parts of the ancient world to tattoo the owner's name on the hands of their slaves. Here in Isaiah 44:5 we see the People of God choosing to belong completely to the Lord, writing his name on their hands in a sign of their total belonging to him; a few chapters later (in 49:16), we see that God himself tattoos our names on the palms of his hand. This tattoo was called a "stigmata" (referenced in Gal 6:17 and the NAB footnote there). With this context, it's clear that the wounds of Christ, foretold seven hundred years before his birth, were a mark of his complete belonging to you, his total surrender, his willingness to become a slave (Phil 2:7) for you. Those wounds remain imprinted upon his risen flesh, an everlasting sign that he is yours.

246 | *Ezekiel 1–3*
Isaiah 45
Mark 3:1–19

"Son of man, take into your heart all my words that I speak to you; hear them well." (Ez 3:10)

Ezekiel ministered to the captive Jews in Babylon, the first prophet called outside the Holy Land. With its wild visions and layers of symbolism, his book can be hard to appreciate. But when I struggle, I remind myself that some people love this type of biblical literature. They delight in long descriptions and are captivated by God's majesty and creativity, loving him more because of the passages that I have such a hard time reading. It's true of every part of Scripture. Some people love genealogies, others the descriptions of the temple, others the detailed military history of 1 Maccabees. And there are people who can't get anything out of the Song of Songs, who find Paul tiresome, who don't thrill at the end of Isaiah. I'm so thankful that God gives us different literary genres to speak to the heart of each person. And while I'm not going to stop trying to enter into the passages I find difficult, I feel tremendously consoled that perhaps some of these words weren't written for me, but for somebody else who is so grateful for them.

247

Ezekiel 4–5
Isaiah 46
Mark 3:20–35

"'Oh no, Lord GOD!' I protested." (Ez 4:14)

I love Ezekiel's heart here at the end of chapter 4. He was a priest separated from the temple, the only place on earth where the People of God could draw near to him by offering sacrifices. With a vocation he could never hope to live out, Ezekiel must have been even more concerned with following the law. It was the way he could cling to normalcy, cling to God and faith and hope that he and his people would return to worship again. So when God himself told Ezekiel to become unclean as a sign to the people, Ezekiel was overcome. He just couldn't do it. I'm sure he would have if the Lord had pressed the issue (as he did with Saint Peter in Acts 10:9–16), but our gentle God loved him in his scrupulosity and preserved him from that suffering.

248 | *Ezekiel 6–8*
Isaiah 47
Mark 4:1–25

"I was crushed by their adulterous heart which has departed from me." (Ez 6:9, NKJV)

How painful it is to read Ezekiel 6:9 and realize that all sin is truly adultery committed against the God who loves us as a bridegroom. How painful to realize that punishment for sin (that is, the consequences of sin) is God allowing our hearts to break over our adultery so that we might repent and return to the lover of our souls. Different translations shed light on different angles here. In the New King James Version, the Lord says that the people's adulterous hearts crushed *him*, while the New American Bible speaks of God breaking our adulterous hearts. Sin does both, of course, but the pierced heart of our God pours his blood upon us so that our broken hearts draw us back to him. Lord, break my heart so that I might cling only to you.

249 | *Ezekiel 9–11*
Isaiah 48
Mark 4:26–41

"Mark an X on the foreheads of those who grieve and lament over all the abominations." (Ez 9:4)

The New American Bible, Revised Edition, translation of Ezekiel 9 says that an X was marked on the foreheads of those who remained faithful to the Lord and were heartbroken at the idolatry that surrounded them. It seems that the mark here referenced (tau) was made in the shape of a cross at the time. Those who followed the Lord were marked with the cross. That mark saved them from death, in a second Passover that pointed forward to the ultimate rescue of God's people from death. This was six hundred years before Christ, but God was laying a foundation for the salvation he would win for us on Calvary.

250 | *Ezekiel 12–13*
Isaiah 49
Mark 5:1–20

"Can a mother forget her infant? … / Even should she forget, / I will never forget you." (Is 49:15)

Isaiah 49:13–16 sings of God's earth-shattering love for you. His love is so wildly beautiful that all of creation rejoices because of it, even the mountains and the sky. Sometimes we can't sense that, no matter how powerfully the Lord proclaims it. We sit weeping that the Lord has forgotten us. But our God promises that he could never forget us. And then he points out to us how he has proven this love: He has written our names on the palms of his hands, like the name of a master on his slave. The wounds that bear our names are before him always, as he looks in heaven upon his wounded hands and feet and side and proclaims again that you were worth it. You are worth living for. You are worth dying for. You are worth the manger, the flight into Egypt, the years of drudgery. You are worth ridicule, betrayal, torture, and death. You are worth coming back for. You are worth remaining a prisoner of love in the Blessed Sacrament for. You are loved. You are fiercely, wildly, ceaselessly, unconditionally, passionately, permanently loved.

251 | *Ezekiel 14–16*
Isaiah 50
Mark 5:21–43

"But I will remember the covenant I made with you when you were young." (Ez 16:60)

Ezekiel 16 is my favorite chapter of Ezekiel. Here the Lord describes his desperate love for us. He acknowledges how broken we were without him but reminds us that he bathed us with water and anointed us with oil through baptism and confirmation — that we became his. And as his beloveds, we are stunningly beautiful because of his splendor. But the passage doesn't stop there, with God delighting in his redeemed beloved. After that, the fall. Verse after verse after verse of depravity, forty-five verses detailing the ways that we have run from him and the evil that we have done. Still, it ends with love. It ends with a covenant enacted by the one who loves us just as much in our sinfulness as he did at our purest moment. He will forgive because he cannot stop loving. And by his grace, we are that radiant, captivating bride adorned with gold and jewels again.

252

Ezekiel 17–18
Isaiah 51
Mark 6:1–29

"Do not fear the reproach of mere mortals / or be terrified by their insults." (Is 51:7, NIV)

In both Mark and Luke, we're told of Herod's attention to Jesus only after the disciples got to work. It seems it was their faithfulness, the power of their prayer, the witness of their trust that caught his attention. I wonder what it would take for the Herods of today to take note of us and wonder at Jesus. What radical forgiveness, what prophetic witness, what life-changing generosity? Our Church is certainly doing this work, but it often gets lost in the shadows cast by our judgment and cruelty and selfishness. How can you as an individual live differently so that the Church as a whole draws even people like Herod to look at Jesus? There is, as we know, great danger in drawing the attention of such a one as Herod. But there is also the possibility that a soul will be saved.

253 | *Ezekiel 19–20*
Isaiah 52
Mark 6:30–56

"Take courage, it is I, do not be afraid!" (Mk 6:50)

The statement that Jesus "meant to pass by them" may be confusing at first, but the language Mark uses is the language of theophany, of God revealing himself to his people as in Exodus 34:6, 1 Kings 19:11, and Job 9:11. Jesus' intention was not to walk past them at a distance but to reveal himself to them, walking on the crests of the waves as only God can (Jb 9:8). It's particularly moving because Jesus was in prayer on the mountain when "he saw that they were tossed about while rowing" (Mk 6:48). There with the Father he could see them and come to them in their need, not only to save them but to reveal himself to them. He took this moment of terror when he seemed so distant and made it an opportunity for them to see his glory. The apostles had learned in 4:35–41 that he could protect them from the elements when he was with them. But now they were in the midst of a storm and he wasn't there. Still he saw them. Still he came to them. Still he saved them. He'll do it for you, too.

254 | *Ezekiel 21–22*
Isaiah 53
Mark 7:1–23

"He bore the punishment that makes us whole, / by his wounds we were healed." (Is 53:5)

Take some extra time to sit with Isaiah 53 today and see how many places point forward to the passion of Jesus. Then take it one step further and see how many things don't make sense about anyone else: that giving his life means "he will see his descendants in a long life" (v. 10, NAB), that his wounds heal us, that his sacrifice will win pardon for those who have offended. Here we have the Beloved of God who was obedient even unto death and then was vindicated, saving his people by a death that seems not to have ended in death.

255 | *Ezekiel 23–24*
Isaiah 54
Mark 7:24–37

"Though the mountains be shaken / and the hills be removed, / yet my unfailing love for you will not be shaken." (Is 54:10, NIV)

How tender and loving is Isaiah 54? The prophet tells us that God is our husband, our redeemer who brings us back to himself with great tenderness and who receives his bride with enduring love. I have long loved verse 10, this unabashed declaration of the never-ending love of God. But a few years ago I began to read the beginning of verse 11 as the completion of verse 10 (NABRE): "… the Lord who has mercy on you, O afflicted one, storm-battered and unconsoled." He sees us in our brokenness and in our mess and still insists that he will never, never stop loving us. Even if you've run off, made yourself feel forsaken and abandoned, he's waiting with tenderness. He's longing to take you back, offering enduring love to heal your broken heart. How blessed are we to know this God, to hear this promise of love and rejoice that we are beloved even when we are broken and afflicted, incapable of feeling it.

256 | *Ezekiel 25–26*
Isaiah 55
Mark 8:1–26

"My heart is moved with pity for the crowd." (Mk 8:2)

Chapter 8 of the Gospel of Mark recounts Jesus' return to the territory where he had healed the demoniac in chapter 5. It seems that the demoniac had done his job after Jesus told him to announce all that the Lord had done for him (Mk 5:19). Again, Jesus' heart was moved with pity for the hungry people; this time, four thousand Gentiles. He worried that they would collapse on the way, using the same verb as in Hebrews 12:3 (there translated "grow weary"). The Eucharist, our share in the passion of Christ, keeps us from growing weary and losing heart. How often do we forget the wonders God has done and doubt his ability to provide? How often do we seek strength in what fails to satisfy while his body and blood are offered to us each day?

257 | *Ezekiel 27–28*
Isaiah 56
Mark 8:27–38

"These I will bring to my holy mountain / and give them joy in my house of prayer." (Is 56:7, NIV)

What a beautiful message of welcome Isaiah offers to those who had so long been excluded from the People of God, the foreigners and eunuchs who were forbidden entry into the temple, allowed to come close but always held at a distance. It ought to call to mind those members of our own community who feel excluded. I think particularly of LGBTQ+ people, many of whom have heard the Church's teaching and expect to be rejected — often are rejected. And even when they are welcomed, they frequently feel so excluded and misunderstood, so hopeless in our Church culture. To them God offers a welcome and promises something better than sons and daughters, better even than the great gift of family life: himself. Eternity. Joy in the house of the Lord. If you feel unwelcome in God's house because of your ethnicity or sexual orientation or disability or past or mental illness or addiction or marital status or anything at all, let the Lord offer this welcome to you. Let him bring you to his holy mountain and make you joyful in his house of prayer. I'm sorry we haven't always been loving, but I promise that you are loved.

258 | *Ezekiel 29–30*
Isaiah 57
Mark 9:1–32

"Jesus took him by the hand, raised him, and he stood up." (Mk 9:27)

The Greek verb translated "raised" in Mark 9:27 is used nearly one hundred times in the Gospels. It's sometimes used to describe resurrection from the dead, of course, but more often these smaller resurrections. Spend some time today praying about all the resurrections you need in your life. Do you have it in you to hope again? What does it look like to hope with detachment, begging God for resurrection while accepting that he might leave that particular tomb sealed?

259 | *Ezekiel 31–32*
Isaiah 58
Mark 9:33–50

"If you pour yourself out for the hungry ... / then shall your light rise in the darkness." (Is 58:10, RSV2CE)

If you didn't feel convicted while reading Isaiah 58, go back and read it again. Remind yourself that as important as fasting and prayer are, they are worthless if we fail to live as God commands, with radical love for our neighbors. More than that: fighting for justice brings healing to those who fight, not just to those for whom they fight. The Corporal Works of Mercy are essential to the Christian life. How does my life in Christ push me to fight for the release of those bound unjustly? To share my bread with the hungry? To shelter the oppressed and the homeless? What change is necessary in my life to make my fasting acceptable to the Lord? This doesn't mean we have to fight every battle. But our God calls us to live for justice. What small (or radical) change can you make in your life to be a person whose life brings about justice?

260 | *Ezekiel 33–34*
Isaiah 59
Mark 10:1–31

"Jesus, looking at him, loved him." (Mk 10:21)

One beautiful way to study Scripture is to compare the different accounts of stories that appear in multiple Gospels. Look for the differences and see what they might tell you. Only in Mark's Gospel are we told that Jesus looked at the rich young man and loved him. Some people believe that Mark may have been the rich young man. When writing his Gospel all those years later, they think, he remembered how Jesus had loved him even when he was ready to turn away. Perhaps it was just this look that made a saint of him. Mark's Gospel is also the only one that says Peter "*began* to say" that they had given up everything for Jesus. Which likely means that Peter, in telling the story to his secretary Mark, admitted that when he had started to brag about the sacrifice he'd made, Jesus had interrupted him. For all Peter thought he had given up a lot, he still hadn't given up himself. It would take the rock bottom of denying Jesus, the eye contact after the cock crowed, to convince Peter finally to stop trying to rule his own life.

261 | *Ezekiel 35–36*
Isaiah 60
Mark 10:32–53

"He threw aside his cloak, sprang up, and came to Jesus." (Mk 10:50)

Imagine being Jesus here. You're on your way to the cross. Your dearest friends, men who have seen you cast out demons and give sight to the blind, are unwilling to listen when you talk about the suffering you're about to experience. Their response? A demand. Were they even listening? You're talking about being crucified, and they're calling shotgun. They're arrogant, insisting they can go wherever you go. Then the others overhear and are irate. You keep loving them, reminding them that you did not come to be served but to serve. Into all this comes a suffering man seeking to draw near to you; they try to shut him up so that he won't bother you. It's like they don't know you at all! But then imagine the joy of seeing blind Bartimaeus jump up and run to you, and the wonder on their faces after you restore his sight. Imagine the joy of being with these foolish men and women, joy that comes simply because you love them so much. Imagine the joy Jesus feels when you draw near to him, even when you're just as much a fool as they were.

262 | *Ezekiel 37–39*
Isaiah 61
Mark 11:1–19

"Will you doubt, then, the Lord's power, when I open your graves and revive you?" (Ez 37:13, Knox translation)

I wonder how many of the crowd of Jews who saw Jesus open Lazarus's grave and watched Lazarus rise and walk out of it were standing there, mouths agape, thinking of Ezekiel 37:13. This above all else was a proof that the Lord was walking among them, our shepherd God who had come to look after his sheep. Isaiah promised that the Messiah would be a tender servant of the Lord, bringing comfort and healing and freedom; his power would be for liberation. Even when Jesus drove people out of the temple area, it was out of love, to make room for people to worship the Lord. The Gospel of Matthew tells us that once the temple area had been cleansed, people in need of healing approached (21:14), though those in power were irate. Consider all the things Jesus needs to clear out of your life so there's room for you to come to him and be healed. Then imagine rushing to him and bringing him all your brokenness, all that's in need of resurrection. Imagine him opening your grave and calling you to rise.

263 | *Ezekiel 40–42*
Isaiah 62
Mark 11:20–33

"As a bridegroom rejoices in his bride / so shall your God rejoice in you." (Is 62:5)

If we can sit with Isaiah 62:2–5 until we truly believe that God is speaking this truth over us, I think it will change everything. Take some time today to read it as God's word to you, a promise that you are not forsaken or desolate. You are the delight of the Father. You are the beloved of Christ, your Messiah, who rejoices in you as a bridegroom rejoices in his bride. How would your life change if you lived as though that were true? If you really believed it?

264 | *Ezekiel 43–44*
Isaiah 63
Mark 12:1–27

"Why do you let us wander, O Lord, from your ways?" (Is 63:17, NAB)

The language of the tenants, "Come, let us kill him" (Mk 12:7), is reminiscent of Joseph's brothers in Genesis 37:20. That time, too, God worked the (intended) death of the beloved son for good. "Even though you meant to harm me," Joseph later said, "God meant it for good, to achieve this present end, the survival of many people" (Gn 50:20). How much the more so in the death of Jesus foretold by this parable. As you continue your second reading of the Gospels, reflect on how much more you understand them having already read much of the Old Testament. Though connections like today's might still not come easily without a good commentary (or even the cross references given in your Bible), there are layers of meaning that you'll catch now that you didn't see before. Make a note of some of these going forward, thanking God for all that he's teaching you through his word.

265 | *Ezekiel 45–46*
Isaiah 64
Mark 12:28–44

"The Lord said to my lord, / 'Sit at my right hand.'" (Mk 12:36)

Jesus almost never used the words *Christ* or *Messiah*, but in all three Synoptic Gospels he introduced the topic of the Messiah by asking this question, with a quotation of Psalm 110. Those who knew the Scriptures well must have been thinking of the words of that psalm, where God said to the Messiah that he must sit on a heavenly throne at God's right hand, indicating equality. Psalm 110:3 tells us that the Messiah was begotten by God before creation, while verse 4 speaks of the Davidic king as a sort of priest. I wonder what gears started turning in the minds of those who listened to Jesus — how much they began to understand of his true nature that day.

266 | *Ezekiel 47–48*
Isaiah 65
Mark 13:1–23

"I will rejoice in Jerusalem / and exult in my people." (Is 65:19)

Isaiah proclaims God's love with great power again here. I'm always struck particularly by the second half of verse 18 and the first half of verse 19. But I replace "Jerusalem" and "God's people" with the second person: "For I am creating *you* to be a joy and a delight. I will rejoice in *you* and exult in *you*." Imagine what it would do to our lives if we really could believe that that's how God sees us.

267 | *1 Peter 1–2*
Isaiah 66
Mark 13:24–37

"Love one another intensely from a [pure] heart." (1 Pt 1:22)

Read in isolation, 1 Peter 2:19–25 could easily be used as a tool for spiritual abuse. But when read in the context of the Bible's insistence upon justice and the defense of the oppressed, it becomes something different. Certainly, there is an invitation to treat people with reverence even when they are abusive. But I wonder whether Peter was saying that if you *have* to suffer, you must suffer in a way that shows people the transformative power of the Gospel — envisioning a situation where justice was impossible. I know he wasn't envisioning a Church complicit with chattel slavery. Or genocide. Or forced sterilization. Or millions of Christians debating people's tones of voice while ignoring injustices perpetrated against their marginalized neighbors. The invitation to suffer without bitterness is not meant to force others to endure suffering without helping them, nor is it an insistence that people tolerate an abusive situation for themselves when there is another option. Leaving people to their abuse (and coddling the abusers) is not the radical love called for in 1 Peter 1:22, nor is it genuine meekness or holiness. The call to holiness is never in opposition to the fight for justice.

268

1 Peter 3–5
Daniel 1
Mark 14:1–21

"Above all, let your love for one another be intense, because love covers a multitude of sins." (1 Pt 4:8)

The First Letter of Peter is full of so many beautiful verses that are hard to absorb when you read three chapters together. If you have time, go through and read this selection again and wonder at the Peter you know from the Gospels writing a letter like this. Arrogant, impetuous Peter writing about beauty and gentleness and compassion and reverence and love while rejoicing in suffering and humility and trust. Grace really is amazing.

269 | *Haggai, Zechariah 1–2*
Daniel 2
Mark 14:22–52

"Abba, Father, all things are possible to you. Take this cup away from me, but not what I will but what you will." (Mk 14:36)

O sweet Jesus. Staring a horrific death in the face, he looked to the one who could save him and spoke not with formal resignation but intimate desperation: Abba. He wasn't just gritting his teeth and consenting to his death but trusting in his loving Father, speaking from his certainty that the Father delighted in him even as he stood at the brink of torture and death. Lord, give me a heart so trusting in you and your love that I look up at you like a child gazing at her all-powerful Father. Even when you tell me no.

270 | *Zechariah 3–6*
Daniel 3:1–45
Mark 14:53–72

"But even if he will not, you should know, O king, that we will not serve your god or worship the golden statue which you set up." (Dn 3:18)

The Book of Daniel tells the story of a young prophet deported from Jerusalem a decade before its destruction and set up at the court of Nebuchadnezzar as a sage. Daniel was a model of a faithful Jew following the Lord during the Exile, as were Hananiah, Azariah, and Mishael. These three are the focus of today's story; threatened with a fiery death, they continued to trust in God. I often pray with Daniel 3:17–18, where the three young men stood before certain death, the king taunting them and insisting that God would not be able to save them. *Perhaps he will not choose to save us,* they responded (their language not intended to imply that God was incapable). *But whether or not he chooses to save us, we are his.* Whether or not God answers my prayers, I am his. If he wants to offer me health and joy and peace in this world, I will praise him. If I suffer alone and unloved, I will praise him. Blessed be the name of the Lord.

271 | *Zechariah 7–9*
Daniel 3:46–100
Mark 15:1–20

"The fast days ... will become occasions of joy and gladness." (Zec 8:19)

Zechariah was speaking to the Jews who had returned to Jerusalem from exile to rebuild the temple with the governor Zerubbabel. They were likely still haunted by the trauma of Jerusalem's fall, even if only from stories their parents had told. What seems to be a minor modification of Jewish practice in Zechariah 8:19 is actually a proclamation of hope and healing. These days of fasting commemorated the fall of Jerusalem, the destruction of the temple, the murder of the last governor of Jerusalem, and the beginning of Jerusalem's final siege. Now, God called his people to rejoice on those days, to celebrate their past suffering because ultimately it brought them to joy. It's awfully hard to look back at evil we've endured and recognize how God was working even then. It *does not* mean that God desired your assault or accident or heartbreak; it means that sometimes we get a glimpse of the good God can bring out of evil. God can turn our agony into a cause for joy. If nothing else, the cross promises us this: Even when our lives seem only abandonment and desolation, God is still God, and Sunday is coming.

272 | *Zechariah 10–11*
Daniel 4
Mark 15:21–47

"Let the Messiah, the King of Israel, come down now from the cross that we may see and believe." (Mk 15:32)

Thank God for unanswered prayers. Here they were, standing at the foot of the cross, demanding that Jesus come down. And he could have listened, could have done what they asked. One has to wonder whether Jesus might really have been tempted by this demand that he be a Messiah without a cross. Had he listened, we would not have been saved. I don't imagine that they were praying with any sincerity, but they were asking God for something all the same. And because he loved them, he said no. Perhaps there are prayers that I offer earnestly, desperately, that would turn out just as badly for me as that would have turned out for all the world. Praise God that he is a Father and not a butler, that he answers our prayers according to our greatest good and not always our deepest desire.

273 | *Zechariah 12–14* *Daniel 5* *Mark 16*

"I received these wounds in the house of my friends." (Zec 13:6)

What a profoundly Messianic passage we have here in Zechariah. In 12:10 they pierce through a man whom they will then mourn as an only son; 13:1 speaks of the fountain that purifies (like the water from the side of Christ); 13:6 describes the wounds on his chest received in the house of his friends; chapter 14 tells of the battle by which God becomes king on the Mount of Olives (as Jesus did through his triumph over temptation in the agony in the garden); and, finally, 14:21 foretells the emptying of the temple of all merchants. This whole book has been about rebuilding the temple, but it culminates by speaking of a promised one who is greater than the temple.

274 | *Esther* A–2*
Daniel 6
Luke 1:1–38

"May your God, whom you serve continually, deliver you!" (Dn 6:16, RSV2CE)

Esther was a type of Mary, a strong and beautiful woman who was given royal dignity so that God might save her people through her. But the fact that Esther's ability to save her people all hinged on a beauty contest, that she was trafficked and abused by a powerful man, and that she's often read as timid and easily cowed can make this book difficult for some. As you read, consider all that Esther suffered and marvel that she continued to trust in God. Meditate on her courage in choosing to stand with her people when she might have held her tongue rather than risk her neck. Pray along with her, holding up oppressed communities throughout the world. And praise God that he can use each of us exactly as we are.

*An important note on Esther: In the NABRE, the numbered chapters come from the Hebrew text and are shared by Protestants and Catholics alike, while the chapters with letter headings are found only in the Greek text; they are accepted by Catholics but not by Protestants. Interestingly, if you read only the text that is shared by Catholics and Protestants, God is never mentioned in this book. The Catholic sections, however, have beautiful testimonies of faith and powerful prayers.

275 | *Esther 3–C*
Daniel 7
Luke 1:39–80

"Behold, with the clouds of heaven / there came one like a son of man."
(Dn 7:13, RSV2CE)

This chapter of Daniel is essential for our understanding of the implications of "Son of Man" as Jesus' title for himself. Daniel saw "one like a son of man" who, to his mind, was a symbol of all Israel but also of its king. Though distinct from the Ancient One, who clearly represents God the Father, Daniel's son of man also was able to come on the clouds (as only God does) and rule an everlasting kingdom, the fifth kingdom from Daniel 2, the unending kingdom not made by man that would replace all other kingdoms. This means that the "son of man" must be God coming in the likeness of man. Imagine how shocking and devastating and delightful it must have been for the Jews of Jesus' time to begin to make these connections, particularly after the Resurrection.

276 | *Esther D–5*
Daniel 8
Luke 2:1–21

"I proclaim to you good news of great joy." (Lk 2:10)

The language of the angel in this familiar Gospel story is extremely subversive. The angel makes a proclamation of *evangelion*, which was the announcement made by a conquering king of the "good news" that he now reigned over the people. The angel's proclamation also declared that this infant was Savior, Messiah, and Lord. Just the use of this last title for anyone but Caesar could be viewed as treasonous. And then the angel was joined by a heavenly host, a word generally used for an army. The ancients who read this passage (immediately preceded in the text by the dangerous names of Caesar Augustus and his governor Quirinius) saw a gauntlet thrown down, a newborn baby challenging the Roman Empire to a battle that even its army's extensive training couldn't win for them: a battle fought by legions of angels. The newborn Messiah had entered into our world with the appearance of weakness, but his kingdom would outlast all empires, and his triumph would be not only over unjust regimes but over sin and hell and death itself. "Good news of great joy" indeed.

277 | *Esther 6–E*
Daniel 9
Luke 2:22–52

"Think, what anguish of mind thy father and I have endured, searching for thee."
(Lk 2:48, Knox translation)

Joseph must have felt so inadequate. He misjudged God's plan. He couldn't find a safe place for the Nativity. He couldn't afford a good sacrifice. He heard God only when sleeping. And in his final appearance in Scripture, he lost Jesus. But God was using every bit of that. In Joseph's uncertainty, we learn how to listen for God and how to admit that we were wrong. In Joseph's failure to provide as he wished, we come to trust that God can do glorious things in unpleasant circumstances. In Joseph's poverty, we learn that God is pleased with the humblest offerings. In Joseph's silence we remember that God delights in who we are, not in what we know or say or accomplish. In Joseph's fear and flight, we learn that God is working even in our trauma. In Joseph's loss and grief, we learn how to live when God seems absent, how to seek him, how to rejoice in finding him. Praise God for the witness of a man who, in being uncertain and mistaken and inadequate and afraid, was exactly who God asked him to be.

278 | *Esther 8–F*
Daniel 10
Luke 3:1–22

"Do not fear, beloved. Peace! Take courage and be strong." (Dn 10:19)

The historical minutiae at the beginning of Luke 3 might seem irrelevant — details useful only to scholars. But Luke is situating the story of Jesus very clearly in history to declare to us that this is not a myth but a historical account of a real human person. Pope Benedict XVI says of this passage, "It was not with the timelessness of myth that Jesus came to be born among us." Whatever objection you make to the person of Jesus, let it not be doubt as to his existence; the historical record simply will not allow it. Luke reminds us of this truth while fixing our eyes on another: the promise of Calvary. With the mention of Pontius Pilate, the cross casts its shadow over the life of Christ, and we are reminded once again that our God came into this world not merely to live for us but also to die. Even in these details, the Spirit is speaking courage and peace into our hearts, just as much as when the Lord spoke words of peace to Daniel.

279 | *Ezra 1–2*
Daniel 11
Luke 3:23–38

"These are the inhabitants of the province who returned from the captivity of the exiles." (Ezr 2:1)

Ezra was the priest-prophet whom God used to rebuild his people. In 458 BC, he led the second wave of Jews back from Babylon (after the first wave under Zerubbabel in 538 BC) and encouraged faithfulness to the Torah in a religious revival that set the tone for Second Temple Judaism (the period between the rebuilding of the temple around 520 BC and its destruction in AD 70). His book covers the history of the returned exiles from the first through the third wave of return (under Nehemiah in 445 BC). It's easy to skim the names in Ezra, especially since we had a genealogy in Luke today, too, but these names matter. Each name represents a family that was willing to leave behind the comfort of captivity to rebuild the city of God. Fewer than fifty thousand returned, of (likely) hundreds of thousands of Jews in exile. The rest preferred the relative ease of Babylon. They were offered home and freedom, an end to the exile that had broken their people, but they preferred to numb their pain and settle for counterfeit comfort rather than fight through to the other side and inherit the kingdom. Don't we all?

280 | *Ezra 3:1—4:23*
Daniel 12
Luke 4:1–13

"No one could distinguish the sound of the joyful shouting from the sound of those who were weeping." (Ezr 3:13)

The "peoples of the land" referenced throughout Ezra are the Samaritans. Perhaps their attempt to join in building the temple in chapter 4 was genuine; perhaps it was a ruse. But the Jews hated them so much that they wouldn't allow them to share in the worship of God. This led to later hostility from the Samaritans, which was returned by the Jews, going on and on until our merciful God made the two one in Jesus. Having refused the aid of their separated brethren, the people began to rebuild the temple under the leadership of Zerubbabel. Notice the juxtaposition of sorrow and joy in Ezra, the tension between those who delighted in God's triumph as the foundations of the temple were laid, and those who lamented the loss of the previous temple. The old men knew that this new temple would never compare to the one that had been a wonder of the world. The young ones who did not know what they had lost saw only the beautiful thing God was doing. How can we stand in this tension, lamenting what ought to be while rejoicing in what is?

281 | *Ezra 4:24—6:22*
*Daniel 13**
Luke 4:14–44

"They suppressed their consciences; they would not allow their eyes to look to heaven." (Dn 13:9, NAB)

Lord, have mercy. How have we fallen so far when we have been given such a story in Daniel 13? How have we ignored the cries of survivors in favor of the "pious" and respected? God, give us the spirit of Susannah to resist, to speak truth, to bring charges. Give us the spirit of Daniel to listen to survivors, to fight for them, whatever it might cost. Give us the wisdom of the elders who listened to the young Daniel. Let us not be bystanders, assuming the virtue of the outwardly virtuous even when we hear the testimony of their victims. Lord, have mercy on those of our priests and bishops who have suppressed their consciences, turned their eyes from heaven, and grown evil. Have mercy on the relatives and friends of survivors who refused to believe them. Have mercy on survivors. Bring healing. Bring justice. Bring peace.

*Daniel 13 and 14 are also found only in Catholic canon of Scripture.

282 | *Ezra 7–8*
Daniel 14
Luke 5:1–26

"They left everything and followed him." (Lk 5:11)

In Luke's account, Peter had seen Jesus heal his mother-in-law, but that hadn't captured his heart. If he hadn't seen other healings, he'd certainly heard about them, but that wasn't enough. It took Jesus barging into Peter's life at the end of a long and miserable night, a carpenter telling a lifelong fisherman how to fish. Peter was exasperated and exhausted, pointing out that Jesus' idea was a bad one but going along with it so as not to be rude. And when it turned out to be a good idea, and Peter (recognizing his weakness) had to call to James and John for help (and draw them to Jesus because he was willing to be needy for once), Peter fell on his knees before Jesus and shouted at him to go away. In the only moment of humility that we see from Peter until the passion, he recognized that he didn't have what it took to be a saint. This whole passage is about Peter's inadequacy — the foundation that his discipleship (and ours) is built on — and the irresistible magnetism of Jesus, whose very presence led a man as proud and self-sufficient as Peter to abandon everything and follow.

283 | *Ezra 9–10*
Wisdom 1
Luke 5:27–39

"You, our God, have made less of our sinfulness than it deserved." (Ezr 9:13)

I always wonder about the wives and children at the end of Ezra. Perhaps Ezra required their husbands to pay for their care and insisted on a written bill of divorce so the women could remarry. Or perhaps he saw them as Gentile scum and left them to fend for themselves. Given that there are no details about their protection, I expect it was the latter. Ezra was a great hero, a second Moses, the father of post-exilic Judaism. That doesn't mean he got everything right. The Jews knew they should never have intermarried with the peoples of the land. But once they'd made that choice, they ought to have fulfilled their obligations to their wives and children. Sometimes our leaders have just intentions but terrible execution. Sometimes our saints were extraordinarily holy — with some enormous areas of bigotry. It's much easier to imagine that our heroes are immaculate, that their canonization (or even ordination) means everything about them is perfect. But with the exception of Jesus and Mary, there is always brokenness and sin mixed in. When God in his mercy makes so little of our sinfulness, it's not an invitation to admire injustice.

284 | *Nehemiah 1–3*
Wisdom 2
Luke 6:1–26

"The goldsmiths and the merchants carried out the work of repair." (Neh 3:32)

It looks like just another list of names, but pay attention to some of the details in Nehemiah 3. Nehemiah was the governor of Israel, working around the same time as Ezra. But while Ezra was desperate to rebuild the faith of the people, Nehemiah was working to rebuild the walls of Jerusalem and return it to its glory as God's holy city. His work crew was made up of an absolute mishmash of people, many of whom had likely never done any heavy labor in their lives. There were goldsmiths and perfumers, priests and Levites, merchants and even the daughters of one of the leaders. Many of this motley crew likely felt either overqualified or ill-qualified for this work. But it was essential because it was the will of God. However inadequate they were, he knew how to use them. Hard as the work was, they persevered. If God is calling you to something, he will use you for his glory. Even when the task seems far beyond you or far beneath you, with God, nothing is impossible — and nothing is unimportant.

285 | *Nehemiah 4–5*
Wisdom 3
Luke 6:27–49

"For the fruit of noble struggles is a glorious one." (Wis 3:15)

What a foreshadowing of the triumph of the cross we see in Wisdom 3:15. It is so deeply (though not uniquely) Christian to rejoice in suffering for the sake of the good that it accomplishes. Wisdom speaks of this fruit of suffering while discussing childless women and eunuchs, people who were on the margins of Jewish society, seen as cursed or as outcasts. Even today, such people may often feel lonely and unrooted, their lives seemingly fruitless. That feeling isn't universal, of course, but I think every one of us has had a similar experience of struggling through the loneliness and futility of life. And here we're told that the fruit of that struggle is a glorious one. The fruit of feeling that you don't belong, of being rejected by the People of God (as eunuchs were), of wondering if your life makes any difference. When united to the cross, when embraced for love of God, that fruit is glorious.

286 | *Nehemiah 6–7*
Wisdom 4
Luke 7:1–28

"Lord, do not trouble yourself, for I am not worthy to have you enter under my roof." (Lk 7:6)

Imagine Jesus' amazement at the centurion's faith. Can you picture it? His slow smile, the wrinkles around his eyes, the raised eyebrow, the single tear. So astonished was he that he gave us the centurion's words to speak to him again and again at every Mass, before that moment of deepest intimacy when we receive him in the Eucharist. And as he hears them from our lips, he's once again amazed at the centurion, amazed at us. Can you think of something about you that Jesus is amazed by? Your persistent faith amid suffering, your generosity, your heartfelt repentance, your creativity, your passion for justice? Can you imagine his face as he looks on you with wonder and awe? Can you see in his amazement how passionately he loves you?

287 | *Nehemiah 8–9*
Wisdom 5
Luke 7:29–50

"Do not be saddened this day, for rejoicing in the Lord is your strength!" (Neh 8:10)

The People of God had lost so much of their identity and their faith over the years of half-hearted observance in the promised land and then over the years of exile, divorced from temple worship and the celebration of their holy days. When Ezra read them the Torah here in Nehemiah, they began to weep. Perhaps some were weeping for joy, but the exhortation not to be sad shows us their grief as well, their anguish at the ways they had failed God, at all they hadn't known. But the call of God, even the conviction of sin and the call to repentance, is always a call to deeper joy. What if we let the word of God wreck us as it wrecked them? What if we chose to rejoice in it as they did?

288 | *Nehemiah 10–11*
Wisdom 6
Luke 8:1–25

"They came to promise, and swear that they would walk in the law of God."
(Neh 10:29, DRA)

The people in Nehemiah had just finished hearing about all that God had done for them, how he'd continued to love them even when they turned from him again and again, how he was their savior in the midst of their sin. And what did they do next? They committed to changing their lives. Our relationship with God always has to lead us to action. To generosity, to forgiveness, to healing, to chastity, to a genuine repentance that changes us. If your faith only affects the time you spend at church or in prayer, it is in vain. We see this need to bear fruit expressed in Luke's parable as well. What a gift that God sows so prodigally, not limiting himself to the soul that's ready to receive him but lavishing grace on even the most hardened hearts. May we be equally generous, irrationally so, in preaching the Gospel.

289 | *Nehemiah 12–13*
Wisdom 7
Luke 8:26–56

"I pleaded and the spirit of Wisdom came to me." (Wis 7:7)

It's tempting to vilify the Pharisees, but much of what they did and believed really was an earnest attempt to follow after God. Remember that the Jews understood the Babylonian captivity to have been a punishment for their failure to keep the Sabbath (Neh 13:17–18; Jer 17:19–27). Not only was Sabbath observance the way they kept their covenant with God, then, but it was also a matter of national security. When we make the Pharisees caricatures, we run the risk not only of anti-Semitism but also of denigrating and dismissing well-meaning people who practice the faith differently from us. People's veils or hands raised in praise or kneeling to receive communion or praying in tongues might tempt you to put them in boxes and ascribe all sorts of bad intentions to them. But even the ones who are judgmental or arrogant or unconcerned with truth or opposed to the pope are often genuinely seeking God. May he give us the wisdom to honor what is true, good, and beautiful in people we don't agree with.

290 | *Judith 1–3*
Wisdom 8
Luke 9:1–27

*"Nebuchadnezzar the king had commanded him to destroy all the gods of the earth, that he only might be called God." (Jdt 3:13, DRA)**

The Assyrian army was an utterly devastating force, mowing down every nation in its path. Reading Judith 2 leaves very little room for hope for anyone who would oppose Nebuchadnezzar or Holofernes. But the Jewish or Christian reader can see the chink in Nebuchadnezzar's armor: He believed himself to be God. In 2:1, he spoke of taking revenge on the whole world, reminiscent of the flood of Genesis. In 2:5 he called himself the lord of all the earth (NRSVE). In 2:12, he swore by his own life (a claim of divinity) and insisted that he would triumph by his own power. And in 3:8, we see that it was his plan to destroy all other gods so that he alone would be worshiped. Despite his show of power, Nebuchadnezzar's downfall was inevitable. Nobody can ape the power of God without reaping the consequences. Now we just get to settle back and watch how a weak member of a weak nation would be the cause of the great king's destruction.

*3:8 in other translations. Here I matched the spelling of Nebuchadnezzar to what's accepted in English, not to the Douay-Rheims Version.

291

Judith 4–5
Wisdom 9
Luke 9:28–50

"Master, it is good that we are here." (Lk 9:33)

Pope St. John Paul II said, "The Church contemplates the transfigured face of Christ in order to be confirmed in faith and to avoid being dismayed at his disfigured face on the cross." Jesus took these apostles up the hill of Tabor to show them his glory so that when he led them up the hill of Calvary they would remember and believe, so that they would see past Good Friday into the promised joy of Easter Sunday because they had been given a foretaste. What are the Tabor moments in your life? What are the glimpses of glory you've been given, the spiritual consolations, the answered prayers? What are the moments when you could look to the Lord and say, "Master, it is good that we are here"? Write them down and pull the list out when you feel overburdened by the trudge up Calvary or the agonizing emptiness of Holy Saturday. Let the joy of the past point you to the promise of what is to come.

292 | *Judith 6–7*
Wisdom 10
Luke 9:51–62

"I will follow you, Lord, but ..." (Lk 9:61)

I wonder how many of us would keep following Jesus if we really understood just what he's demanding here, just how much the Gospel requires that we relinquish control. And yet. While the call to follow Jesus is an invitation to take up our crosses, it's also an invitation to a love affair beyond all imagining. The crosses we're given may be heavy, but they're formed to fit our shoulders, to strengthen us as we walk alongside him bearing a burden so much smaller than his.

293 | *Judith 8–9*
Wisdom 11
Luke 10:1–24

"You are the God of the lowly,
the helper of the oppressed,
... the savior of those without
hope." (Jdt 9:11, NAB)

The desperate confidence of Judith's prayer resonates with me so deeply. Here was a woman with no earthly reason for hope, whose home was besieged by the world's most powerful army, whose future held the promise only of suffering and death. She knew there was no way out. But while she was powerless, she served an all-powerful God. So she volunteered to do the impossible. And then she prayed from the darkness to a God who can bring light. She knew that the God of Israel is a wonder worker with a heart for the helpless, and she begged him to save his people. I love that she knew she had something to offer. I love that she didn't fawn over the leaders but corrected them, calling them to trust in the God they claimed to serve. I love that before she acted, she prayed. And I adore her prayer, especially verses 11 and 12. These words are so faithful, so hopeful, so desperate. What a prayer to pray in this broken world of ours.

294

Judith 10–11
Wisdom 12
Luke 10:25–42

"You punished them with such solicitude and indulgence, / granting time and opportunity to abandon wickedness." (Wis 12:20)

Wisdom 12:20–21 invites us to consider how God treats the wicked with such solicitude, pleading for them to return to him, offering them time to repent, and gently leading them home. When they do not know him and haven't accepted his laws, he is profoundly gentle in trying to draw their hearts to him. The need for severity comes with those who know exactly what he requires, who congratulate themselves on their adherence to his law and still rebel in their hearts and their lives. Though we may think we know which category a person belongs in, we can't ever be certain, which is why it's generally best to speak the truth with gentleness and compassion and trust God to sort it all out.

295 | *Judith 12:1—14:10*
Wisdom 13
Luke 11:1–28

"Blessed are you … above all the women on earth." (Jdt 13:18)

Judith stands as one of the most profound types of Mary. At the hour of her people's greatest need, Judith struck at the head of their enemy and won them freedom just as Mary, by her faithfulness, struck at the devil's head. This is most evident in Judith 13:18, where Uzziah said, "Blessed are you … above all the women on earth." When Elizabeth said this to Mary, she was referencing both Jael (Jgs 4:17–22) and Judith, women who struck at the head of the enemy of God's people. Like Mary, Judith is no demure caricature of feminine docility. For Judith, biblical womanhood involved physical strength as much as beauty and virtue and wisdom. Each of us — male and female — is called to be like Mary. The diversity of Marian types makes it clear that Christians aren't required to force ourselves into any one personality type or lifestyle. Rather, to model ourselves on Mary means obedience and faithfulness, regardless of exactly how that's expressed.

296 | *Judith 14:11—16:25*
Wisdom 14
Luke 11:29–54

"Her beauty captivated his mind, the sword cut through his neck." (Jdt 16:9)

Judith is one of the reasons that I find Catholic feminism so compelling. Here we have a daring and beautiful and ruthless and brilliant leader who is extolled in this song of praise for all of those things. The witness of Judith helps us to read Proverbs 31 in a life-giving way rather than a confining one, because we see such diversity of holy femininity throughout Scripture and throughout Church history. In a vacuum, any one of these stories might serve only to make Christian women feel inadequate. But when you read of Abigail's diplomacy and Judith's cunning and Esther's terror and Ruth's trust and Leah's anguish and Martha's anxiety and Lydia's leadership, you begin to see that there is space in the annals of holiness for every kind of woman and every kind of man. There is room for you as God made you. Take some time with this hymn and reflect on the positive attributes that you never would have expected to be extolled in a hymn to biblical womanhood.

297 | *Malachi, Obadiah*
Wisdom 15
Luke 12:1–34

"What you have whispered behind closed doors will be proclaimed on the housetops." (Lk 12:3)

Luke 12:3 ought to leave us feeling discomfited: "Therefore whatever you have said in the darkness will be heard in the light, and what you have whispered behind closed doors will be proclaimed on the housetops." I have often been convicted by the realization that the Lord hears my snide remarks and clever put-downs. I have often considered that my dearest saint friends cringe when they hear the way I talk about people. I have never been convicted enough to change. Lord, have mercy.

298 | *Joel*
Wisdom 16
Luke 12:35–59

"Yet even now, says the L*ORD,*
/ return to me with your
whole heart." (Jl 2:12, NAB)

Joel 2:11–17 brings me such hope. Every October when I read it and every Ash Wednesday when it's proclaimed from the ambo. The connection to Lent can make it seem like an invitation to dour repentance, a demand that we flagellate ourselves to earn the love of God. But really it's a plea from the one who loves us at our lowest point. In Joel we have verse after verse after verse of misery and well-earned punishment leading up to this passage of entreaty, where the Lord begs us to return to him. And though we return with fasting and weeping and mourning, it's the breaking of our hearts that makes it possible for him to enter in. All the rest is just a symptom of a heart that is turned back to the Lord. The trouble is that sometimes we have the symptoms without the underlying cause, because we don't truly believe God can love us in our brokenness — or that we're broken in the first place. May God, in his mercy, spare us. May he convict us of his love and invite us to repentance once again. May we return to the Lord with our whole hearts.

299 | *Jonah 1–2*
Wisdom 17
Luke 13:1–17

"Jonah made ready to flee to Tarshish, away from the Lord." (Jon 1:3)

Jonah was sent to Nineveh to preach to the Assyrians who had destroyed the kingdom of Israel only a few centuries earlier. When God called Jonah to offer his mercy to the Ninevites, Jonah refused. He didn't want them saved. So he went down to Joppa, went down into the hold, and went down into the sea, because running from God's will always pulls us toward hell. His conscience silenced, Jonah slept through the storm, then offered to be thrown into the sea rather than repent, because he preferred death to mercy. But the storm was a gift of God's mercy just as much as the lifesaving fish. And because God's rescue often seems worse than our danger, the unconvinced and unconverted prophet complained. But he also recognized (begrudgingly, perhaps) that he'd already been rescued, even in the belly of the fish. He prayed in the past tense about his deliverance even as he lay in that tomb, trusting that God was working in and through the darkness. This time of darkness was formative, and in his prayer we see that his suffering was bringing him closer to God.

300 | *Jonah 3–4*
Wisdom 18
Luke 13:18–35

"I have a right to be angry — angry enough to die." (Jon 4:9)

Having realized that he couldn't run from God's will, Jonah went to Nineveh, but it doesn't sound like he did much preaching. He didn't tell the people to repent; he just said that they would be destroyed. He would rather have died than have to see the Ninevites saved, and when they repented, he was livid, praying for death because he was too angry to live. We may think we can't identify with Jonah. But do you want your political opponents to be blessed? Do you want your abuser to find repentance, healing, and joy? Are there people whose deep conversion would make you bitter? I think most of us are more like Jonah than we want to believe. Jonah saw something even more miraculous than his encounter with the fish: the conversion of a city whose wickedness was legendary. His only reaction was misery. When God tried to show him how unreasonable he was being, Jonah sat pouting next to his hut, refusing to go inside while lamenting the lack of shade from the plant. Jonah was, in many ways, a tantruming toddler before the merciful God whose love he couldn't possibly understand. So are we.

301 | *Job 1–3*
Wisdom 19
Luke 14

"The LORD gave and the LORD has taken away; / blessed be the name of the LORD!" (Jb 1:21)

If you're uncomfortable with the beginning of Job, know this: It's totally okay to read the conversation between God and Satan as a rhetorical device intended to explain God's decision to allow Job to suffer. Catholics believe that the Bible is true as the author intended it to be read (taking genre into account), not necessarily that every word is a literal description of historical events. The beginning of Job reads very much like a parable, a story written to make sense of Job's suffering. Regardless, Job is a profound book, inviting us to reflect on suffering and the problem of evil, on where we find our value and our identity; on the inadequacy of our theologizing in the face of people's lived experiences; on the role of friendship (for good or for ill) in the life of one who suffers; and finally, on the way that suffering well makes it possible for us to encounter God even more profoundly.

302 | *Job 4–7*
Sirach Foreword, 1
Luke 15:1–10

"A friend owes kindness to one in despair, / though he has forsaken the fear of the Almighty." (*Jb* 6:14)

Like many who are hateful in the name of Jesus, Eliphaz said a lot of true things. He used very biblical language. But that doesn't make this the right response. He wasn't listening to Job — he was just applying a theological truism to Job's life without any concern for its applicability or helpfulness. Truth spoken with cruelty or without respect to the situation can be abusive and can drive people from Christ. If a woman is being abused and I say to her, "Jesus was silent in the face of his abusers," that is a cruel and violent thing to say. It's a true statement, but the way I've used it contributes to her oppression. My refusal to hear her pain and respond to her need takes the truth of Jesus' submission and makes it a bludgeon damaging the beloved of Christ. As you read this book, try to see yourself not just in the suffering Job but in the self-righteous friends who were too busy having all the right answers to mourn with him.

303

Job 8–10
Sirach 2
Luke 15:11–32

"When you come to serve the Lord, / prepare yourself for trials." (Sir 2:1)

I cannot tell you the number of times I have survived because I have Sirach 2:1–6 memorized. It's a promise that the service of God will bring trials, and it's a word of encouragement to accept suffering, to be patient in crushing misfortune. The juxtaposition of "crushing misfortune" (in the NAB) and "patience" is a reminder that we're being asked to suffer as Christ did. Humiliation so often seems like a crucible, but God is present to those who hope in him, as Sirach promises. Even the proclamations of woe later on are more like a coach giving his quarterback a quick shake, telling him to focus and it will be all right. These warnings are to people who refuse to bear up under hardship and discipline (Heb 12:12), to those who don't trust God, to those who have lost hope. There's something about "woe to you who have lost hope!" in conjunction with this promise of suffering (and of God standing beside me in my suffering) that makes me feel I can bear up.

304 | *Job 11–14*
Sirach 3
Luke 16:1–15

"Though he slay me,
yet will I trust in him."
(Jb 13:15, KJV)

This is a difficult parable, but I think Jesus was asking, "What would you do to feed your children? What steps would you take, what corners would you cut, how would you be willing to humiliate yourself? What do you do to earn money or fame or comfort? Why don't you sacrifice like that for me?" The dishonest steward chose to betray his master in order to ingratiate himself with his debtors, which wasn't virtuous. But he was making a break from one thing so that he could throw all his energy and trust into another. Do we do that when it comes to Jesus? Job's speech today ends with him insisting that all his suffering would be bearable if only there were a promise of eternity (Jb 14:14–15). We have that promise. Do we accept that suffering in the face of the much greater good awaiting us? Do we choose to run after Jesus, whatever the cost? Or are we trying to live with a foot in each world, serving two masters and betraying them both?

305 | *Job 15–17*
Sirach 4
Luke 16:16–31

"From the needy do not turn your eyes." (Sir 4:5)

Did you know that this is the only parable in which a character is named? Perhaps it was to show that while the world thought Lazarus worthless, Jesus called him by name. Perhaps it was to show that the rich man (traditionally called Dives) was not ignorant of Lazarus's plight. He knew Lazarus was there. He even knew his name. But he did nothing to help him. And when their roles were reversed, and he was calling out the cry of a beggar, "Have pity on me!" Dives still didn't address Lazarus. He demanded that Lazarus be sent to serve him. But that was impossible. And it was useless for Lazarus go back and warn Dives's brothers. Because, in some very clear foreshadowing, they would not be persuaded even if someone were to rise from the dead. Not this Lazarus, not the dead Lazarus whom Jesus would raise in John 11, and not Jesus himself. Who is Lazarus in your life — the person or group in need whose suffering you ignore?

306 | *Job 18–19*
Sirach 5
Luke 17:1–19

"For I know that my Redeemer lives, / And He shall stand at last on the earth." (Jb 19:25, NKJV)

We're so used to the command to forgive that we don't realize how absolutely devastating Jesus' insistence in today's Gospel passage is. If a man sins against you seven times in the same day, you have to forgive him. Every time. The apostles were so overwhelmed by this that the only thing they could do in response was beg for faith. It takes extraordinary faith to forgive like this, but such faith (and such forgiveness) is possible through grace. It's just as miraculous as a mulberry tree being uprooted and put in the sea, but it's possible. It was even possible for Job in his grief. It might seem shocking that in the same speech Job rails against God's injustice and cries out his longing to be in God's presence, but it's a perfect image of the complexity of grief. We who mourn so often sit in the tension of anger and grief and hope and trust, loving God desperately as we beat our breasts over what he's allowed. It's a hard place to be. It's a holy place to be. Your Redeemer lives. You will see him. In the end his love will heal it all.

307 | *Job 20–21*
Sirach 6
Luke 17:20–37

"At least listen to my words, / and let that be the consolation you offer." (Jb 21:2)

Job is all of us in 21:2, begging the person who keeps responding with potential solutions or platitudes or bad theology intended to console, "Stop! Just listen!" It's something we need to hear when we try to explain away other people's pain, when we try to excuse those who've hurt them, when we insist that it wasn't racism, misogyny, or prejudice, when we haven't walked in their shoes and can't know how it feels. Listening without trying to solve or explain or even console can be maddening, but it is a powerful witness to the truth of the Gospel when we we're willing just to sit with people in their pain rather than insisting on trying to drag them off the cross and into Easter Sunday. At those times, we stand like Our Lady of Sorrows, consoling them just by keeping them company. It's a very difficult place to be, but there is so much grace there.

308 | *Job 22–24*
Sirach 7
Luke 18:1–14

"But he beat his breast and said, 'God, be merciful to me, a sinner.'" (Lk 18:13, New Jerusalem Bible)

I know most of us have a hard time looking at those Pharisees who opposed Jesus and seeing ourselves. But there's something so familiar about the arrogance of this prayer, something I've heard again and again from people insisting that they are the most Catholic. I wish we could look with wonder at the deep faith of those who don't quite fit into this immaculate world view, all the addicts and the sex workers and the wounded and the angry, at the people who haven't darkened the door of our churches in years but pray with deeper sincerity than many daily communicants. What if we looked at our own lives and saw not our accomplishments but only overpowering grace? What if we imagined what we might have been without his grace at work in us? What if we looked at those who aren't Catholic in the specific way that we're Catholic, or those who aren't Catholic at all, or those who are so easy to condemn and dismiss, and saw not something to be pitied but the beloved of God, in whom he delights, whose faith may even put ours to shame?

309 | *Job 25–28*
Sirach 8
Luke 18:15–43

"Lord, please let me see." (Lk 18:41)

The very first thing he saw — maybe ever — was the face of Jesus. Imagine.

310 | *Job 29–31*
Sirach 9
Luke 19:1–27

"He ran ahead and climbed a sycamore tree in order to see Jesus." (Lk 19:4)

What sort of man must Jesus have been? How kind, how funny, how strong, how wise? What kind of man makes a guy like Peter leave everything behind? Convinces a snob like Nathaniel, a practical woman like Martha, a Zealot like Simon to love him unreservedly? Today's Gospel always leaves me wondering, longing to see the face of a God who had this effect on Zacchaeus. Zacchaeus was a tax collector, a traitor to his people, who made his fortune oppressing them on behalf of the occupying force — not entirely unlike a Nazi collaborator. But even before Jesus looked his way, Zacchaeus was so drawn to him that he surrendered his reputation by running through town and climbing a tree in hopes of catching a glimpse. And when Jesus called him, he left behind his life of extortion and handed himself over completely to the God-man he'd barely even met. Do you know that Jesus? Because when we meet that Jesus, it changes everything. It's less an ideology and more a wild adventure, a love affair. Pray today that you would see Jesus as he truly is — and leave everything behind to follow.

311 | *Job 32–34*
Sirach 10
Luke 19:28–48

"Why are dust and ashes proud?" (Sir 10:9)

After the initial setup, the Book of Job gives us thirty-five chapters of Job's friends blaming him or trying to explain away his suffering or offering him platitudes or refusing to listen to him. Most of us just want to get to the resolution and finally hear God speak out of the storm. But this delay is deliberate. It's easy to skim through these debates without seeing ourselves in the friends of Job. When we draw these chapters out over many days, we're able to reflect on the ways we respond to people's suffering and uncertainty. There ought to be some self-recrimination for people of faith who read these words. This agonizing interlude also helps us truly to identify with Job, to feel abandoned and alone, desperate for some word from the Lord. Without these many chapters, I don't know that we would be ready for the response of God that's coming in a few days. Without living through the loneliness and fear and long stretches of silence from God, perhaps we wouldn't be ready to receive him when he finally shows himself in our suffering.

312 | *Job 35–37*
Sirach 11
Luke 20:1–19

"Do not find fault before making thorough enquiry; / first reflect, then give a reprimand." (Sir 11:7, New Jerusalem Bible)

What would your social media interactions look like if Sirach 11:7–9 were your rule of life? What about your conversations? Which of these maxims is hardest for you to adhere to?

313 | *Job 38–39*
Sirach 12
Luke 20:20–47

"Where were you when I founded the earth? … / While the morning stars sang together / and all the sons of God shouted for joy?" (Jb 38:4a–7)

Finally, God spoke. Read in isolation, his response seems like the same argument Elihu made: God's ways are not our ways, and Job couldn't possibly understand what God was doing. But Elihu was voicing a theory. When God spoke to Job out of the storm, he was offering him a *relationship*, not an ideology. Imagine God speaking to you in the depths of your greatest suffering. Even if he didn't answer your questions as you'd hoped, the fact that he'd turned his gaze on you would change everything. In this moment, I don't think God was putting Job in his place. I think he was consoling Job, showing him the bigger picture. In listing a hundred different things he was in control of, God was showing Job that he was at work in Job's suffering, too. Imagine God gently showing Job all he'd done, all the beauty he's brought out of destruction, and then murmuring, "Sweet boy, don't you see that there's nothing I can't turn to good? There's no desolation that I can't make fruitful." Even then, this resonated with Job only because he heard it from God himself, because he finally knew him personally.

314 | *Job 40–42*
Sirach 13
Luke 21:1–19

"Now my eye has seen you. / Therefore I disown what I have said, / and repent in dust and ashes." (Jb 42:5–6)

Job 42 is so marvelous, so honest and real about the confusion of grief and the difficulty of relationships, even a relationship with God. Job had known *about* God, but now he *knew* him. He'd seen God and marveled at his power and providence, and now he regretted his ranting and railing. Though he'd had every right to speak honestly to God in his search for answers, he was also right to seek healing in this relationship after he spoke with such anger. It feels like any loving relationship where one person is devastated by grief, lashes out, and later apologizes. In most cases, the other person insists that they have nothing to apologize for. But the grieving person needs to apologize, for their own sake and for the healing of the relationship. Also, note: While we read that Job received so much more than he had lost, this is not a suggestion that the loss of his children was negligible. While sheep and camels and oxen can be replaced, no amount of new children could make up for the ones Job lost. And I don't think God could be callous enough to expect that they would.

315 | *2 Peter*
Sirach 14
Luke 21:20–38

"Be eager to be found without spot or blemish before him, at peace." (2 Pt 3:14)

The Second Letter of Peter speaks about false teachers, about the way that we become slaves to whatever drives us. It's a hard message to read in a Church so full of corruption. But into this world of sin, our first pope speaks the word of God, promising the persistence of the Spirit in the Church, promising his constant intercession, and reminding us that this is no myth, no elaborate scheme designed to protect the corrupt and aid them in the abuse of their power. Whatever might be going on in the Church now, we are the bride of the one whom Peter saw radiant on the mountain, the bride of the beloved Son with whom the Father is well pleased. If we fix our eyes on this, as on a lamp in the darkness, we will prevail. It can be so, so hard to love such a broken Church. But Christ did it first and best.

316 | *Ecclesiastes 1–3*
Sirach 15
Luke 22:1–38

"Vanity of vanities! All things are vanity!" (Eccl 1:2)

Until you figure out the point of Ecclesiastes, it is simply baffling that this book is in the canon. It's a depressing meditation on the utter futility of everything, showing us what despair there is in a life without God. Ultimately, it's the dilemma to which the rest of the Bible is an answer: a soul-shaking doubt of God's existence (or at least our ability to know him). Traditionally, it's said that Solomon wrote the Song of Songs when he was young and in love; Proverbs after he was given the gift of wisdom; and Ecclesiastes at the end of his life when he was despairing in his sin. If we read Ecclesiastes on its own, it's impossibly depressing. But if we read it as the scene into which the Incarnation bursts, the dark, monochromatic series of uninspired grays that will be touched by the rainbow light of joy that comes with the opening of heaven's gates, it's a beautiful reminder of all that we've been saved from. Solomon sought meaning and joy in wealth, pleasure, and even wisdom and found them all unsatisfying. Only God satisfies.

317 | *Ecclesiastes 4–6*
Sirach 16
Luke 22:39–71

"As he came forth naked from his mother's womb, so shall he return, and shall take nothing away with him of his labour." (Eccl 5:15, DRA)

It is stunning to compare Ecclesiastes 5:15 (verse 14 in the NABRE) to Job 1:21. Solomon and Job were saying the same thing, that we enter the world with nothing, and we leave the world with nothing. But Solomon said it to voice his despair, while Job said it to proclaim his trust in God. Neither knew the promise of eternal life. Both had been inordinately successful and wealthy. Solomon spoke as one who had experienced the satiation of every appetite and the hollowness such satisfaction leaves in its wake, while Job had been plunged into the depths of impossible suffering and learned to trust in God even there. Solomon had turned to false gods, driven by lust and likely curiosity. Job had clung only to God. It's not the circumstances that matter but the attitude, the choice to trust in God even when the world seems intent on dragging you into despair. When you could be a Solomon, be a Job instead.

318 | *Ecclesiastes 7–8*
Sirach 17
Luke 23:1–32

"No one can comprehend what goes on under the sun. … no one can discover its meaning." (Eccl 8:17, NIV)

Solomon is an interesting contrast with Job again in today's reading from Ecclesiastes. Both men sought to understand the bleakness of this world. Both were unsatisfied by the wisdom that was presented to them. But for Job, it was because he wanted to *know* God, not just to know *about* God. Wisdom wasn't enough for him; he wanted relationship. For Solomon, it's because he was only interested in answers, but all the answers in the world are no substitute for knowing God intimately. At the end of Ecclesiastes 8, Solomon talks about how unknowable God is because he is too vast for our comprehension. But Job saw God's greatness and power and infinity not as a barrier to knowledge but as an invitation to enter into the mystery. Which one are you? When you don't understand, can you seek to rest in the unknowing? Or is your faith a purely intellectual pursuit?

319 | *Ecclesiastes 9–12*
Sirach 18
Luke 23:33–43

"Jesus, remember me when you come into your kingdom." (Lk 23:42)

The good thief is the only person in the Gospels to address Jesus simply by name, with no title. It might be because he had no familiarity with the man, hadn't heard the stories, wasn't trying to curry favor as those who called him "Teacher" or "Son of David" or "Lord" might have been. He was looking at a broken, defeated man and somehow believed that Jesus was on his way to take his throne. This familiarity isn't meant to show disrespect. It's expressing intimacy. This man who had been justly condemned for wicked deeds, who had no right even to look on the face of Jesus, was given unimaginable grace in this moment, not just to recognize Jesus but to love him. We tend to think that we can judge other people's souls based purely on their actions, but the good thief shows us how often evil deeds cloak a soul that is ripe for divine intimacy. That's why we can't judge others (even if we can decry actions) — because we can never know the state of their soul.

320 | *Song of Songs 1–4*
Sirach 19
Luke 23:44–56

"Arise, my beloved, my beautiful one, and come!" (Sgs 2:10, NAB)

I long to hunger for Jesus the bridegroom the way Solomon's bride hungered for him, to find his love more delightful, more intoxicating than wine. I read his terms of endearment: "you whom my soul loves"; "most beautiful among women"; "my beloved"; and I know who I am. Certain of being so well-loved, I can speak with confidence of my beauty as the bride does, can proclaim the goodness of my bridegroom to everyone around me. And as I seek to believe his words, I hope to live in such a way that at the end of my life I will hear him call me to arise and come. This bridegroom laden with frankincense and myrrh, covered with a glory cloud, was crowned by his mother as he came to win my heart. How blessed I am to know how beautiful he finds me. What an incredible, unimaginable mercy that I ravish his heart. Whether you're a man or a woman, married, single, or consecrated, you're called to belong to Jesus, the bridegroom who longs for your love. If you haven't spent much time with this book, please go back and read it until you hear how he loves you.

321 | *Song of Songs 5–8*
Sirach 20
Luke 24:1–35

"Where has your lover withdrawn / that we may seek him with you?" (Sgs 6:1)

Though the Song of Songs is about a consuming love, at the center of the book is desolation, loneliness, and loss. The bride was reluctant to turn from her own pursuits to her beloved; when she finally turned to him, she found him gone. She wandered through spiritual darkness and desolation, but even in her feelings of abandonment, her longing for the bridegroom led others to want to know him. They saw how rooted she was in his love even when she felt no consolation, and her heart for him made them wonder why he was worth loving. Having heard her testify to the one who is all delight, the people listening also began seeking him. Her spiritual darkness caused her to run after the Lord with all she had. Her honesty about that desolation didn't scandalize those around her but made them seek him, too. God is working in our darkness when we're (prudently) honest about our struggles. Lord, let us speak of you in such a way that others long to know you even when you seem distant. Let us find our identity in your words even when your voice seems faint.

322 | *1 Maccabees 1–2*
Sirach 21
Luke 24:36–53

"Whoever refused to act according to the command of the king was to be put to death." (1 Mc 1:50)

The Jews were being targeted once again, their temple desecrated, their people forced to apostatize. We're so accustomed to seeing ourselves as the heroes of the Scriptures that it's easy for us to over-identify with the persecuted Jews here, to equate the difficulties of being a Christian in the West today with abuse along the lines of the Maccabees'. Instead, let's take the profound suffering we're reading about as an invitation to pray for those who are experiencing systematic, state-sanctioned persecution. There are Christians (and Muslims and Jews and LGBTQ+ folks and members of oppressed racial and ethnic groups) enduring similar violence and cruelty and disenfranchisement right now. Sometimes all we can do is pray. But sometimes we can donate or advocate. We can educate ourselves and write our representatives. At the very least, we can refuse to look away. May our reading of 1 and 2 Maccabees challenge us to work for the liberation of the oppressed alongside the God who is always working to set his people free.

323 | *1 Maccabees 3–4*
Sirach 22
John 1:1–18

"A man named John was sent from God … so that all might believe through him." (Jn 1:6–7)

There is an ancient tradition that John the Evangelist was the bishop of Ephesus, a town that was evangelized by a man who didn't know the fullness of the truth about Jesus but knew John the Baptist (Acts 8:24–25). So when John the Evangelist introduced the person of Jesus, he rooted his writing in the witness of John the Baptist to ground his people in what they knew. He geared his evangelization toward the strengths and needs of his audience, and because of that the name of John the Baptist has been read at millions upon millions of Masses. This Gospel is read at the end of every Mass in the Extraordinary Form, which means John the Baptist's witness is proclaimed daily around the world, and all because John the Evangelist knew that his people would be moved by his inclusion. Evangelization is always personal, the Gospel always proposed according to the needs of the individual. That doesn't mean that we leave anything out or ignore hard truths; it means that we see how the truth speaks to the specific deep need of every human heart, and we propose that desperately needed love and healing and mercy and clarity first.

324 | *1 Maccabees 5–6*
Sirach 23
John 1:19–51

"Here is a true Israelite.
There is no duplicity
in him." (Jn 1:47)

There's so much richness in these encounters. Andrew and the unnamed disciple (traditionally John) awkwardly followed Jesus, desperate to be near him though they had no idea what to say when he spoke to them. Philip needed only to hear Jesus say "Follow me" to leave everything behind and become an evangelist, bringing Nathanael along. Arrogant and dismissive Nathanael was so sure that Jesus couldn't be worth anything. Then suddenly he was calling Jesus the Son of God and the king of Israel, just because Jesus said he'd seen Nathanael under the fig tree. It's clear that Jesus was speaking very specifically into some need or brokenness of Nathanael's. What would Jesus have to say to you to break down your walls with a single blow as he did for Nathanael? What lies would he have to fight? What truths would he have to name? Nathanael needed Jesus to declare that there was no duplicity in him. What do you need to hear?

325 | *1 Maccabees 7–8*
Sirach 24
John 2:1–12

"The mother of Jesus said to him, 'They have no wine.'" (Jn 2:3)

How beautiful is Mary's prayer here? She didn't tell Jesus what to do or how to do it. She didn't sit there trying to orchestrate exactly how he was going to fulfill her will. No demands. No plans, No explanations. No expectations. She just told him their need and trusted him to take care of them. One of the most powerful things that we can do when we're petitioning the Lord is just to hold our needs up before him, just to pray the name of the person for whom we're interceding, to present our lack to him and trust him to respond according to our needs and his mercy. Can you trust God enough to intercede without giving him a to-do list?

326 | *1 Maccabees 9–10*
Sirach 25
John 2:13–25

"If our time has come, let us die bravely for our brethren, and leave no cause to question our honor." (1 Mc 9:10, RSV2CE)

The fall of Judas Maccabeus is tragic. He had been the heart of the Jewish people, leading them in battle and also in prayer. But here, at his last battle, he refused to respect the apprehension of his men, not because he trusted in God's strength but because he refused to look like a coward. His pride drove him into battle and led him to death. He was doing the same thing he'd been doing for years, but his goal was no longer service to God. It was his own glory. And the people had become so accustomed to praising him that in death they called him the savior of Israel, giving a man the title due to God alone (Is 43:11). What areas of your life look virtuous externally but have been corrupted from their original intentions? Who do you look to as your savior? The savior of your country or your business or your future or your family? Can you remove those people from their thrones in your heart?

327

1 Maccabees 11–12
Sirach 26
John 3:1–21

"Jonathan tore his clothes ... and prayed. Then he went back to the battle and routed them, and they fled." (1 Mc 11:71–72)

The First Book of Maccabees is a tremendously difficult book to read if you're not paying careful attention (perhaps even taking notes to keep track of the different nations and rulers and usurpers). If you have a mind for ancient military history, trying to outline all the alliances and betrayals of 1 Maccabees might be a fruitful undertaking. If not, keep reading, but focus on looking for one takeaway each day. Today, for example, you might marvel at Jonathan's power to repel the enemy single-handedly (11:70–72). Or you might notice the Jews' assertions that God is enough for them and they have no need of alliances (12:9, 15). Or that they make those claims while looking to the nations for protection. You might begin to worry about the People of God trusting in pagan rulers for protection (remembering Is 36:6). And you might see the groundwork for Roman occupation being laid here in their request for Roman aid. Even without a strong sense of which leaders belong to which nations, there is much to be gleaned from 1 Maccabees.

328 | *1 Maccabees 13–14*
Sirach 27
John 3:22–36

"Wrath and anger are hateful things, / yet the sinner hugs them tight."
(Sir 27:30, NAB)

This last verse in Sirach 27 is so convicting: "Wrath and anger are hateful things, yet the sinner hugs them tight" (NAB). I know I have a tendency to cling to anger — not just to feel it and try to move on, but to recite a litany of grievances, to tell them again and again to different people who will amplify my anger, or just to list them off in my head as a reminder that I'm in the right. Anger might not be your particular temptation, but you likely have pet vices. What are the hateful things that you hold tight to? Things that corrupt your soul but bring you so much pleasure that you don't even always realize how destructive they are? How can you allow the Lord to loosen your grip on these vices?

329 | *1 Maccabees 15–16*
Sirach 28
John 4:1–42

"Ptolemy had sent men to kill him also. On hearing this, John was utterly astounded." (1 Mc 16:21–22, NAB)

The First Book of Maccabees is a confusing book of military history, but at the heart of it is a feeling of powerlessness even in the brief periods that the Jews were at peace. Their nation was a pawn used by political powers eager to further their own ends, whatever the cost. The People of God often find themselves in a similar position: fawned over by the powers-that-be when we're useful, betrayed when we outlast our usefulness. We've gotten used to being swindled by those who need us for a season; but unlike the Jews here, we don't realize how often we're being used. When we're living for the Gospel, embracing all the uncomfortable positions we must embrace to be Catholics, there will never be a political party or movement into which we'll comfortably fit. We need to remember that we are Catholic before we are American or Irish or progressive or conservative or whatever. Perhaps then we can stand courageously, refusing to bow before the worldly powers that we think will deliver us, standing for truth regardless of the consequences.

330 | *Jude*
Sirach 29
John 4:43–54

"To the one who is able to keep you from stumbling and to present you unblemished and exultant, in the presence of his glory." (Jude 24)

What a beautiful image Jude 24 offers us: Jesus Christ, who is able to keep us from stumbling. Jesus Christ, who will present us unblemished before the Father. Jesus Christ, the one who will bring us, exulting, into his glorious presence. Jesus Christ who redeems, transforms, purifies, and saves even those of us who stumble all the way.

331 | *2 Maccabees 1–2*
Sirach 30
John 5:1–30

"Lord God, … who are awe-inspiring and strong and just and merciful, who alone are King and are kind." (2 Mc:1:24–25, RSV2CE)

The Second Book of Maccabees isn't a sequel, but a completely different book with a completely different author; it is more a series of stories and spiritual reflections than a military history. From the very beginning, we see this different tone, as the opening blessing prays that those who read it will have "a heart to worship him and to do his will readily and generously" (2 Mac 1:3, NAB) that God will hear their prayers and be with them in times of trouble. Then in 1:24–25, we find a beautiful prayer of praise, crying out how good God is. Can you pray like this today, praising God for who he is regardless of your circumstances?

332 | *2 Maccabees 3–4*
Sirach 31
John 5:31–47

"If you had believed Moses, you would have believed me." (Jn 5:46)

When you're finding the Old Testament difficult to read, it helps to look at the end of John 5: "If you had believed Moses, you would have believed me," Jesus said. It's true of the entire Old Testament: It's all about Jesus. And though we may not see exactly what each passage is trying to communicate to us about the Lamb of God, let us become men and women of the word — even the difficult parts.

333 | *2 Maccabees 5–6*
Sirach 32
John 6:1–21

"Although he disciplines us with misfortunes, he does not abandon his own people." (2 Mc 6:16)

The Second Book of Maccabees is so good for perspective. *This* is persecution. And as they saw their temple desecrated, their law outlawed, their men turned against one another, and their women murdered alongside their children, the Jewish people chose to trust. Though they had no idea what the particulars of the Resurrection would be, they believed that this life was not the end (as we'll see repeatedly in tomorrow's moving account). They believed that God was using their misery to draw them back to him. And because of that, they had joy. Though they couldn't yet look to the model of Jesus' death, they were able to suffer in peace, to suffer with joy because of the hope they had in the God they loved so well. They knew that he would not abandon them, no matter what he allowed them to suffer. How much the more should we be able to carry the cross, knowing the One who carried it first and best.

334 | *2 Maccabees 7–8*
Sirach 33
John 6:22–59

"Never lord it over any human being, / and do nothing unjust." (Sir 33:30)

Biblical passages about slavery always make me deeply uncomfortable. It's impossible as a modern American to hear "slavery" and not picture chattel slavery in the Americas with all its attendant horrors. But I think this passage from Sirach makes it evident that slavery in the ancient Near East was a different thing. Imagine a book of proverbs written to nineteenth-century plantation owners saying, "Never lord it over any human being"; "treat your slave like yourself"; "deal with him as a brother." It's unthinkable. It might be better if we had different language to talk about slavery in the ancient world. It was situational (prisoners of war, debt slaves, criminals) rather than hereditary; it was rarely viewed as a permanent situation (in Israel slaves were to be freed every seven years); and it didn't declare the enslaved person to be less than fully human. Though slaves were often abused and mistreated, it wasn't inherent to the institution as it was in chattel slavery. It seems to have been rather closer to indentured servitude than to the slavery we know from our American history textbooks.

335 | *2 Maccabees 9–10*
Sirach 34
John 6:60–71

"He who fears the Lord is never alarmed, never afraid; / for the Lord is his hope." (Sir 34:14, NAB)

What a wretched spectacle from Antiochus. He was so desperate for healing that he was offering one bribe after another to the God of the universe — he who wants for nothing. He was lying to himself so thoroughly that he might even have believed that he was quite well, even as worms writhed through his flesh. And in all his posturing, all his promises, all his vows that he would become a Jew, there is not a word of contrition. All he needed to be healed, to be saved, was to ask for mercy. It's the one thing he couldn't do.

336 | *2 Maccabees 11–12*
Sirach 35
John 7:1–13

"Therefore he made atonement for the dead that they might be delivered from their sin."
(2 Mc 12:45, RSV2CE)

In 2 Maccabees 12:45 we read the best scriptural support for purgatory; it's also a powerful invitation to pray for the dead and trust in God's mercy. These fallen men were idolaters who lost their lives as a consequence, but still their comrades begged the Lord to save their souls. It's easy to write people off, thinking they were so holy they couldn't possibly need our prayers in death, or thinking they were so wicked or so distant from the Church that prayers could do no good. But our most direct scriptural passage about praying for the dead encourages us to offer prayers for absolutely anybody, whatever the apparent state of their soul in life. Pray for the villains of history, even the villains of biblical history. We can't know whether they repented in their last moments or whether they're still in need of our prayers in purgatory, but what an incredible thing it would be to see cruel and vicious men and women transformed by grace and radiant with the Father's glory in heaven.

337 | *2 Maccabees 13–14*
Sirach 36
John 7:14–36

"A deceitful character causes grief." (Sir 36:20, NAB)

My heart breaks over the fate of Nicanor. He was one of Judas Maccabeus's closest friends, an enemy who became an ally, a brother who encouraged Judas to marry and have children. I imagine them almost like David and Jonathan in their love for each other, a love so hearty that Judas immediately realized when something was wrong with Nicanor. But for all Nicanor loved Judas, he loved himself (his life, his position, his comfort) more. And when he was asked to choose between his dear friend and his treacherous king, he chose to betray Judas. We who remember 1 Maccabees 7 know just how little he would gain, dying in battle against the friend he had forsaken. Had he chosen honor and friendship over loyalty to a black-hearted tyrant, he might have lived. They might have fought side by side and defeated Demetrius. Instead, Nicanor betrayed his friend, blasphemed against God, and died, leaving the sorrowing and furious Judas to display as a trophy the severed head of the one he had loved.

338 | *2 Maccabees 15*
Sirach 37
John 7:37–52

"Most important of all,
pray to God / to set your
feet in the path of truth."
(Sir 37:15, NAB)

There's some really beautiful discernment advice from Sirach here. First he tells us all the people we mustn't consult when making a decision (notably those with vested interests one way or the other). Then he encourages us to seek counsel from godly people, to use reason and our conscience to weigh our options, and finally — most importantly — to pray, asking God to place us in his will (even if he doesn't necessarily reveal it to us). Which of these steps do you find most challenging?

339 | *Acts 1:1—2:13*
Sirach 38
John 7:53—8:11

"You will receive power when the holy Spirit comes upon you, and you will be my witnesses." (Acts 1:8)

Most translations render Acts 1:1 as referring to "all that Jesus *began to do and teach*," as in the NIV. Luke wants us to see Acts as a sequel to his Gospel; Jesus is still the main actor, but now he's working through his followers by means of the Spirit. Before his ascension, Jesus sent the apostles out to "Jerusalem, throughout Judea and Samaria, and to the ends of the earth" (1:8), a directive that also serves as an outline of the Acts of the Apostles. They began by praying together (with Mary), established apostolic succession (with Matthias), and then experienced the outpouring of the Holy Spirit. Even this is reminiscent of Luke's Gospel; Jesus' promise of the Holy Spirit in 1:8 echoes Gabriel's words to Mary at the Annunciation — word for word but for the tense of the verb. Throughout Acts, we'll see healings, resurrection, speeches, and imprisonments that call to mind the stories Luke told of Jesus in his Gospel. The apostles' presence in the world is distinct from God's Incarnation, of course, but the meaning is clear: Jesus remains present in his Church.

340 | *Acts 2:14—3:26*
Sirach 39
John 8:12–30

"What I do have I give you: In the name of Jesus Christ of Nazareth, rise up and walk.'" (Acts 3:6, NKJV)

Who would ever have imagined that brash, impetuous, arrogant Peter could become such a man as this? And not two months after he had denied Jesus three times. Peter, who tried to correct Jesus, who bragged about giving up his boat. Peter, who chopped off a man's ear, who was reconciled to Jesus and immediately turned jealous eyes on John. This Peter now converted three thousand men with one homily. He trusted so completely in God's healing power that he raised a crippled man to his feet, then directed the wonder and awe of the crowds to God in another brave and brilliant and compelling speech. He took no credit. He was no longer his own man. He was still in need of renewed conversion and increased maturity, as we'll continue to see, but he was transformed. This is what the Spirit can do in our lives. It's often a far slower process than it was with Peter, but it's possible for every one of us. Like Peter, he can make us more fully ourselves and more fully his. Come, Holy Spirit!

341 | *Acts 4–5*
Sirach 40
John 8:31–59

"All day long, both at the temple and in their homes, they did not stop teaching and proclaiming the Messiah, Jesus." (Acts 5:42, NAB)

Already we begin to see the Christians' different roles. Some were boldly proclaiming, some working miracles, while others spent their time serving at table or distributing to the needy. There's even an ancient tradition that the rabbi Gamaliel was a secret Christian in later years, baptized by Paul but continuing to serve as a member of the Sanhedrin as a sort of hidden leaven in the world. What united them wasn't the way they served but their willingness to be content with the role they'd been given. Except Ananias and Sapphira. Had they been humble enough to acknowledge that they didn't dare give up all their possessions, there would have been no trouble. Instead, their lies destroyed them. The Church can work with addicts and murderers and adulterers and even apostates, once they're willing to acknowledge their shortcomings. It's deception that's so dangerous, a veneer of holiness concealing corruption that destroys lives and souls and whole parishes. If you're struggling with persistent sin, ask for help. I know it's terrifying, but it may well save your soul — and the souls of those who admire you.

342 | *Acts 6:1—8:3*
Sirach 41
John 9

"He said, 'I do believe, Lord,' and he worshiped him." (Jn 9:38, NAB)

The healing of the man born blind is so different from the other healing miracles, notably because Jesus appears at the beginning and then disappears for almost thirty verses. During that time, we see the man go from a disinterested recipient of this miracle to a follower of Jesus, all in the Lord's absence. Never having seen him. He had an encounter with Jesus, then had to bear up under opposition from the world. And the longer it took, the more devoted he became. First he called Jesus a man (v. 11), then a prophet (17), then said he was from God (33). Finally, having fought past one doubt after another in Jesus' absence, he encountered him again and worshiped the one he now called Lord (38). Conversion often happens like this: a flashy experience, followed by God's apparent distance and silence — not because he doesn't desire to be with us but because he knows this is what we need to be fully his. Had Jesus stood there grinning at this man after the miracle, perhaps the man would have pushed him away. Because he was hard to find, the man pursued him and finally became his. Maybe that's happening with you, too. Keep fighting.

343 | *Acts 8:4—9:43*
Sirach 42
John 10:1–21

"Laying his hands on him, he said, 'Saul, my brother, the Lord has sent me.'" (Acts 9:17, NAB)

God, who works all things for good, used the martyrdom of Saint Stephen to disperse the Christians throughout Judea and Samaria (as Jesus had instructed in Acts 1:8). It ought to astonish us that Philip the Deacon went straight to Samaria, the capital city of the despised ancestral enemies of Judah. This profound openness to reconciliation marked the Church (at its best moments) from the beginning. Ananias was told to present himself before a brilliant and powerful persecutor of the Church, a man who had been responsible for the imprisonment of countless Christians. And though Ananias voiced his fear to the Lord, he went. In courage and obedience and trust and mercy, he walked up to the terror of the Christians and called him brother. He spoke the name of Jesus to him and welcomed him into the Church. Barnabas, too, was willing to take risks for a man he had every reason to hate and fear; because Barnabas believed that grace changes people, the Church embraced Paul, and the world was never the same. There was a time when everybody knew Christians were willing to accept absolutely anyone. How can you help the Church earn that reputation again?

344 | *Acts 10–11*
Sirach 43
John 10:22–42

"God has shown me that I should not call any person profane or unclean."
(Acts 10:28, NAB)

Stubborn Peter was trying to be faithful, but faithfulness was going to require openness and flexibility, even more than while Jesus had walked with him. His refusal to eat unclean foods is reminiscent of Ezekiel's protestations many centuries earlier (Ez 4:4). But while God had capitulated then, allowing Ezekiel to maintain his ritual purity, he refused to do so here; it was essential that Peter understand that Christians weren't bound by the ritual laws of the Old Covenant. Mercifully, God used this vision to free Peter to go to Cornelius, while using Cornelius to help Peter understand the vision. When Peter realized what God was doing in the heart of Cornelius (not just a Gentile, but a Roman centurion, an oppressor of the Jewish people), he finally understood the vision and his new role in making the Church not just a sect within Judaism but a whole new creation, the People of God united from every nation. For once, he was catching up to the work of the Spirit rather than running out ahead of God and needing to be reeled in.

345 | *Acts 12–13*
Sirach 44
John 11:1–54

"Jesus wept." (Jn 11:35)

Sweet Saint John. Imagine him writing these words, frail and elderly and approaching the end of his life at last. Imagine how his breath caught in his throat as he remembered the tears of God. Imagine the consolation that memory must have brought over the years as he received word of the death of each of his brother apostles in turn. Imagine him, betrayed and uncertain and rejected and ineffective, feeling every one of the emotions we feel and clinging not just to Jesus but to the memory of this moment, when abject grief was so glorious. I think John shares this memory with us because he spent so many more years serving the broken and wounded People of God than the other evangelists did. The more we love people in their pain, the gentler we become and the more we cling to a God who suffers alongside us.

346 | *Acts 14:1—15:35*
Sirach 45
John 11:55—12:19

"The house was filled with the fragrance of the oil." (Jn 12:3)

That detail in John 12:3 — "the house was filled with the fragrance of the oil" — testifies to the power of this moment, the strength of this memory so deeply ingrained in John that the smell could bring it all back. There was Mary, in all her vulnerability. There was Jesus, his eyes filling with tears of joy as his beloved made an offering so costly it could only have been her dowry, tens of thousands of dollars' worth of ointment poured out as a gift to him. And there, too, was the traitor. John's friend. The one he had walked with and slept beside. The one who had caught John's eye and smirked, perhaps, each time Peter's foot was in his mouth, who had eased tensions between Simon the Zealot and Matthew the Roman collaborator. Did it still break John's heart, all those years later, to think of Judas? Did he miss him? Had he forgiven? When he told the story, did his breath catch in his throat as he spoke of Mary's act of generosity and the selfishness that destroyed Judas?

347 | *Acts 15:36—16:40*
Sirach 46
John 12:20–36

"Then he brought them out and said, "Sirs, what must I do to be saved?"" (Acts 16:30)

Paul and Silas's jailer was unconverted by the stories he'd heard of their miracles, unconverted by their preaching, by their evident joy in the midst of hardship. And when an earthquake blew the doors off the jail and pulled the chains loose, even that miracle couldn't touch his heart. No, he was converted by love — by the fact that Paul and Silas stayed. They knew what trouble he would be in if they escaped, so they looked freedom in the eye and chose captivity. They even convinced the other prisoners to do the same. That's what converted the jailer. God can draw people to himself through miracles or wisdom, but most often people come to know him because we love with his love. That's what changes hearts. That's what makes saints.

348 | *Acts 17–18*
Sirach 47
John 12:37–50

"Some began to scoff, but others said, 'We should like to hear you on this some other time.'" (Acts 17:32)

When Paul preached so brilliantly to the Athenians, in a clever speech perfectly crafted to appeal to the curiosity of this philosophy-loving crowd, he didn't preach Jesus. Oh, he mentioned the Resurrection, but he skipped the crucifixion and left out the saving name of Jesus. And while a handful of people converted, most politely put him off, interested but not changed. Paul went from Athens to Corinth, where he meditated on his failure. He had done everything right but had no success. Suddenly he realized his glaring omission. Some years later, he would write to the Corinthians of his resolution to preach Jesus: "I resolved to know nothing while I was with you except Jesus Christ, and him crucified" (1 Cor 2:2). All our clever theology, our pat answers, our brilliant homiletics with expertly chosen anecdotes and analogies — it's all worthless if we don't preach Jesus the God-man, if we don't speak his name and introduce people to him, if we don't proclaim his cross.

349 | *Acts 19–20*
Sirach 48
John 13:1–20

"Jesus answered and said to him, 'What I am doing, you do not understand now, but you will understand later.'" (Jn 13:7)

Peter was trying to be humble by refusing to let Jesus serve him, but disobedience is arrogance even when it looks like humility. He did the same thing when corrected, ignoring Jesus' authority in favor of a piety that demanded more than the Lord had offered. There was pride and self-righteousness and false humility and disobedience here, but at the heart of this exchange was something deeper and more painful: Peter didn't trust Jesus to love him well. He wanted to choose how God loved him. Peter couldn't stand to be vulnerable, couldn't handle the intimacy, couldn't let God love him the way God chose. So much of the suffering in our lives comes from fighting against the goodness of our God who is trying to love us. Here's how St. Teresa of Ávila put it: "You see, the gift our Lord intends for us may be by far the best, but if it is not what we wanted we are quite capable of flinging it back in his face. That is the kind of people we are; ready cash is the only wealth we understand." It isn't always easy to let God love you the way he wants to love you.

350 | *Acts 21:1—22:29*
Sirach 49
John 13:21–38

"He … proceeded to tell them in detail what God had accomplished among the Gentiles through his ministry." (Acts 21:19)

What a perfect expression of authentic humility here in Acts 21:19, when Paul spoke of all that God had done for the Gentiles through Paul. There's no false modesty here, pretending he had nothing to do with the fruit his work had borne. But he was profoundly aware that God was the one laboring; Paul was only an instrument, willing to be in the right place and let God work through him. What parts of our lives do we take too much credit for? Not enough?

351 | *Acts 22:30—24:27*
Sirach 50
John 14

"Do not let your hearts be troubled or afraid." (Jn 14:27)

All through John 14, Jesus was speaking to our anxious hearts. "Do not let your hearts be troubled or afraid," he said, knowing what a battle it would be. He knew that the world would try to rob us of our peace. He knew that anxiety would rage within us — the clinical kind as well as the situational. And he didn't tell us to be happy in some glib way, as though it were simply as easy as choosing to smile, as though we could blithely pray away all fear and dread. No, he told us to fight. He told us he would be with us, never leaving us as orphans. He told us that his apparent absence was only so that he could bring us to himself. He promised us the Holy Spirit. And then he told us once again not to let anxiety win. There will be days when it seems bound to conquer you, but cling to him who loves you as the Father loves him. Keep fighting. He is with you.

352 | *Acts 25–26*
Sirach 51
John 15:1–10

"As the Father loves me, so I also love you. Remain in my love." (Jn 15:9)

He prunes the ones that are bearing fruit. Pruning is healthy and necessary and — if you're the branch — hard and painful and terrifying. But the God who was about to go to the cross for his people was not interested in a prosperity Gospel, unctuously insisting that those who loved him enough would get whatever they wanted. No, he had made it clear from the beginning that following him would involve suffering, not just as a consequence of persecution but because he is able to sanctify and purify us through hardship. This would be an impossible promise to accept if he didn't follow it with that reassurance that makes all pain bearable: "As the Father loves me, so I also love you." He loves you with the same love that the Father had for him before the world began. If he truly loves you with the kind of love that set the galaxies spinning, his pruning can only ever be for your good. Suffering allowed by that love can be endured. Suffering that leads us to his love is worth it. So worth it.

353 | *Acts 27–28*
Hebrews 1
John 15:11–17

"Keep up your courage, men; I trust in God that it will turn out as I have been told." (Acts 27:25)

Paul was so rooted in the Lord that he had absolutely no fear. He knew that God would take him to Rome to proclaim the Gospel to the household of Caesar, to establish the Church in the heart of the world and watch it begin to spread down every road. So when things didn't go according to plan, he didn't worry. When he was set on the path to martyrdom, he rejoiced. When the soldiers ignored his advice, he submitted. When they were about to be shipwrecked, he celebrated Mass (taking, blessing, and breaking the bread in Acts 27:35, but not sharing it with the pagans there with him). And when they washed up on the shore of Malta, he saw in his wrecked itinerary an opportunity to preach the Gospel to a country that remains Catholic to this day. Despite a personality that might naturally have been inclined to seize control and rail against ruined plans, Paul had learned that God is always working, even in our ruined plans. What promises has God made you that you can depend on, no matter how bad your circumstances get?

354 | *Revelation 1*
Hebrews 2
John 15:18—16:4a

"To him who loves us and has freed us from our sins by his blood ... to him be glory and power forever." (Rv 1:5–6)

Revelation is not the easiest book of the Bible to read. With all the apocalyptic imagery (which is certainly not intended to be taken literally), you will be grateful for your footnotes or a good study Bible. But even if you find this genre off-putting, with its talk of dragons and green horses and many-eyed lambs, remember that these are likely the last words of the last living apostle. This vision is the last public revelation offered to the Church by Christ, the words written by a man who'd spent his youth walking with Jesus and now, in his old age, wanted to speak of nothing but "him who loves us and has freed us from our sins by his blood." Even if there are images that are utterly baffling to you, search for the word the Holy Spirit is speaking to you.

355 | *Revelation 2*
Hebrews 3
John 16:4b–15

"Yet I hold this against you: you have lost the love you had at first." (Rv 2:4)

These messages of Revelation are personalized notes of encouragement and correction to specific ancient churches, of course, but they also make excellent examinations of conscience. Are you zealous but without love? Fearful in the face of suffering? Compromising with evil? Tolerating and promoting false teachers? Which of the rebukes in this chapter (and the next) hits closest to home? For me it's Revelation 2:3–4: "You have endurance and have suffered for my name, and you have not grown weary. Yet I hold this against you: you have lost the love you had at first." How often do we congratulate ourselves on our orthodoxy and delight in what we have suffered for "the truth" when our lack of compassion breaks God's heart? I always used to read this as a condemnation of those whose faith had lost its passion, but I realize now that feelings aren't commanded or even expected. This love that was lost is an act of the will. Are we so focused on being "good Catholics" that we content ourselves with that without giving God our hearts? Without loving our neighbors? Without reckless generosity?

356 | *Revelation 3*
Hebrews 4
John 16:16–33

"Because you are lukewarm, neither hot nor cold, I will spit you out of my mouth." (Rv 3:16)

Revelation 3:16 was my very favorite Bible verse when I first came to know Jesus. I wanted more than anything to be passionate about my faith, to be wildly in love with the Lord. I filled the margin of this page with other verses talking about complacency and half-hearted faith, other Scriptures to meditate on when I was wearied by my failure to live entirely for the Lord. Perhaps I'm such an intense person that faith for me was always going to be everything or nothing. But it seems to me that God answered my desperate prayer, giving me a heart that earnestly longs for him even when I don't live as I should. I am many things, but I am never lukewarm. Praise the Lord for answered prayers.

357 | *Revelation 4–5*
Hebrews 5
John 17

"Worthy is the Lamb that was slain." (Rv 5:12)

Even a very cursory familiarity with Biblical imagery will help in our reading of Revelation. The Lamb is, of course, Jesus. But the image John describes is something out of a nightmare, a lamb covered with horns and eyes. But seven is the Biblical number for fullness or perfection; horns symbolize strength; and eyes symbolize knowledge, which means this is the unblemished sacrificial Lamb who is omnipotent and omniscient. Before him bow the twenty-four elders — the heads of the tribes of Israel and the twelve apostles, who stand for all those who have died in the Lord. They worship the Lamb eternally, always holding up the prayers of the faithful before him, our intercessors before the throne of God. And for all eternity, his praise is sung by those "in heaven and on earth, and under the earth" (Phil 2:10). We, too, participate in this heavenly adoration every time we come before him at Mass, placing our sovereignty over our own lives before him (casting down our crowns before his throne — see Rv 4:10) and giving him control over our lives.

358 | *Revelation 6–7*
Hebrews 6
John 18:1–27

"Shall I not drink the cup that the Father gave me?" (Jn 18:11)

Jesus' power is just incredible. It's not merely the fact that speaking the divine name (I AM) knocks a mob of soldiers and civilians to the ground, but the fact that he could so easily have stopped them in their tracks and yet chose to submit in silence instead. This is meekness: power under control. This is holiness: surrender to the Father's will. But it didn't make any sense to Peter, no matter how many times he'd heard Jesus foretell his betrayal and death. After witnessing this display of power and submission, after trying to defend his Lord and being reprimanded, after his confusion pushed his courage out of the way and left him running in fear, poor Peter didn't know who he was supposed to be or what he was supposed to do. It's a lot to take in, a lot to experience. Maybe we ought to be more sympathetic about his denial.

359 | *Revelation 8–9*
Hebrews 7
John 18:28–40

"What is truth?" (Jn 18:38)

Irony is a prominent feature of John's Gospel and is particularly evident in today's passage. These leaders of the Jews were so concerned about remaining ritually pure that they required the procurator to come outside to confer with them, rather than deigning to enter a Gentile building; meanwhile, they were conspiring against an innocent man to put him to death (whether or not they knew he was innocent) and incurring far greater defilement. Pilate looked at the way, the truth, and the life, and asked, "What is truth?" Jesus, whose life hung in the balance, is presented as utterly in control, while powerful Pilate was unable to free a man he several times proclaimed to be innocent. And finally, Barabbas (whose name means son of the father) was freed instead of the true Son of the Father, who was far more a revolutionary than Barabbas was. From the very beginning, the Bible turns all that we think we know on its head, and never more than in the Incarnation.

360 | *Revelation 10–12*
Hebrews 8
John 19:1–30

"A woman clothed with the sun, with the moon under her feet, and on her head a crown of twelve stars." (Rv 12:1)

There were no chapter divisions in Scripture until the thirteenth century, and no verses until the sixteenth. Try to ignore these breaks as much as possible, particularly with Revelation 11:19, which ought to be read with Revelation 12. When John was writing, the Ark of the Covenant had been gone for seven centuries, since Jeremiah hid it in a cave on Mount Nebo (2 Mc 2:4–5). Its loss was devastating to the Jewish people. So if John had seen the Ark in the sky (attended by lightning, an earthquake, and a hailstorm), he would not have announced this and then placidly changed the subject. He would have proclaimed it with great jubilation. If we read it without the chapter break, we see, "I saw the Ark of the Covenant, a woman clothed with the sun!" Mary is the Ark of the Covenant, as we'll understand even better when we study the Ark in Hebrews tomorrow. Suffice it to say that the woman crowned with stars, pursued by the Evil One, and made mother of all believers is much more than she seemed — as John himself well knew.

361

Revelation 13–14
Hebrews 9
John 19:31–42

"In it were the gold jar containing the manna, the staff of Aaron that had sprouted, and the tablets of the covenant." (Heb 9:4)

Though Exodus 25:16 only tells us of the tablets of the ten commandments being placed in the Ark of the Covenant (the locus of the presence of God in the midst of the Israelite people), Hebrews tells us of two other sacred items added to the Ark in the decades following its construction: the staff of Aaron and a piece of manna. Aaron's staff had miraculously bloomed to show that his authority came from God; Numbers 17:21–25 tells us that it was then placed before the commandments. The manna was added to show God's faithfulness and willingness to sustain his people. Thus, in the original Ark we find the words of God, a symbol of the first high priest, and the miraculous bread from heaven. The womb of Mary contained the Word of God, the Great High Priest, and the true Bread from Heaven, making her the new Ark of the Covenant, the one specially prepared to contain the presence of God — the one John saw crowned with twelve stars.

362 | *Revelation 15–16* *Hebrews 10* *John 20:1–18*

"You need endurance to do the will of God and receive what he has promised." (Heb 10:36)

It's rather lovely that 362 days into this project we're told, "You need endurance to do the will of God." But there's more to that endurance than merely committing to a practice like this and following through (even if it takes you more than a year). Yes, there is profound grace that comes of faithfulness to our spiritual disciplines. But spiritual endurance also means perseverance under persecution (as Hebrews reminds us) and supporting others who suffer. It means clinging to Christ when he feels distant. It means offering him our suffering even when that suffering threatens to crush us. This invitation to suffer well isn't just a call to the cross but a call to the empty tomb; we persevere knowing that the one who loves us has promised us eternity. Any suffering is bearable if at the end of it we will hear him say our name as he said Mary Magdalene's outside the tomb. But for that, we need endurance. Not visions. Not delight in prayer. Not a brilliant intellect. Not moral perfection. Endurance.

363 | *Revelation 17–18*
Hebrews 11
John 20:19–31

"He went out, not knowing where he was to go." (Heb 11:8)

Abraham didn't receive what had been promised (Gn 12:1–3). Though he had many descendants at the time of his death, of Isaac's line there was only Isaac. The only land he owned was the field he was buried in. And nobody much saw him as a blessing. Still, he believed that the one who had made the promise was trustworthy. So he who had gone out "not knowing where he was to go" left this world the same way. But with his eyes on the God he had tried to follow, he trusted. The difficult thing about trusting as Abraham did is remembering that the promises God has made us aren't the same promises he made to Abraham. Abraham was promised land and descendants and a heritage as a worldwide blessing. He was, essentially, promised success. We're not. God has promised us far more: unceasing love, unfailing mercy, peace, joy. He has promised us himself, we who are strangers and sojourners, who follow him in faith, not knowing where we are to go, who fail and mistrust and attempt to seize control of our lives again and again. Still, he offers himself.

364 | *Revelation 19–20*
Hebrews 12
John 21:1–14

"Consider how he endured such opposition from sinners, in order that you may not grow weary and lose heart." (Heb 12:3)

The saints exist to turn our gaze to Jesus, who endured the cross "for the sake of the *joy* that lay before him" (Heb 12:2). You were that joy. The thought of you strengthened him to bear up under torture. And why did he suffer so brutally? Not because such pain was necessary for our salvation. Not to impress upon us the enormity of our sin or to weigh us down with guilt. No, he endured so that we would "not grow weary and lose heart," so that in our most trying moments we could look to him in the garden, at the pillar, on the Via Dolorosa, on the cross, and know that if he could go on, so can we. And then, that last little jab, the gauntlet thrown down: You may have fought against sin, but not to the point of shedding blood. Stop congratulating yourself. Look at the witnesses that surround you. Look at the one who died for you. Remember what you are called to. Keep going.

365

Revelation 21–22
Hebrews 13
John 21:15–25

"He will wipe every tear from their eyes, and there shall be no more death or mourning, wailing or pain." (Rv 21:4)

What a beautiful trio of readings to finish out this year. John speaks to us of reconciliation with Christ, reminding us that ours is not to compare ourselves with others but to trust and follow Jesus. Hebrews exhorts us to strive for virtue, while sending us off with a touching blessing. And Revelation cries out the promise of what is to come, a promise we can hear so much more clearly after spending a year soaking in the word of God. We know that the radiant, glorious bride described here isn't just the Church but each one of us. Each of us is the beloved our God has pursued through the marriage covenant of Exodus, the poetry of the Song of Songs, the acclamations of love of Isaiah, the prophetic marriage of Hosea, the wedding at Cana, the marriage bed of the cross. We've been promised that our mourning would turn into joy (Ps 126; Is 35; Is 51), that he will wipe every tear from our eye (Rv 7; Is 25). He has promised a new Jerusalem (Rv 21:10), a new temple (Rv 21:22), a new Eden (Rv 22:1–2). And he who makes all things new will make us new. He keeps his promises. Maranatha! Come, Lord Jesus!

Timeline of the Bible
From Creation to the Time of Christ

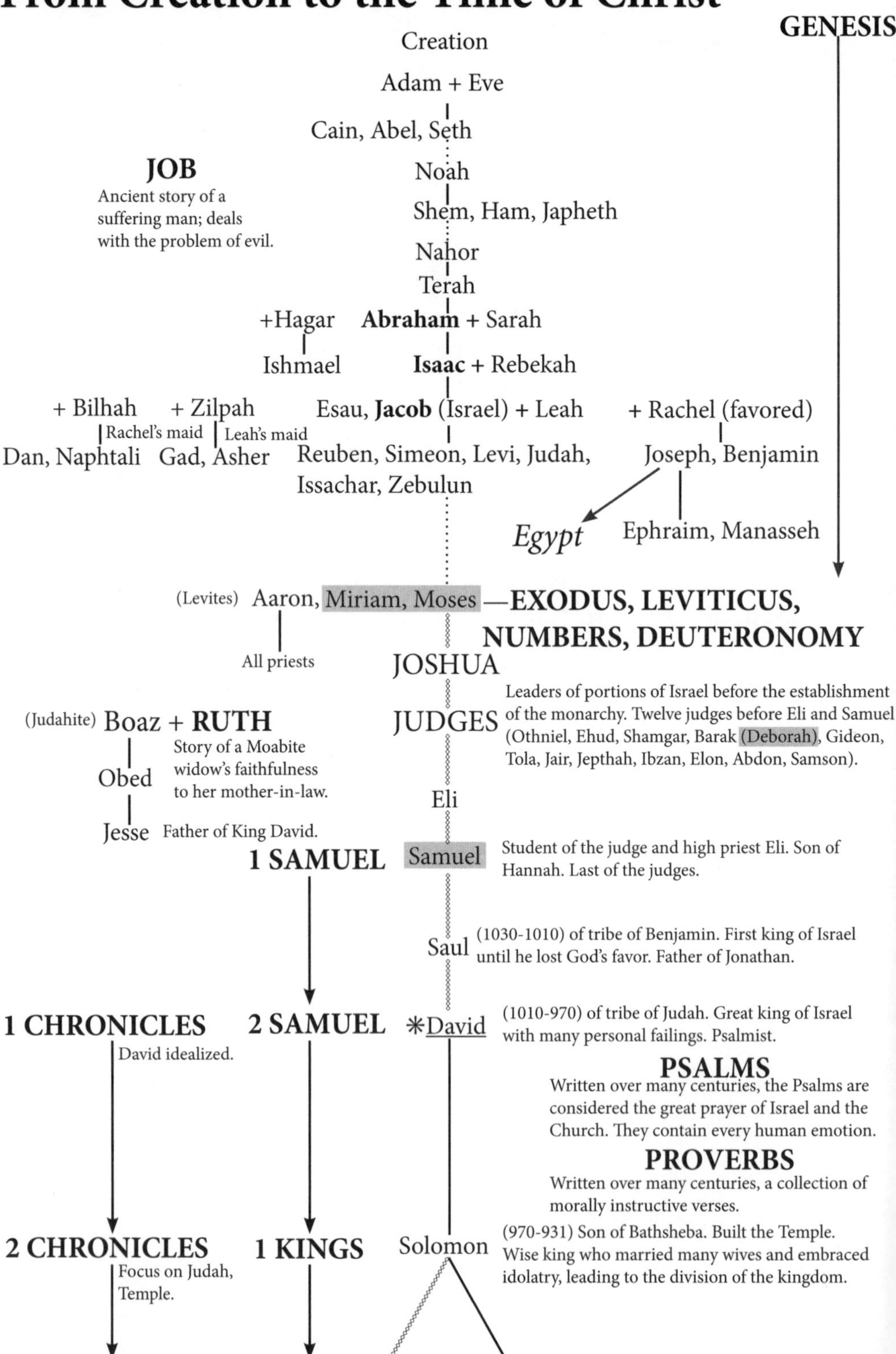

| Line of immediate descent

⋮ Line of descent with intervening descendants removed

Line of non-hereditary power

Patriarch

Ruling Nation or Foreign Monarch

Prophet

King

(King with reign of ≤ 3 years)

✳ Good King

BOOK OF THE BIBLE

All dates are approximate and B.C.

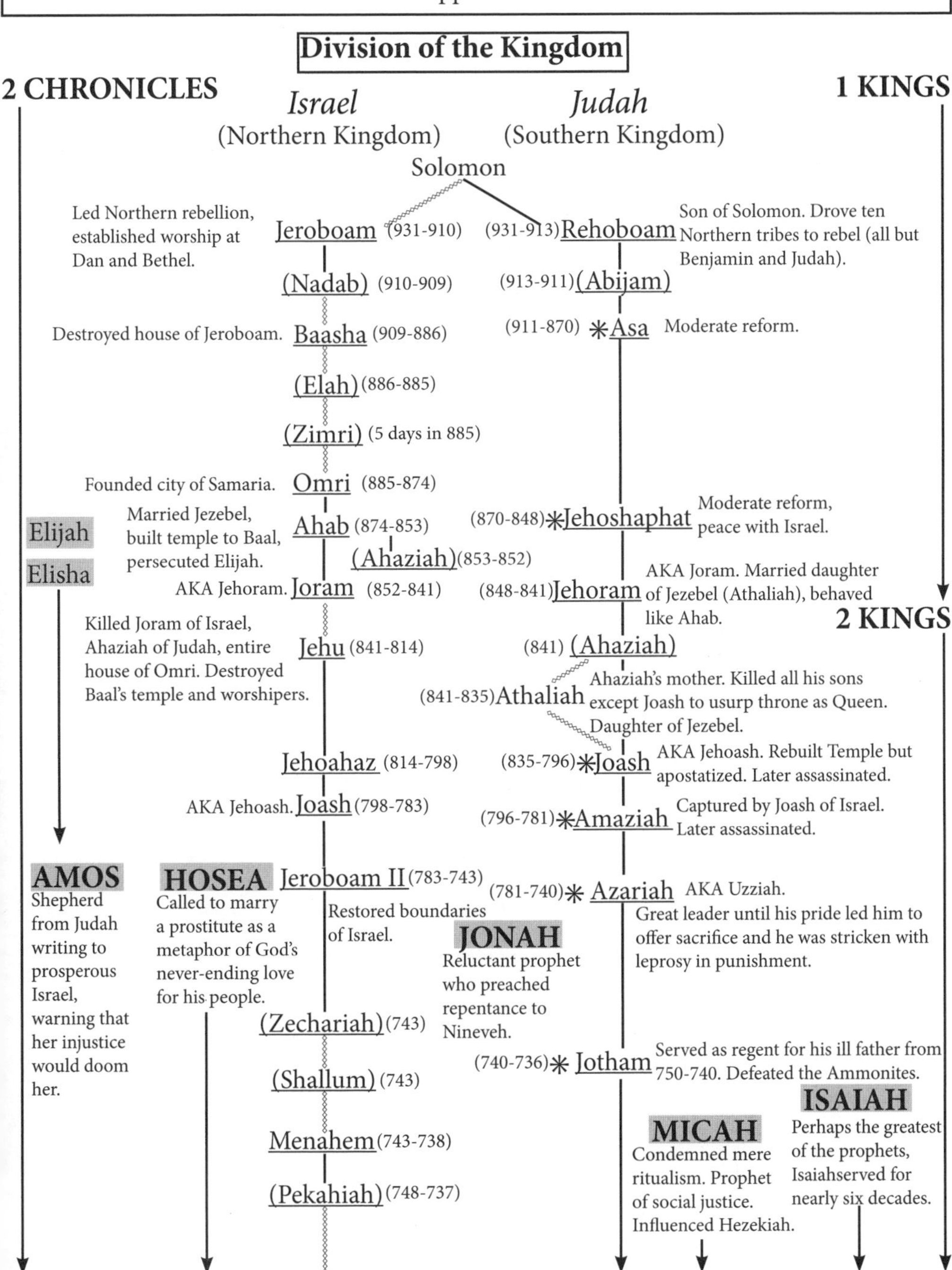

2 CHRONICLES and 2 KINGS

Israel

HOSEA

Pekah (737-732)

Hoshea (737-732)

Assyria

Assyrian Exile–722

- Exiled Israelites were replaced by foreigners who intermarried; their descendants became the Samaritans.
- **TOBIT** exiled in Assyria. His son Tobiah journeyed with the Archangel Raphael.

ZEPHANIAH
Coming Day of the Lord. Unjust punished, repentant restored through Messiah.

HABAKKUK
Reassured Judah that God uses our suffering to bring about victory. Foretold Babylon ("Chaldeans").

EZEKIEL
First prophet to be called outside the Holy Land. Judah deserved punishment, must acknowledge that the Lord is God. Promise of a new spirit and a new covenant. Described the new Temple.

JEREMIAH
Described God's heartbreak at Judah's faithlessness, foretold Captivity, promised restoration. Begged people of Judah to submit to Babylon, not flee to Egypt. Failed.

Judah

MICAH **ISAIAH**

Ahaz (736-716)
Fought with Assyria against Israel, lost. Heinous idolater.

*Hezekiah (716-687)
Major reform—restricted worship to the Temple. Fought Assyria (under Sennacherib).

Manasseh (687-642)
Worst king of Israel (though he repented). Put pagan altars and idols in the Temple.

(Amon) (642-640)

*Josiah (640-609) Major reform—found the book of Deuteronomy (622)

NAHUM
Foretold fall of Nineveh (612).

(Jehoahaz) (609) Deposed by Pharaoh.

Jehoiakim (609-598) Installed by Pharaoh.

Jehoiachin (598-597) Deported to Babylon.

Zedekiah (597-587)

Babylon

Babylonian Captivity–587

- Judah's elite taken to Babylon.
- Jerusalem destroyed.
- **LAMENTATIONS** (acrostic poems mourning loss of Jerusalem) composed by remnant in Judah.
- Many (including Jeremiah) then emigrated to Egypt.

BARUCH
Scribe of Jeremiah. Wrote to encourage exiles.

Nebuchadnezzar

Belshazzar

Darius the Mede

Cyrus of Persia 538—sent Jews back (under Governor Zerubbabel), started to rebuild Temple, restored sacred artifacts.

DANIEL
Encouraged faithfulness in Babylon, demonstrated the superiority of the God of Judah

| Line of immediate descent
: Line of descent with intervening descendants removed
Line of non-hereditary power
Patriarch
Ruling Nation or Foreign Monarch

Prophet
King
(King with reign of ≤ 3 years)
* Good King
BOOK OF THE BIBLE

All dates are approximate and B.C.

The Restoration: Judah Post-Babylonian Captivity
Return to the Promised Land

Cyrus

Darius I of Persia (522-486)

Renewed work on the Temple (520). Temple finished around 516.

Xerxes I of Persia (486-465)

AKA Ahasuerus. Husband of **ESTHER**, a Jewish woman who saved her people by interceding with the king when Haman tried to destroy them.

Artaxerxes I of Persia (465-423)

Stepson of Esther. Stopped the rebuilding of Jerusalem. Nehemiah then persuaded him to allow it.

EZRA Spiritual leader of returned exiles. Priest who encouraged fidelity to the law, established Second Temple Judaism; considered a second Moses.

NEHEMIAH Political leader of returned exiles. Governor who rebuilt walls of Jerusalem beginning around 445.

Various Persian rulers (423-332)

Macedonia (332-305)

Ptolemies of Hellenistic Egypt (305-198)

Seleucids of Hellenistic Syria (198-141)

Hasmoneans (140-63)

Jewish descendants of the Maccabees who ruled Galilee and Judea with (pagan) Samaria in between.

Rome (63 into the Common Era)

JUDITH Brave widow who killed Holofernes, the enemy general. (Date of the story's setting is uncertain.)

HAGGAI
First post-exilic prophet. Exhortation to finish Temple to avoid God's wrath.

ZECHARIAH
Exhortation to finish Temple for the Messiah.

OBADIAH
Prophesied against Edom, promised reunification of Israel and Judah.

MALACHI
Message of judgment to complacent people living in Judah before Nehemiah's arrival.

JOEL
Call to repentance before apocalyptic Day of the Lord.

ECCLESIASTES
Vanity of the world, fulfillment through obedience to God. Attributed to Solomon, the date it was written down is uncertain.

SONG OF SONGS
A love poem attributed to King Solomon—an allegory of the love between God and his people. The date it was written down is uncertain.

SIRACH
Primarily moral and spiritual maxims.

1+2 MACCABEES
History of the revolution against Greek rule led by the priestly family of Judas Maccabeus (from 167-141).

WISDOM
Moral maxims in praise of God and His wisdom.

Scripture Versions Cited

Scripture quotations marked (DRA) are taken from the Douay-Rheims 1899 American Edition Bible.

Grail Psalter: From *The Psalms: A New Translation* © 1963 The Grail (England) published by HarperCollins.

The Jerusalem Bible © 1966 by Darton Longman & Todd Ltd and Doubleday and Company Ltd.

Knox Bible, The Holy Bible: A Translation From the Latin Vulgate in the Light of the Hebrew and Greek Originals by Monsignor Ronald Knox. Copyright © 1954 Westminster Diocese.

New International Version®, NIV®. Copyright © 1973, 1978, 1984, 2011 by Biblica, Inc.™

The New Jerusalem Bible, © 1985 by Darton, Longman & Todd Ltd.

New King James Version. Copyright © 1982 by Thomas Nelson, Inc. Used

About the Author

Meg Hunter-Kilmer is an itinerant missionary and storyteller who travels the world telling people about the fierce and tender love of God. She is a Fellow of the Sullivan Family Saints Initiative in the McGrath Institute for Church Life and the author of two books about the saints: *Saints Around the World* (an international saint storybook for children) and *Pray for Us: 75 Saints who Sinned, Suffered, and Struggled on Their Way to Holiness.* When she's not obsessively googling obscure Saints, trying to convince people to read Scripture, or driving appalling distances while listening to audiobooks on double speed, she loves watching the Olympics and spending time with her nieces, nephews, and godchildren.